MOTHERGHOST

Other Books by Eclipse Neilson

The Moon in Hand: A Mystical Passage
Wing & Bough

MOTHERGHOST: A JOURNEY TO THE MOTHER

A MEMOIR

by

Eclipse Neilson

Published by Star Meadow Press

StarMeadow Press

A subsidiary of
Rowe Conference Center
Kings Highway Road
Rowe, MA 01367
Phone (413) 339-4954
www.rowecenter.org
Retreat ~ Relax ~ Relate ~ Reflect ~ Revitalize

ISBN: 978-0-9779818-2-3

Note to readers: Some of the names and identifying details
of people mentioned in this book have been changed.

Printed in the United States of America

Library of Congress Cataloging-in-Publication Data (applied for)

I dedicate this story to Isis.
She who picks up the pieces,
whose lap is the throne of heaven,
whose heart holds her child forever.

CONTENTS

MOTHER III: THE GROWING-UP YEARS, 1967-1974

MOTHER IV: FINDING MY FAMILY, 1974-1983

MOTHER V: BECOMING ECLIPSE, 1983-Present

THE MOTHERGHOST VI:

THE MYSTICAL REALM, 2000-Present

EPILOGUE   237

Acknowledgments

I would like to thank those who have offered their support and insight over the years, both in words and in action. Creating a life has as many components as does writing a book about one's life. My friends have reflected back to me my story and some have corrected the commas and semicolons for me. Thank you.

Wonderful professionals have helped launch different phases of this book. I thank Jane Bernstein, whose exuberant belief in the manuscript and skilled editor's encouragement began my path toward publication. Cynthia Bolling of CMB Editorial Services rescued me from a writer's dark spin. Her gentle heart's response to my words and her professional editor's eye for improvement gently moved me through the birthing process of *Motherghost*. Heather Alexander of Foxfyre Designs has employed her skills in graphic design to make everything look great and feel beautiful. To Jayleigh Lewis, who quietly and skillfully, word by word, brought a valuable clarity to the story. Felicity Pickett, Director of Rowe Camp & Conference Center, has provided ongoing support of my spirit expression, bringing light and hope on my path in a very real and practical way.

I am also grateful to Star Meadow Press, which grew from and is supported by the spirit of Rowe Camp's WomenCircles. May it continue to be a vessel for the visionaries among us. And as always, I express my gratitude to the spirits of the meadow, who call me by name and lead me through everything I do.

Thank you all for being you.

INTRODUCTION
Mother Imprints

As far as we can discern,
the sole purpose of human existence
is to kindle a light in the darkness of mere being.
–Carl Jung

My mother was a woman with many masks and many gifts. Just before she gave me away, in a silent act of desperation, she drew upon the folk traditions of her grandmother's old country. She enacted a sacred rite with me, passing on a legacy that had been handed down to her from mother to child for centuries. She stood in front of a mirror, holding my tiny hand tightly, while staring at our reflection. She looked directly into my eyes and whispered ancient words that sealed a prayer into my heart, and meticulously, with mystical skill, she imprinted an image of mother and daughter–Goddess and child forever.

This one act of my mother's became a piece of a puzzle–a profound mystery of the heart that remained with me into adulthood. All my life I hungered for the answer to where I might belong. As an adult I searched for my mother. I yearned to stand together with her once again. I wanted to face her . . . eye to eye, heart to heart . . . soul to soul. I believed I could heal my broken heart if I could find her. But I discovered it wasn't that easy. She was nowhere to be found and my feelings of betrayal became deeply rooted.

I have learned that our birth mother's imprint is the most powerful influence we will ever experience, whether our mothers were present in our childhood or absent; good, bad, or even indifferent, its mere existence cannot be denied. When a mother holds her baby in her arms and lovingly whispers a blessing, or offers a secret wish for her child's future, her intention remains subconsciously in the heart of her child forever. Within this silent exchange between mother and child, a light, a faint reflection of love–infinite with possibilities–emerges. This is the same mystical light that Jung refers to. It is the Motherghost. It is the love we all seek in moments of vulnerability. It is the bond that artists have attempted to capture for thousands of years. The earliest image of a mother holding her child dates back to 6,000 to 4,000 BC and speaks for itself of the importance of mother love.

I've learned to face the mother bond that I was handed. I've wrestled with it, tried to reject it, and ultimately I have grown from the lessons it taught me. I did not have a chance to ask what my mother's blessing was for me. The moment closest to what I describe as the mystical imprint–the precise second when time pauses to take in the precious exchange–was the moment I realized that my mother was going to leave me forever.

And so, my story is about what happened when my mother bond went askew, causing my young heart to break into a trillion eternal moments. The life I could have had, the mother bond that could have thrived, simply shattered, and all that was left for me were faint reflections–stars in the distance of some vast universe. Yet it is exactly among those fractured reflections I discovered the healing light of the Motherghost.

Mother I
The Life of Robin
1950-1954

Fitting the pieces together

CHAPTER 1
The Reflection
When I Lost My Mother

As a young child my past had always been a secret that was known only to a select few: my adoptive family the Neilsons and the social service agency that handled the adoption. All the vital facts about me like my birth certificate, where I was born, who my parents were, why they gave me up for adoption—all the answers to my questions about my earliest years—were in a large manila envelope locked away in a file cabinet in the adoption agency in Manhattan. And according to New York State law in those days, adopted children were not permitted to know anything about their biological parents. It was not permitted in the early fifties, when I was first put up for adoption, and it was still not permitted when I was twenty and desperate to know. The law was the law and there was no way around it. The best one could do, if adopted, was live on memories, but if, like me, you had no memories, you had nothing but an inexplicable longing to hold on to. Though I could not identify my feelings as grief, a heavy sadness weighed on me throughout my childhood. There was no face—no voice—just a dull ache that would throb in my chest in the most enigmatic moments.

My birth name was Robin: the name of a child I once was, a child who held tightly to an image of herself in a mirror with her mother. My adoptive family changed my name to Marcy. Many years later, the name Eclipse was given to me by a spirit guide in a dream. These days, my son calls me Mom and others call me Eclipse. Marcy Neilson is only a name on an old passport.

My life before age three is only a scar. A memory. A truth whispered by a lost child who has put the fragments together in a way that works. I have lived all my life with deep, unresolved feelings of looking for where I might belong and feel accepted. It is as if I have been waiting all these years to find the part of me that did not let go of my mother's hand the day she walked out of my life forever.

When I grew older, I understood how complicated and extraordinary the effect that the mother bond, broken or intact, has on a child. This, along with a deep yearning for the lost pieces of myself, inspired my search for my mother. Had my mother taken parts of me away with her the day she left me behind? Or was I too crushed to remember our bond? I wanted to understand where I came from, what traits I had inherited, and I wanted to belong somewhere. I wanted to stand face to face with my mother again.

I was just under two years old when my birth mother, with no warning, put me into a foster home. Then into another foster home. My memories are very clear beginning with the day I met the Neilsons. By the time I was almost four, the papers were signed and I was legally adopted by Frances and Winthrop Neilson, a wealthy, very social, very eccentric New York City couple who loved to wine and dine the celebrities of the world. The Neilsons gave me everything: expensive clothes, boarding school in Switzerland, piano lessons, sailing lessons, tennis lessons, horseback riding lessons, trips to Morocco, Spain, France, Germany. But they took away everything, too. They took away what I knew about myself. They replaced my identity with what they wanted me to be, and that was Marcy. In short, I was brainwashed. What they didn't give me—probably couldn't give me—was a sense of being accepted and understood. And so, little Robin became a ghost—a forgotten memory locked within my heart.

The Neilsons were uneasy with my past. They implied that my past, my life, my mother, my father, all were regarded as a disgrace in their social circles. I was adopted, and in the fifties that fact needed to be hidden. In some distorted way they treated me as if I had come from the wrong side of town—unwanted and dirty. My identity was to be erased once and for all.

Having no identity as a child, I learned to watch people carefully. I listened to voice inflections. I observed hand gestures and the way people held their bodies as they talked. I looked deeply into people's eyes. But people didn't become real to me until I closed my eyes and I saw them with my heart. I know that I often felt the extremes of a situation. I felt the unspoken vulnerability within any given moment or any person. Because of my acute sensitivity to people, I learned to observe people and events around me from a distant place inside me.

This special way I had of perceiving people and the world took root before I was adopted. It began the last night that I lay in bed with my mother, Stephanie. Something happened to me that changed me forever. Even at such an early age, I felt alone in the world in that moment and discovered a deep sense of myself. It was an understanding that goes beyond words. After a trauma, some children have a kind of deadness in their eyes; others carry a profound, unexplainable resilience. Something different happened to me that night. Even though I was too young to actually know what "destiny" meant, I knew in the depths of my being that I had a future. This feeling has always stayed with me, and it has helped me through many difficult alone moments in my life.

***

I know that I was different as a child. And from my earliest years, even before the Neilsons adopted me, I had had strange experiences. While

I don't know if they even existed, those unexplainable flashes haunt me. What I do know is this unique trait of mine unsettled my adoptive mother, who often tried to squelch my "fantasies," as she called them. Within a short period of time I had learned to keep my experiences to myself. I did not tell her that I saw a young child weeping inside her or that the man next door was always angry or that I could sometimes hear my brother crying when I looked at him. No. I kept quiet. I felt safer alone, away from those who did not understand me.

I was a child who loved trees and climbed to the top of them. I gave names to all the very special ones, and from the top of the old beech tree I often watched the birds around me, which I could identify by name at a very early age. I was not like other little girls who played with dolls; more often I was lying in the bright sun, nose to the ground, studying the ants. I talked with animals and I often pretended I was one of the many goddesses from the Greek myths; maybe I was Artemis, the Greek Goddess who protected the animals; or Persephone, who lost her mother; or Athena, who had no mother and became the great warrior who battled injustice.

Under the moonlight one night, quite by chance, I saw the Fairies—not the ones we see in Disney or in books, but The Wee Folk or what the Irish named the Special People. They appeared as soft lights filling my room. This is when the spark of magical resilience inside me began. That moment in my life as a child brought me exactly what I needed in those days—the Fairies brought me a feeling of belonging and a way to survive in the most difficult of times. This was my bit of perfect joy, and it never left my life.

CHAPTER 2
The Will
I Am the Daughter of Stephanie and Alfred

My journey to discover the pieces of my life and identity, and where they fit into my story before the Neilsons adopted me, began the day a strange letter arrived—a letter that would ultimately change everything that I had accepted as reality. At the time, I had settled into a life with a responsible but underpaid job as an art teacher in a private girls' school.

I was tired that evening as I trudged home from work. My heart felt heavy for some unexplainable reason, and, as I always did in moments like those, I sought solace in the beauty of the sky. That evening a soft salmon glow filled the heavens. I sighed from its simple beauty as I looked to the West. It was hard to ignore the splendor of pastel colors, and so I paused and leaned up against the old sycamore tree for a moment. I let the gentle twilight hues caress me.

When I pulled a letter out of the mailbox and saw its return address—Caring Times Children's Service, the adoption agency that had placed me with my adoptive family—it jolted me. I had never received any mail from them before. I knew that whatever the letter said, something strange was about to happen to me. In growing anxiety, I immediately opened the envelope and slowly marched up the squeaky stairs to my third-floor apartment. I stopped to catch my breath at the landing and began to read:

Caring Times Children's Service
Susan C. Spears
Executive Director

Miss Marcy Neilson
c/o Winthrop Neilson
15 Gramercy Park South
New York, New York 10003

November 1, 1971

Dear Marcy:
We would very much like to talk to you because of some information we have recently received from a Canadian source. Will you please call so that we can arrange an appointment?
I look forward to seeing you again after these many years.

Sincerely,
(Mrs.) Beverly P. Smith
Caseworker

I was almost four years old when my adoption papers were signed, so I vaguely remembered the name Beverly Smith. I fixed my eyes on the words: "We would very much like to talk to you because of some information we have recently received from a Canadian source." What information? What could it be? My mind raced with all kinds of possibilities.

As I reread the letter slowly, I felt something happening–something changing inside me. It struck me that I'd been waiting all my life for a letter like this–a letter, a phone call, an *anything* that would tell me who I was and where I had come from. And maybe where my real mother, my real father was? Somehow I knew that this letter was going to help me solve this puzzle. It felt as if at last I was putting down a very heavy load.

The next morning, before leaving for work, I called Caring Times and asked for Beverly Smith. After giving the receptionist my name, Marcy Neilson, I was put on hold for a few moments before being put through to Beverly Smith. This was the same Beverly Smith who was part of my history, a history hidden in a file folder in a locked file cabinet.

Beverly Smith told me that a gentleman from Toronto, a Mr. Phipps, trustee for a Canadian estate, had made inquiries about my whereabouts and would like to meet with me. Beverly Smith suggested that we meet as soon as possible.

The events that followed changed my life forever. I went to the adoption agency in New York City and I met Beverly Smith. Then when I went back a second time, Mr. Phipps, the trustee who was representing my deceased birth father's estate, interviewed and cross-examined me. Sitting in that office with the stern-faced lawyer and the long-forgotten social workers, I seemed to be living simultaneously in two time zones: the present and the past. Mr. Phipps, a well-dressed man with a trim mustache, was in the present, putting me through an elaborate process of identification. As we talked and I answered questions, the antique bronze clock's pendulum grew louder with each minute. I began reliving the past. I felt strange emotions growing inside me. A heavy feeling weighed in my heart, as if I were mourning someone or something. I did not really know what I had lost, but I could feel a small child inside me crying.

The room we were in looked almost too familiar as my lost memories started waking up. I recognized the mahogany desk and the green leather chairs. It was exactly the same office it had been almost twenty years ago when my birth mother sat beside me, held my tiny hand in hers, and then signed the papers that gave me over to a series of foster homes. And later my mother sat here again to sign the papers that gave me up for permanent adoption. It was the same Beverly Smith sitting across the desk from me now, looking older and more tired, but still the same woman of long ago, with pale blue eyes, blond hair, and a prominent nose. I closed my eyes for a moment to see if I could retrieve an old memory. I felt queasy and uncertain about what was happening inside of me, but my adoptive family had raised me to be reserved and gracious, and so I sat up straight like a young lady and smiled. I kept my feelings hidden.

Frances and Winthrop Neilson, who had adopted me all those years ago, were also present, heightening the tension of the meeting even more. The parents I no longer spoke to because I could not let go of my childhood wounds. Frances smiled as I went and sat down at the other end of the long wooden table. It was awkward seeing them, but I was polite. After a period of questions and answers, the lawyer paused, cleared his throat, stood up, and, extending his hand to me, said, "Well, my dear, I am convinced that you are indeed the person we are looking for." He then took out a large, legal-looking document from his briefcase, held it up, and began to read in a very formal tone: "To my daughter, Robin Claire Mulock, daughter of Stephanie Muriel Le Bow Mulock and Alfred Mulock. . . ."

I was to inherit a substantial sum from the estate of my father, Alfred Mulock aka Alfred Mulock Rogers. I . . . Marcy . . . Or was I really Robin Mulock? I had been listening to the lawyer's words in a state of profound shock. Alfred Mulock was dead, and I was confused as to why I felt so sad for a man I had never known. But I was to find out that Alfred Mulock was a man I, as Robin, had known for a little while. In addition to the permeating sadness—and far more stunning than the idea of the inheritance—was the name Robin. Not Marcy. Robin. It was the first time since my adoption sixteen years ago that anyone had used my birth name. Robin. I will never forget the impact of hearing my name once again. It was riveting. Astonishing. Frightening. And above all, deeply painful.

As I sat in the office that afternoon taking this information in, my first thought was, could my adoption have been a mistake? As a child I had secretly comforted myself by believing there had been a mix-up of some sort. Then over the years I let go of my memories and simply wondered whether I had been the unwanted mistake. The question of what really happened in my past began to pull against what I had believed to be true. I felt that my truth lay hidden somewhere in the dark spaces between what was real and what was not. It suddenly hit me that what the Neilsons had forced me to believe about myself for over twenty years was false. I turned to them for an explanation. They said nothing. Mother patted Father's arm, smiled at the lawyer, bypassed my glare, and looked away. They had been caught in a lie.

What happened at that very moment was extraordinary—my early life, which had been invisible to me, broke through the veil of time. The present dissolved and a flood of memories exploded in my mind. Suddenly my buried self, sleeping for years, was awake. A tidal wave of feelings and memory fragments washed over me and a fierce inner drive, like the current of a river crashing over smooth stones, pulled me along. I am going back to find me, I thought. I am going back to find my lost pieces and most of all my mother. I felt that I might faint or even worse—throw up.

I all but forgot where I was. I was back in Robin's past. A brief feeling that I belonged somewhere and to someone filled my heart. I repeated to myself over and over, "I'm Robin. I'm Robin. Not Marcy. Robin is my name. Robin . . . daughter of Stephanie."

CHAPTER 3
My Name Is Robin
I Am My Mother's Ghost

As a child I was subtly led to believe that I was born without a beginning. My adoptive parents never mentioned anything about my life as Robin–the child I was before they adopted me. In their mind I had no life before my arrival into their family as Marcy–it did not exist–nor had I.

For some dark reason I was to forget my beginnings. But why? When I was four years old, I was told that my birth mother and I had never been together after my birth. There had been no mother bond. I accepted this as truth.

At the reading of my father's will, hearing the lawyer refer to me as Robin was profoundly liberating. Along with my name returning, I remembered what had happened. Why it had happened. How it had happened that day long ago when I lost my name.

To this day I remember the events with painful clarity. It was a few days after my arrival in the Long Island house of the Neilsons. My new mother, Frances Neilson, said to me, "Now you have a real name. It's Marcy. As I told you, your mother didn't really love you. We do and from now on your name is Marcy. Marcy Neilson. You are not Robin anymore. Robin doesn't exist."

My reaction to this was to say, "No! I'm Robin." For days after that first encounter, I made it a habit to stand in front of the full-length mirror in the master bedroom of the house and point at my mirror image in the same manner that she had pointed at me, saying over and over, "You're Robin. Robin. Robin is your name."

One afternoon while I was at the mirror, my new mother came into the room looking for a pair of white gloves. She found the gloves, put them on, and paused. Instead of leaving the room, she stood silently for perhaps a half minute, watching as I stood before the mirror, pointing at myself.

"You're Robin. Robin. Robin is your name," I repeated. Then she walked slowly over to me. Kneeling down beside me, she quietly corrected me. "No, sweetheart, not Robin. I'm tired of this." She looked hard into my eyes. "Your name is Marcy. Marcy. Marcy Neilson is your name. Remember that." Then she stood up and walked away.

I grew angrier as I watched her walk out the door. I yelled after her, "No. No. I'm Robin. I am Robin. That's what my Mommy called me. Robin!"

My new mother again paused, listening to me in silence, her back to me. Before I could say another word she turned sharply and glared at me. Then she marched over to where I was standing and bent over. She placed her face squarely in front of mine. She took my chin in her hand and squeezed tightly. Looking at me, eye to eye, she said in a precise, cold tone, "I am your mother. You have no other mother. And your name is Marcy. Marcy Neilson. There is no Robin. You are Marcy. You will remember that." The look in her eyes terrified me. I nodded.

"Good," she said softly, still staring at me for a long moment. It was a stare that every child of hers knew. It would make anyone shudder. Then she straightened her gloves and dress, turned again and walked out the door.

At that moment, panicked by her furious eyes, I gave up my name. And with that surrender, I slowly and unconsciously gave up Robin's past and the people and things that Robin had loved. It all slipped through my fingers like a handful of sand. My memory of my real mother, my real father, faded and was soon lost to me. After that, neither Frances Neilson nor anyone else in the Neilson family ever used the name Robin. All that remained was a deep feeling of loss—and of fear—within me. Robin was gone. I was Marcy Neilson.

Until the reading of my father's will.

What I knew at the time of the reading of the will was that my father was dead. As for my mother? I knew nothing. She could be living anywhere. If I were to meet her I wondered what I would call her. Mom? Mother? Stephanie? Muriel? What? I think I used to call her Mommy or Momma. But that was before Robin's world ended. Before I became Marcy.

Still, she had to be somewhere, I thought. For years I had felt her presence in a very strange way, but after the reading of the will, my feelings grew and I became obsessed with finding her. I began searching for her unceasingly, as unsettled ghosts are often said to search for something, for anything, to prove that once they'd been alive. I hungered to know my mother, to know what she was like. I needed to know if she was still alive. Was she rich or was she poor? Married or single? Did she have more children? Did I have sisters or brothers? Or both? Was it because she stopped loving me that she gave me away? Or had she never loved me enough? Was this the reason for the pain I carried inside? I needed to know. I needed to stand face to face with my mother. I wanted to find my mother's love.

∗∗∗

Although I've come out looking a bit like my mother, and I stand like my father, I have none of my mother's or father's career ambitions in theater. My mother and father were both stage struck and met in a Stella Adler drama class. They were both Method actors, using an acting technique where the desired emotion is brought forward from deep within the resources of the psyche and then given release with, hopefully, the performance of a lifetime.

It was the forties in Manhattan, where actors hung out in cafes, drinking and comparing notes, celebrating, and reviewing the latest openings of off-Broadway plays. They were young dreamers, ready to sell it all for that one big break—the break that would put their name in lights. But until that glorious moment they simply partied at the local corner bars and restaurants. They gossiped, wrote poetry, made music, talked politics, and schemed about how they would become all that they dreamed of becoming. They were shining stars yet to sparkle.

Alfred and Stephanie associated with people whose names later became well known, like Beatrice Arthur, Sean Connery, Luther Henderson, Sergio Leone, Henry Fonda, Bob Hope, Bing Crosby, Gordon Scott, and more. They were the glamorous people who had worked on projects or movies with my parents.

The memories I have of my life long ago with the two of them come back to me now in a random way, sometimes opening old wounds, sometimes giving me momentary comfort. One may doubt the accuracy of the memories of a child, but the small child within me lives on, as it does within all of us, carrying the memory of rain-drenched days when she belonged to a family she loved, no matter how briefly. Children remember far more than adults like to admit, even to themselves. And children will forgive a chaotic family life if, despite the chaos, they still feel loved.

I have checked my memories of my mother and father with relatives and friends who knew them well. I have put the pieces together as they have come to me in flashes and dreams. Where there are empty spaces between the flashes I have told the story as I imagine it to be. Some will question its accuracy and the timeline might be off, but this is the story that lives in me and has spurred me to share my journey to what I lost so long ago. To further expand the reach of my memory, I have used techniques practiced in many tribal cultures, which are described as Calling in the Ancestors. The meditations are profound and are special ways of making contact with the beloved dead. They are preserved today in countries across the world because they have proved their value.

Yet, long before I learned these techniques, before the reading of my father's will, before I knew the truth about my past, reminders of my real father and real mother would come back in sporadic "sightings"–in dreams of scenes, smells, voices, songs, and faces. And with it all would come unbearable feelings of loss and fear.

These reminders welled up one day when I went to the movies with my parents. It was *Butterfield Eight*. I have compared photos of my mother that people sent to me with Elizabeth Taylor, and I think she reminded me of my mother. I also sat behind some woman whose perfume nauseated me.

Sometimes I imagine it might actually have been my mother sitting there. I will never know. But I am sure it was my mother's perfume the woman was wearing. The dread I felt sitting through that movie was unbearable. The feeling has never left me.

When I would ask my adoptive mother about my dreams, she'd shrug and smile and say, "Marcy, you are very inventive. You have dreams about people who you never knew."

Her made-up stories about my beginnings continued throughout my childhood. Was she trying to protect me? No, I think she was trying to protect herself. Once I asked her if she was sure I had never lived with my mother, because who then was the woman I lived with before she adopted me? And who was the blond-haired man who lived with the woman? He used to sing a song with me. Who was he? At that point, my new mother would get angry. "Marcy, how could you remember anything like that? If you do remember a woman, it had to be a foster mother who you lived with before I picked you out to be my daughter. I've told you and told you, you were placed in a foster home at birth. Your birth mother and father didn't want you. I wanted you. I'm the only real mother you've ever had."

But I'd *had* a real mother, Stephanie, and a real father, Alfred, who was the one who named me Robin because he, with his ancient Anishinabe blood, found solace in the woods and loved the birds that returned each year in the spring. I am the daughter of a father who was very tall, very thin, with very blond hair and the bluest eyes I've ever seen. He was handsome, and I learned from others that he was a "charmer." At the same time, he was a man constantly tormented by terrible inner demons. But with my short experience of knowing him, he was a man who, at least with me, was gentle and tender, happy and grinning as I stood in his lap giggling and ruffling his hair. My dearest memory is bouncing on his knee as we sang together. Sometimes he would stop in the middle of our singing, stare at me with his very blue eyes, and I would giggle. Then a big grin would light his face and that was the signal. Off we'd go singing our song as loud as we were able. "O h h h, the bop bop robin goes bop bop bopping along. . . ." No matter what else he might have felt, with me he behaved as if he were happy–until that last day.

Sometimes he would carry me around as he talked. His voice was deep and raspy and calming. I would lay my head down on his shoulder. I loved him. I felt that we belonged together.

As for my mother, I know I am the daughter of a beautiful woman with almond-shaped eyes and hair that fell to her shoulders. Standing beside my father, even in high heels, she looked small and fragile. But her looks were deceptive. I was told that my mother was much tougher than my father.

Wildness was in my father's nature, and when he was drinking, there were furies tearing at him. He'd fly into violent rages, hurl chairs, and slam doors. He would shout at my mother, often. She was the reason for his outbursts. And she, in turn, would break glasses, storm around, throw things.

When my mother was angry, I've been told, her voice grew high-pitched and shrill. At those times, her anger frightened me. I think that's why I've always hated high-pitched voices and any form of dramatic outburst.

My father created his own inner chaos but the battles with my beautiful, demanding mother drove him even more deeply into his private hell. He was depressed or furious a good deal of the time. I know that many of their arguments were over money—the millions my father would inherit someday. My father came from a very famous Canadian family, listed in a Toronto paper as one of the top eight families in the country. To this day there are streets, hospitals, parks, and university halls named after them.

My mother knew what she wanted in life, besides love, and wrote in a letter to her sister, "We have estimated that there is at least one million dollars that we are to inherit some day. . . ."

On that last day I believe that an argument started over money, and I imagine the yelling went something like, "I'll never let you get it." My mother would have fought back, yelling, "Keep your money. Damn it. Get out of here!"

"I will," he would have answered in a resentful, deep voice. "And you'll never get a dime of it," he would have yelled, laughing drunkenly. "Not one single dime. I'll make damn sure of that." And that is exactly what he did—he left her with no money. The front door slammed, and then there was silence in the apartment. It was so quiet it felt as if someone had died.

I am told that he'd vanished in that way before, that he would leave for days, sometimes after bouts of drinking, and sometimes he'd just disappear. Usually my mother lived with his disappearances calmly, as if she knew he'd be back.

The next day we left the apartment for a while, and later that afternoon, when we arrived home from our outing, my mother opened the door to our apartment very quietly, almost as if she were an intruder who'd stolen the key. Slowly she sidled inside and looked around. I followed her and looked around too. Even now I can feel the eerie stillness of the apartment. My mother walked quickly to the bedroom, paused in the doorway, took a deep breath, and looked around again. At last she went in, and I followed. I watched her check in the closet and pull open the bureau drawers. The closet was bare. The bureau drawers were empty. My father was gone.

My father was born into a Canadian family of great wealth and cultivation, which had influenced his actions and style of living. All of this was in his blood. His grandfather was postmaster general of Canada. This grandfather's face was on a Canadian postage stamp and in the news, his portraits in university halls. My father had been raised with the benefits of expensive boarding schools, servants, beautiful homes, and trips abroad. My father's family supported the arts and bought the Royal Alexandra Theatre. His mother raised him to appreciate painting, music, and theater. It was natural, given his background, that he wanted to be a poet, a writer, an actor.

I don't know if it was his potentially large inheritance or his natural charm and good looks that first attracted my mother–probably a bit of each. I have been told that a poor man would never have attracted her.

My mother's family–unlike my father's–was modestly educated, Jewish, and resolutely middle class. My mother, I am told, was brilliant and graduated from high school at age sixteen and college by age twenty.

My mind works differently; I naturally want to go deep inside and seek great wisdom, but I know my inquiring intelligence comes from both my mother and my father. My mother loved theater, just like my father, and was probably a good actress. But I think she loved the theater primarily for the fame it might bring. When my father married my mother, I suspect his family was far from pleased. Their beautiful, white, WASP son marrying a Romanian Jew. How could he do this to them? They showed their displeasure by holding him on a very tight financial leash. To spite them, my father threw away what little money he had and lived as if he were always flat broke. There were times when my parents couldn't pay the rent and had no money for food. Many years later, in my search for information on my parents, I found a trunk full of old family letters. One letter from my mother's doctor, to my father's mother, Adele Mulock, is a grim comment on their married life.

> *I realize you do not know their circumstances here in the city and therefore I take it upon myself to write to you. Both your son and daughter-in-law are suffering from lack of nourishment because of insufficient funds to buy adequate food.*
>
> *At present they are living in a squalid apartment on the East Side, paying, I believe, $19.00 a month rent. I am sure you do not know that they are in debt and that they do not even have funds to provide for their daily needs. . . .*

It's true that my father could have done a number of things to earn money to support the family, but he did nothing. That was another of his ways of defying his mother, "showing" her and his father what they were doing to him.

My mother had the same attitude about work as my father. She was an actress, a dreamer–not a stenographer. If she did look for work, it was in acting, which then was uncertain and unreliable. My mother would have felt dishonored and humiliated if she'd taken a nine-to-five office job. I believe that in her mind it would have seemed an acceptance of her in-laws' judgment that she was "lower class" and "not good enough for them." My mother was too proud for that. She would never surrender to my father's family or anyone else without a fight. And yet, after my father left, she worked at a place like the Club Twenty-One, selling cigarettes and cigars.

My mother kept her relationship with her family a secret from my father. They met and married not long after the end of World War II. In those days, I suspect that between the undercurrent of fear of being Jewish and the social stigma that she assumed her heritage would have in the eyes of his white Anglo Saxon family, she never told him that she was Jewish. Instead, she told him that her mother and sister were her foster family. I am sure she loved her mother, but their relationship was strained. I was also told that the slow disconnect between them began the afternoon my grandmother witnessed her oldest daughter Oreilla get hit by a truck. Miraculously, Oreilla only suffered a broken leg, but the sound of screeching brakes and the image of her child lying in the street never left my grandmother's mind. After that day, Oreilla was treated as extra special and was given every gift she ever wanted, including singing lessons and a grand piano. My mother, on the other hand, also never recovered from the accident—her relationship with her mother changed drastically. Where once she had been the cute baby of the family, she became "the hand me down child." For the rest of her life she had a nagging feeling that she was less worthy than her older sister.

The other fact important to my mother's history was that my grandmother was a "good Jewish woman" and would never have accepted my mother's marriage to my father—a Gentile. Because of this, I was told that my mother kept her elopement with my father a secret from her mother. My grandmother died never knowing her youngest daughter was married and pregnant. I was told that when my grandmother grew ill, it was a few months before I was born. As her mother lay in the hospital, Oreilla covered for her younger sister by telling their mother that Stephanie was out of the country, busy working on a film. My Grandmother died believing her youngest daughter was going to be a star. I surmise that my mother struggled with this sad and deeply internal dilemma for the rest of her life. But I believe that to her, it was an act of compassion—an act of letting her mother die in peace—with no worry that her daughter had perhaps made some bad choices.

Sometimes I wonder what my life would have been like if, when he married, my father's family had given him even as much money as I inherited. I think we would have remained a family, with the standard fights that families have, but a loving family. Given my father's violence, and my mother's fearless nature, however, this may be a fantasy.

In any case, the reality was that they didn't inherit any big money, so my father acted as if he were poor. He owned very little: a few articles of clothing, a Gruen watch with a gold wristband, a fishing pole in a canvas case, a few books, a typewriter–nothing more.

After the last terrible fight, when my mother and I returned to the empty apartment, she found that what little he did own was gone. There was nothing of his anywhere, not in the closet, not in the hall, not in the bureau–nothing.

I went back into the living room to wait for my mother while she looked around in the bedroom. Standing alone, I noticed that my father's black typewriter, books of poetry, and scattered papers were gone from his small table where he worked when he was writing poetry.

My father loved reading and writing poetry so much that I think he longed to be a poet even more than he wanted to be an actor. And when the poetic inspiration came over him, he would type for hours, a cigarette hanging from his lips, not stopping to eat or drink. Then he would suddenly pause, take a long puff, exhale slowly, and lean back to read what he'd typed. When he finished reading, he would take a sip from his bottle of bourbon, which always stood nearby, and moments later the quick clicking of the typewriter would begin again. My father wrote as if there were a savage beast inside him fighting to get out.

Today I think that, besides his ongoing war with my mother, my father was always in a struggle with his personal demons, and bourbon was his way of holding them at bay, keeping away his silent dark days, when he would sit in that chair for hours saying nothing, staring into space. He would slip into a deep despair, which was one part of his true illness: untreated manic depression. My father's injuries were internal, and the wounds to his spirit never healed.

Years later, when the day came that he assessed his wounds, he quietly committed suicide by jumping off a balcony on a movie set. His dream of becoming a great actor was over. I was told that as he lay there on the ground, he asked for one more cigarette, while in the background the director, Sergio Leone, quietly instructed the crew to remove his costume before they rushed him to the hospital–after all, as he saw it, someone would have to replace him. My father died on the way. There are times I can see his face staring out at me from the TV, from his last movie, *Once Upon A Time in the West*. Lucky for me, Sergio Leone liked close-ups–many of them–so I can take a good look at my father's eyes–seek his tortured thoughts–try to understand–relate to his last moments. I see his blue eyes, so lost, so angry, and so confused, staring out at me. And sometimes I hear him say, "Don't go this way, Robin–don't go this way. . . ." That look–that stare–was his last scene for real–his swan song–a turning of a moment. It is a close-up unlike

17

any other in any movie—it is the few minutes, captured on film, before his leap into the heavens.

But that long-ago day, as I stood and stared at the empty table—with the books of poetry gone and the typewriter gone—I knew for certain that my father was gone. Tears began to fall down my cheeks, but I shut my eyes tight to stop them. If I cried, my mother, who was already upset, would hear me and come to see what the matter was, so I started to play with one of my toys and acted as if nothing had happened.

Eventually, my mother did walk back into the living room. She reached for her purse, pulled a cigarette from a silver case, tapped it, and walked slowly to the coffee table where a large round ceramic lighter stood. Her hand was shaking as she lit the cigarette. She took a puff, went to the window, and stood with the cigarette between her lips, one arm folded as if clutching her stomach. She stared out the window for a long while, lost in another world. I was very frightened and stayed absolutely still. There was a terrible, constrained grief in our silence, and I wanted to escape my mother's eyes. After awhile my mother took the cigarette from between her lips, gave a deep sigh, and exhaled the smoke. It was as if she were letting my father go. Tears were brimming in her eyes, but her expression never changed.

After my father left, there was no more singing and no more yelling. The house was dead. There was a melancholy about my mother that never went away. Sometimes she was quiet and preoccupied, as if off somewhere dreaming. Other times she'd jump up without warning and frantically pace around the room. I never knew what would happen next. In a fury for no reason that I could see, she might yell at the air and throw things at my father who wasn't there, or behave in other crazy ways. At those times I think she was delirious. Once she picked up a lamp and threw it against the wall. Watching the lamp break into pieces, I was terrified and I screamed. My screaming startled her. She turned and looked at me sitting on the floor. She stared, surprised to see me and surprised to see my tears. She'd completely forgotten I was there. Kneeling, she picked me up and started comforting me. Then to my surprise she began to sob too. This shocked me so much that I started to hiccup between tears. I must have looked comical because, seeing me hiccupping, she stopped crying and began to laugh. I laughed too, still hiccupping, and then we were suddenly giggling together. After that she tenderly wiped the tears from my cheeks and wiped her own tears with the back of her hand. Perhaps that intimate moment with my mother—a moment where we bonded together with humor—is where my gift and love of humor began.

"I'm so sorry, Robin," she said, not looking at me. "I'm so sorry, so sorry. Mommy has too much on her mind. She's so busy she's a little crazy."

Within minutes she'd regained her composure, cleaned away the lamp fragments, and everything was back to normal. It was as if nothing had happened, as if she hadn't thrown the lamp at the wall, or, to be exact, at my father who wasn't there.

About six months after my father walked out, my mother and her sister were sitting at the kitchen table talking about my mother's problems. I am sure that how to pay the bills was still the main topic. Did my mother tell my aunt that she couldn't handle both her career and me? I have been told that my aunt wanted me and I imagine that she suggested that day that she might take care of me. Did my aunt fight to keep me? What I know is that my mother said no.

At the time I didn't know what a foster home was. I thought it was some kind of playgroup. But over the next few days I began to sense something awful coming.

***

I have one memory of my mother that burns in the deepest part of my heart forever. On our last night together, she took me into her bed and held me. With her warm body close and her arms around me, I felt safe. I stayed very still, hoping nothing would change. She was crying silently, and I felt her warm tears rolling onto my hair, but I stayed quiet, pretending to be asleep. The moisture of her tears was like perspiration, accenting the smell of her skin. Lying so close beside her I felt eternity in a way I do not know how to explain.

"Robin," my mother whispered in my ear, breaking the silence. "Remember, Mommy will take you in her heart." She kissed me and murmured, "You will be with me wherever I go."

Listening to her, I knew she was saying, without saying it, that our life together was ending. So began the pain that has lasted all my life.

First I lost my father. Now I would lose my mother. I would become the ghost in my mother's heart.

Come away, O human child!
To the waters and the wild
With a faery, hand in hand,
For the world's more full of weeping
than you can understand.

–William Butler Yeats, "The Stolen Child"

CHAPTER 4
Foster Homes
My Mother Fill-Ins

When I try to recall what happened the next day, it is all jumbled into one big mess. I feel a numbing cold inside me. I've blocked out a lot of what occurred, so everything about that day and the months and years that followed is blurred. That day happened before I was three. I know that because when I was officially adopted, they gave me a new birth certificate that said I was almost four. So I have attempted to craft a story that is created of moments from frightening flashbacks and feelings retrieved from the deepest parts of my past. Are these memories before I was adopted accurate? I do not know. I do not own my past. I blanked it out for many years. My story–my truth–is to be found in a numbered file on a microfilm. I am certainly not the only child who has suffered from an undocumented bad foster home experience. All I have to hold on to are images, voices with broken sentences, distinct smells and chilling–sometimes heartbreaking–feelings.

The one fact I do know is that my mother let me go. She walked out the door and left me behind in a strange world where I knew no one. There was no warning, no consoling, not even an explanation. And worst of all, she never told me the truth. What she did, as painful as it was for her, she did with precise efficiency. It took a long time for the child within me to accept fully what had happened. In fact, it took me years to accept the depth of my loss, and even more years to learn to trust anyone else again.

I remember strange details about the day my mother gave me away. For example, she was wearing a pleated skirt with a white jersey and I had a perfectly ironed light blue dress. I can still feel the puckered material of the pink embroidery cross-stitched on the bodice. I can smell the starched clean cotton. I sat on a bed with my little legs stretched in front of me as my mother carefully tied my white shoes. These are the memories of my mother's love that comfort me. She kept me clean and well dressed: I cling to that as proof that she had cared.

It was raining that morning. When we were a family, my father invented for me a game called The Raindrop Game. I would follow the slide of raindrops down the window with my index finger, then together we would try to predict where a raindrop would break.

This memory prompted me to ask my mother, "Why do some raindrops break and others don't?" She looked at the window and then at me with my cheek pressed against the cold pane of glass. She didn't answer. Instead she said we were going somewhere. She was busy packing my red valise for the trip. She went into the bathroom. She was standing in her stocking feet, brushing her long hair with cowlicks on either side of the bangs and checking her makeup. What stands out the most about the way she looked was the bright red and perfectly painted nail polish on her fingers. This was typical of my mother. She always dressed as though she were auditioning for a part.

When I asked her again about the raindrops, she stopped packing, and even though she looked at me for a long time, her thoughts seemed far away. She took a breath to answer my question, then changed her mind and exhaled it away, saying nothing. Abstractedly, she ran her fingers through her hair and went back to packing. Watching her, I saw tears streaming down her cheeks, and I was sorry I had mentioned the raindrops. The mother I knew then was deeply unhappy. Even then I had the ability to see into other worlds and I could see a shadow cross her face. Perhaps my asking about the raindrops was a reminder of my father who was gone, and of me–the daughter she was about to leave.

After she finished packing my valise, she brushed my hair with long, loving strokes in front of a mirror. When she finished brushing, she took my hand and we stood together for a minute staring at our images. She whispered something into the mirror. It was as if we were looking through an ancient looking glass and into another realm, perhaps to our souls' connection, which remained intact in a timeless place. What I remember most about that moment was the feeling I had that my mother was proud of how I looked.

She turned from the mirror and finished dressing herself, and me. Then we quickly left the apartment, my mother saying, "We're going to visit a very nice lady." I was to find out that she lied.

The woman we were "visiting" wasn't a "nice lady." She turned out to be an evil woman and above all we were not visiting. My mother was leaving me behind. I was being abandoned.

The rain had stopped; she carried my small valise while I clutched my worn pink elephant stuffed under my arm. Today I can still hear the pace and sound of her spike heels clicking on the wet pavement. It is the sound of my mother's walk the day she gave me away.

We paused on the sidewalk where a dark green car was parked, a car I'd never seen before. Once we got in, she drove what seemed to me a very long distance, and we eventually arrived at a row of brick-and-white ranch houses. We were somewhere in a borough of New York–maybe Queens–on a street where the houses all looked alike. The woman who answered the door was tall and skinny with graying hair tied in a knot. She had a haggard look. She smiled faintly when she bent down to talk to me. Instinctively I moved away. Her closeness frightened me and I clutched my mother's skirt. After the greetings, we went inside. Whenever I see a motel, I am reminded of that house. It was furnished with catalogue furniture, but no family snapshots were on the pale green walls. No knickknacks or flowers, or anything to show that it was a home where people lived. It was clean and orderly and smelled of Clorox and furniture polish. There was no trace of anything to alarm an outsider and no hidden cameras to expose the secret horrors that awaited me.

During the uneasy visit, my mother and the woman, who perpetually smiled, talked. I didn't listen to what they were saying but played on the floor with tinker toys until I sensed my mother was preparing to leave. I looked around and I was right. She had gathered her keys and purse and was standing up to go. I jumped up to run to her, thinking we were going home. The woman stopped me before I could reach my mother. I was initially surprised and I squirmed. She wouldn't let go.

In the midst of this struggle my mother knelt in front of me and said, "Robin, you must stay here. I'll be back tomorrow."

"No," I cried. "I want to go home with you."

"No, Robin. You have to stay here."

"Mommy!" I screamed. "Mommy!"

The woman, still smiling, gripped my arm tightly with one hand and gestured with her free hand for my mother to leave. My mother's eyes were full of tears. She looked at me. Then she quickly turned away and without another word walked out the door. I collapsed onto the floor into a temper tantrum. Sometimes I still hear that helpless child screaming inside me.

I didn't stop screaming until I felt the long cold fingers of my new foster mother carefully squeezing the back of my neck as she pulled me up off the floor. "We will have none of that in this house, Robin," she said calmly.

She carried me up the stairs, still kicking and screaming, to a gray tiled bathroom. Methodically, she turned on the hot water faucet in the tub. I saw the steam rise and drops form on the tiles, and I tried to get away.

"This is what we do to little girls who cry like babies," she said, placing me on the floor and passing my hand quickly under the steaming hot water.

My time with this first foster mother, whom I later named The Hot Water Mom, was a nightmare, and there were more punishments to come. Unfortunately, I know my story is not unique.

***

The memories of this time with that foster mother have often come back to me as flashbacks, as if someone has opened one of many doors and I've stepped into the story. Some moments may have happened differently or

23

are merely wishful thoughts harbored by a lost child, who hoped her mother would rescue her. But the first door I often see belongs to the closet that the foster mother locked me into. The smell of wet wool or old-fashioned shoe polish brings me back to that experience. I pretended the coats were alive, and I even named them The Coat People. They became tall, silent friends hanging in a row, quietly consoling me. Soon I found comfort and safety in the dark space with the coats and galoshes.

On one of my mother's visits to the foster home she brought me a gift of a large pink bear with a soft red muzzle. He had beautiful brown glass eyes and a red ribbon. I called him Pink Bear. He was my best friend. I talked and played with him for hours and I slept each night with my arms around him. I believed he had magical powers.

One afternoon, a few months after my arrival, I remember wedging myself between the wall and the sofa to hide from the foster mother. The rough texture of the material scraped against my cheek. I was scared. I had done something bad but I can't recall what it was. For my foster mother I think it was a macabre game of hide and seek. For me it was a simple act of survival. I waited and hoped she wouldn't find me. But she did find me. I looked up and there she was, leaning against the doorjamb watching me like a bird of prey. She marched over to me, pulled me out from behind the sofa, and dragged me screaming to the closet. She opened the door and pushed me into it.

As I sat there in the dark, I heard the front doorbell ring. I heard the familiar sound of her slippers on the carpet as the foster mother hurried to answer the door. She opened the door and I heard my mother's voice. How could it be my mother? This was not her visiting day, I thought. But I heard my mother and the woman talking. Their voices got louder. My mother's voice grew more demanding. "Where is Robin?" The foster mother started to explain that she was disciplining me.

I heard my mother's high heels go thumping on the carpeted floor. When she opened the closet door, she found me inside, huddled in a corner. I didn't dare look up. The woman came up behind her, still explaining how the discipline was good for children. Hearing her, my mother turned and screamed at her. She picked me up, grabbed my coat, and left with me in her arms. She whisked me out the door, leaving behind everything that was mine, including Pink Bear. We caught a bus at the end of the block. During the long ride, my mother held me close.

"I am so sorry," she said as she rocked me. "I'm so sorry." She said it over and over. "Forgive me, Robin."

I desperately wanted my mother's love. As I settled into the warmth of her arms, I thought, my mommy is taking me home. I am going home.

I was wrong. We didn't go home. Instead my mother took me to Caring Times, the social service agency that had arranged my original placement with the first foster mother. I sat in my mother's lap in the small office, eyeing the new social worker, Joan, who was busy filling out forms. She seemed nice and her voice was very tender and reassuring as she asked my mother different questions. She had beautiful brown eyes that were like those of a young doe. She paused often during the conversation to smile at me. I listened to the talk between Joan and my mother, and I dimly understood that the new foster home would only be temporary. I believe that was the day that my mother conceived the idea of letting me go for good.

"Have you thought of a permanent home?" Joan might have asked.

"No, not yet," my mother might have answered. Joan's gentle attention and kindness made me want to cry.

"Well, I think we will have to think about Robin. The longer we wait the harder it will be for her," she said.

That afternoon, my mother, pressed for time, left me with Joan. I beli eve that she was up for a big part in a new play, and she couldn't afford to be late for the audition.

I held on tightly to Joan's very cool, slender hand as we left the building, and began our trip to a second foster home. Joan seemed to be a quiet kind of person, and as we drove to the new place, she told me—in a very calm, reassuring voice—about my new foster home, where there would be other children and a black and white collie type dog. I never forgot the feeling I had when I was around Joan. She felt like an angel.

In the beginning I was overwhelmed by the chaos and activity of the new place. It was such a contrast to my previous one, where there had been no other children. Instead of a house that was sterile and silent, now there were many children running around in a house full of knickknacks, pets, and lots of toys strewn all over the place. I slept with three other children in a room painted a bright yellow with white trim and red and white seersucker curtains.

I quickly adjusted from my ordeal and within a few days I was running around with the other children. My new foster mother was kind and patient. She had a sweet, lyrical voice and a soft giggle that matched her well-rounded looks, which were a lot like Doris Day's.

Soon after my arrival at the new foster home, my small red valise also arrived. My new foster mother opened it for me in my bedroom. I knew in my heart that Pink Bear was too big to fit into the valise, but I kept hoping he'd been packed with my clothes. But he wasn't. Pink Bear was gone forever. By the time the red valise arrived, the loss of my beloved Pink Bear was greater than the loss of my beloved mother. The split between my mother and me had widened into a chasm, and I no longer reached out for her. My mother was becoming a stranger.

The last time my mother visited me, I went on playing with the other children instead of running to her. And she didn't ask to see me either. Her entire visit was spent with my Doris Day Mom. It was raining during her visit, so I was playing inside the house, near the window at the top of the stairs overlooking the driveway. I could hear the two women downstairs talking, and my new foster mother seemed to be soothing my mother. I think now their conversation had something to do with my mother saying she was giving me up for adoption. But that's a guess. Only one thing about that visit stands out—the exact moment when my mother left. It was a strange experience. Without my Doris Day Mom saying a word, without my mother saying anything, I knew this was the last time I would ever see my mother. And, knowing this, I didn't want to hold her close. There'd always been pain when we said goodbye, but this goodbye I couldn't bear—the "goodbye forever" goodbye.

I'd always known when my mother was about to leave, even when I was in another room or at the other end of the house. I sensed it this time too. Suddenly I jumped up and ran to the window. Looking out, I heard the front door open, and I knew it wasn't one of the children going out in the rain for something. I knew it would be my mother leaving.

Then I saw her. She stepped out the door and ran through the light rain to the cab. A lump came into my throat. I wanted to call to her to come back, not to go, to wait for me, but I did nothing. I stood still. I don't remember if I cried. I just remember that I watched her get into a cab for the last time. And that I could hear the rain as it hit the glass pane—ever so gently.

I turned away from the window and stopped. I wanted to fall down and sob. Instead a dry, stark wave of despair overcame me. I saw a bright, glowing light flickering at the far end of the hallway. And even as I saw the light, I heard a rushing sound swirling around me. I now recognize the sensation as the sound of angel wings. My guardian spirit had come to stand beside me, to give me courage and help me say goodbye to my mother forever.

That day was the beginning of the end of my foster home. In the weeks after my mother's last visit—though I didn't realize it then—I would be put up for adoption.

CHAPTER 5
The Adoption
Mama Can You Find Me?

As with everything else in my first three years, my adoption happened suddenly. One meeting in the director's office to meet Mr. and Mrs. Neilson–known as Frances and Winthrop, who now would be my new parents, and then . . . poof! The foster family life that I had come to rely on was gone.

The experience of leaving my Doris Day Mom haunts me like an empty box that I keep opening. Nothing is there. No name. No scent. No memento. Nothing. I cannot retrieve the moment of the "forever goodbye" with her. I know that I am grateful for the Doris Day Mom. She was only a passing moment in my life, but she held me in her arms and with her special laugh, she calmed my heart.

I do know that I recall that goodbye moment whenever I see a story on the news about an adoption case, where two sets of parents fight over their rights to a single child and I watch the grieving parents as they let go with tears rolling down their cheeks and I hear the child's piercing screams. At those times my heart sinks, and I feel it bleed a thousand moments of my pain.

In contrast, the meeting that led to my adoption felt like an "Oh, by the way" kind of thing, as if they were talking about the weather. It went something like this:

"Robin, this is Mr. and Mrs. Neilson."

"Hello. How are you?" they said. "Nice to meet you. We are your new parents and we will be taking you home tomorrow."

I clung even tighter to Joan's knee and started to twist her skirt nervously in my hand as I looked around the room and saw my new father sitting in a large, dark leather chair in the corner. He seemed to be a simple and gentle man and even though he had very white hair and a well-trimmed mustache and came across as sophisticated, I sensed that he was just as shy as I was and spoke very little.

I watched him quietly watch me, while my new mother busied herself by flirting with the director. Every once in a while, we would catch each other's glance and he would grin nervously at me. Soon, amidst the buzz and chatter of the adults around us, we were playing a secret game of peek-a-boo. First he glanced at me. Then I glanced at him. Then he glanced at me again! Finally, I gave him a shy but real smile. And he smiled back.

"Do you want to blow out the match?" he asked me, while lighting his pipe. He held it out to me. Everyone became silent to see what I would do. I paused, staring at the small yellow flame. Cautiously I marched over to him and gave a big, childlike puff. He struck another match and held it out. I giggled and blew it out again. We all laughed.

"Would you like to sit here with me?"

I looked up at him, and without thinking I crawled right into his lap. It was as if we had known each other before that day.

On the other hand, my new mother was a different story. She sat on the sofa, smiling at me. She was a dead ringer for a young Bette Davis and she had many of the same scary mannerisms and facial expressions. Frances was the opposite of her husband; she wore fancy clothes and had a beautiful emerald band on her finger.

I stared apprehensively at my new mother as I sat on Winthrop's knee. I didn't like her. Not that she had done anything to deserve my rejection. I just didn't like her.

"Make that lady go away," I ordered my new father.

Everyone laughed uncomfortably. Frances pouted a bit, but smiled quickly, as if to brush it off.

"It will take time for Robin to adjust," the director assured her.

"Just give her time and she will be crawling up in your lap, too." They all laughed and nodded.

"Yes. Yes, she will be doing that in no time," Joan said.

No, I won't. No one is going to make me do that, I thought.

"Go away," I said again. "Go away."

***

Frances did not go away. No, quite the opposite. It all happened so fast. By the next day, I was sitting next to her as we drove down the highway toward my new home. I was told that two older brothers, four whippets, a greyhound, a tortoise, and a black cat were waiting for me there.

Frances pulled me close to her. As I squirmed she said, "Your father and I want to talk to you about your name."

I looked up at her.

"Your mother named you Robin and since your mother didn't love you . . . well . . ."

"What?" I interrupted. I glared up at her. She turned and looked down at me and smiled.

"No, she didn't love you. You poor little thing." She squeezed me tighter.

I squirmed more.

"You do know that she didn't love you? Don't you?"

I shook my head no.

28

She laughed.

"After all, she gave you away. Didn't she?"

Silence.

"But we love you, dear."

More silence.

What does she mean my Mommy doesn't love me? I thought. No one had ever told me that before. Joan never told me that. The director never told me that, the foster mothers never told me that. But my new mother was telling me. Frances Fullerton Neilson, with a swiftness akin to cutting a cord, was altering my reality regarding my mother's love. And she was doing it with a tone of cold authority.

I felt myself begin to shut down inside. It felt like a steel door closing. I knew right then and there that I wasn't going to like what came next.

"So, Robin, we want to give you a nice new name to go with your nice new Mommy and Daddy."

I put my hands to my ears.

"We want to call you Marcy."

I was silent.

"It is the name of a beautiful brook near our summer home in the Adirondacks."

"I will take you fishing there," my father said.

"Yes, it is a beautiful place! So now let's hear you say your name," Frances ordered.

Again I was silent.

"Marcy, I am waiting to hear you."

"Marcy," I finally answered with a deep, unsettled loathing. This new name brought only one reality home to me, and that was that my mother hadn't loved me.

About an hour and a half later we turned down a long gravel driveway that led through woods to a beautiful gray and white house with a weathervane on its roof. There were trees and open land everywhere and I quickly noticed that my new world was strange and luxurious compared to my old world. It was a startling contrast and seemed so far away from what was familiar. No city stench. No brick buildings. No other children crowded into small rooms. No diaper pails. No dirty dishes. Nothing. All of it was missing.

When we arrived home my new older brothers, Jock and Wink, awaited our arrival. My brothers opened the front door and out poured all the animals. It was a *grand* welcome. There were many new people and many new sights. Maybe in any other circumstance it would have been wonderful. Instead it was overwhelming. By late afternoon I found myself in my new room sitting on my antique bed, crying hysterically, as I looked around at my new world—the beautifully decorated room with a linoleum floor with nursery rhymes printed on it, the picture of a guardian angel helping children in a storm, the piles of new toys, the pretty clothes. It all meant nothing to me at that moment. On that cold November afternoon with all of the newness, glamour, and glitter, the only thing I could think about was, how would my real mother ever be able to find me?

Mother II
The Neilson Family
1953-1967

For the road to the Faery is strewn with
thorn thickets and glamoury.
This ancient inner path has been long
neglected by an arrogant humanity
and the Fay beings will test the seeker.

—Orion Foxwood, *The Faery Teachings*

CHAPTER 6
Frances
My Adoptive Mother

My mother never did find me. I don't know if she even looked for me or asked how I was doing. I believe she suffered quietly in her own way, because not long ago a friend of my mother's did tell me that in a private moment, just before she died, she said, "I wish I had searched for Robin."

I like to imagine that in those early years, whenever she saw a little girl with dark hair with cowlicks, round cheeks, and piercing dark brown eyes, she would whisper to the child, "Robin, is that you?" It comforts my soul to imagine this.

My truth is that my mother, Stephanie, haunted me throughout my childhood. Sometimes when I saw her it was for real, like when her face appeared in a commercial on TV, on a sitcom, or in a magazine. I would stare blankly at the screen and not remember the face. Instead I would feel nauseous. Then there were times when I sensed that I had crossed paths with her on the street or smelled her familiar perfume at a movie, or maybe I imagined that I saw her when I received an inquisitive glance from a stranger. Though lost to me, my mother was there. Her ghost was a constant nagging–a tugging at me to pay attention and not to forget that I was special. But my new mother–Frances–had another agenda and that was to squelch any fragments of Stephanie's existence that might have remained in my life. I fought hard to keep my real mother alive in my memory, and I fought even harder not to lose Robin. But I lost both.

For me, growing up with the Neilsons was like having a map without helpful keys or reference points. After the roots of the foundation to my origins had been cut away, all I had left was a feeling of emptiness–a dark space, a sealed tomb, a veiled mirror.

From the day I walked into the Neilson family to the day I left them behind, it was always the same. It was always about their plans for who Marcy would become. But who was Marcy? To survive I became, in time, a ghostly reflection of myself. And after much resistance I became Frances' daughter.

***

Who was Frances? Who was this woman who shaped my life, became my new mother, and guided me into adulthood? Who was this woman who for better or for worse created a mother bond with me? I called her "Mother," not Mommy or Mamma.

I have mixed feelings about her because, while we did share some bonding moments when I was a child, she also caused many nightmare experiences for me. She could be dramatically loving, sweetly cunning, and most of all unpredictable. When I look back, I see that I was very young, very lost, and very vulnerable. When I arrived at the Neilsons' home, I needed a mother and Frances had to do. Frances had always wanted a daughter and after giving birth to two sons, she tried very hard to have more children but each ended with a late-term miscarriage. In some strange way, because she so desperately wanted the mother-daughter relationship, I felt sorry for her and tried to please her.

When I talk to my friends about my childhood and Frances, they have no tolerance for what she did to me, and they often ask me, with frustration in their voices, "How can you have mixed feelings and even fondness for her? How can you be so generous?"

I answer, "I was a child needing a mother and she was a mother needing a daughter. Children are more forgiving than adults." But it goes deeper than that simple response, because I know there was more to Frances than most people knew.

Even with Frances, I believe destiny brought us together. Why? I am not sure—but I trust the path my life has taken. It has shaped me and made me wiser. At a very early age, I practiced being brave and simply witnessing others in silence. Frances, whom I called Mother, was a creative woman who helped give me, at times, a world of fantasy and, at other times, moments of horror. I think she intuitively knew about the mystical realms, and in some ways it served as a balance for the conflicting personality that struggled inside her.

We had some strange, mystical experiences together. As, for example, when our dog was killed. High was a white whippet that tragically ran into a protruding wire in a fence and died instantly. One of the gardeners found him that afternoon and reported it to my mother.

"Win, come here quickly," she called down the hall to my father.

"What? What is it, dear?" he asked as he entered the room.

"High has been killed." Her voice trembled with horror. Father looked at her and then at the gardener and then back to her. He said nothing as he bit down on his pipe. He seemed to be searching for an answer.

"You can bury him in the woods," he finally instructed the gardener as he put his arm around Mother's shoulders. Mother's face was ashen. Over the years I noticed that she had a habit of filling a bad moment with all the right expressions and this was one of those times. She looked down at me. "Marcy, why don't you go play outside and ride your new bike," she instructed. She then quietly turned away from everyone and disappeared into the bedroom, closing the door behind her. No one saw her again until that evening.

I kept out of everyone's way, dealing with my grief in the way many children do—with simple acceptance and play. I stayed outside most of the day until it began to get dark. It was a very clear, brisk fall evening and I was beginning to feel sad. High would not be coming home. He was one of our four whippets and a quiet dog. He had been my favorite. Mother had given him to me the day I arrived in the family. It was my dog that had died—not hers.

I was putting my bike away that evening, and I was thinking about High and where he might be. Had he gone to heaven? Or was he still in the ground? I looked up at the sky, hoping he had gone to heaven. Suddenly I saw something extraordinary. Against the early evening sky appeared the beautiful shape of a whippet. It looked just like a paper cutout of the Greyhound Bus logo. The shape was shining like a bright moon and was moving across the sky with a slow but consistent pace. Behind the whippet image were two very large, hazy, round balls. They looked like glowing stars. These two stars were following the moon/dog across the sky. It was all very strange, but as I watched it, I knew that I was seeing something very special. I ran into the house to get Mother.

"Mother, High is in the sky!" I said as I ran into her bedroom where she was lying on her bed reading.

"What are you talking about?" she asked as she looked up from her book.

"Hurry! Come with me," I said as I pulled her hand and tried to drag her outside. She finally put the book down, sat up, and went out to the driveway with me.

"Look! There is High in the sky," I said, pointing up to the image.

Mother looked up and then gasped. I watched her as she gazed up at the stars, clasping her hands to her chest. I smiled.

"Yes, look! Those two glowing lights are the angels taking High to heaven," she said, pointing to the lights.

"They are?" I hadn't thought of that.

"Yes, they are taking him to heaven," she whispered. Tears rolled down her cheeks.

"I want Father to see this too," I said. I quickly ran to my father's studio, where he was working. I burst into the room.

"Father, High is in the sky!" I said as I dragged him away from his desk, down the stairs and outside, where Mother was still gazing up at the sky. Just as Father and I arrived, the last bit of High's body was going behind the dark tree line and the glowing fuzzy stars were following. No one said anything.

***

One day, when I was a teenager, I asked Mother about that evening. "Do you remember the day High died?"

"Yes."

"Do you remember seeing High in the sky?" I looked straight at her.

"No, I didn't actually see him," she said, smiling back at me.

"What do you mean, no?" I was deeply disappointed by her dismissive response.

"Marcy, I can tell you the truth now." She paused, looking for the right words.

"The truth? What do you mean, the truth?"

"You were so insistent and convinced that you saw High, that I just went along with you."

"No. You didn't!"

"Yes, I did."

"But?"

"It was a sad night and it seemed to make you happy." She smiled again.

"But?"

"No buts, Marcy. I didn't see anything." She was getting agitated, as if I were pushing her to reveal some unsettling secret of hers.

"But you saw the angels," I said. "I don't understand why you are denying it."

"No, I did not see the angels."

"I know you did," I insisted.

"No, I didn't." With that, she changed the subject.

I knew she was lying at that moment, because what she had forgotten was a small but important detail. It was something that, to me as a young child, had meant the world. It was a small fact that I had secretly hung on to all my life as proof that it had happened. Also, it had been an intimate moment between us—that night, when she had turned to me and said, "Look. Those two glowing lights are the angels taking High to heaven." Her words had validated what I was seeing. For once, I didn't feel so alone with my psychic gifts.

What she did not remember was that when I had dragged her outside that night, I hadn't mentioned the large fuzzy glowing stars following High. She had seen the angels on her own. I know it. And for whatever reason, she needed to vehemently deny that reality, as if she were afraid to admit what she had seen. Maybe Frances' mother had squelched *her* daughter's psychic gifts, but I would not let anyone do that to me.

36

I wish Frances could have been the woman who, in quiet moments, shared dreams and fairy tales. I would have loved her. We could have experienced the world of fantasy and children's classics; we could have explored the pleasure of world culture and the arts. We did in some ways, but they are the fragmented memories of Mother reading to me, or rescuing a wounded animal, or me listening to her tell a story with an artistic flair. There was so much about her I could have admired. I could have respected her strength—her *joi de vivre*. How it breaks my heart to know it was different.

Mother exhibited unexplainable and sudden behaviors that reflected how truly disturbed a woman she was, but in those days, it was easier to hide psychotic and destructive behavior behind the stoic and well-mannered rules of society. She wanted to love me, own me, make me a little version of herself and even though I often rejected her and was aloof, I longed for a mother. The truth is that neither one of us could love the other in the way the other needed.

She had certain expectations for both of us. This was reflected in my clothes, which were made to order to match hers. In some ways, I served to heal her childhood wounds, but these wounds still festered inside her, and she cultivated a mean streak, which she expressed in the most unpredictable ways. One moment she would be sweet, loving, a mother figure straight out of a picture book. Then the next moment, without warning, she would turn into a nasty, cruel woman who abused me in very discreet and subtle ways.

***

My childhood was not all bad. There were magical moments, when spirits reigned and teddy bears ruled. My mother's Uncle Erin was one of those spirits. His portrait was one of two family icons that stood out among the antiques and knickknacks. He was our family ghost on Mother's side of the family. He was a descendant of the Knights of the Round Table. This austere painting initially hung over the fireplace in the west wing living room. The portrait moved into every new house and apartment we ever lived in, whether it was across the ocean or a few miles away. It was one of those old paintings where the eyes followed you as you walked by; it scared me as a young child. I was always aware of his presence and his subtle influence on our psyches. The family credited him with the unexplainable events that happened periodically, such as water faucets turning on, lights going out, and money appearing from nowhere. Whether the luck was good or bad, we attributed it all to Uncle Erin's presence in the home.

The second icon of great importance was quite different and had the opposite effect on the children. It was dear Chubbins, a turn-of-the-century teddy bear that had belonged to my mother as a child. He was magical and sat with grandeur on the chaise lounge in my parents' bedroom. Chubbins was the symbol of honor and truth in the Neilson family. As children, we would swear the truth by Chubbins, or make promises and, just like swearing on the Holy Bible, no one dared doubt the word of the person making the oath. As strange as it sounds, Chubbins, a teddy bear, held the hidden honor and integrity of the Neilson family.

Mother could be caring, for example, when she brought a starving kitten home, or carried a little Steiff teddy bear in her purse just in case a child needed it in an emergency. And she had her humorous moments, such as the time she bought a very expensive Amazon parrot that bit and swore at the top of its lungs. Mother's face explained it all, when, within an hour of its arrival, it began to swear nonstop. Armando was his name, and he lasted only a day in our proper home. Mother, with her English background, did not tolerate any swearing or bad words.

Her affection often emerged in the afternoons when she read the fairy tales and English classics to me, like *The Secret Garden*, or *The Princess and Curdie*, *Peter Pan*, and *Anne of Green Gables*. I will always be grateful to her for introducing me to *At the Back of the North Wind* by George MacDonald. This one story has remained with me all my life. It was my first glimpse of the Goddess, portrayed as the chilling North Wind, who came and gently led an ailing child to his death. But in those moments, it did not matter what the story was really about because, with a teddy bear under one of her arms and me under the other, we were the model upon which English classics are made.

Mother also taught me about the Goddess, about Persephone, daughter of Demeter, who, just like me, had lost her mother. It was moments like these that made me forget the other times when the storms, and the horrors, changed her demeanor and she became crazed. I know that these tales of heroines and fairies helped guide me out of the dark places of my childhood when I felt alone.

I believe that her glamorous dream world balanced the inner demons that tore at her psyche. I saw the horror that lived inside her. It was a dark secret that gave her migraines. When the inner torment became too much for her, she acted these horrors out on her children.

My mother's room always had a timeless air; the same paintings, furniture, and even the same baby pillows—and the silver-framed photo of Mother, taken when she was in her early thirties—went wherever we lived. As I look back on it, I am once again amazed at how much she looked like a young Bette Davis. Mother's room looked the same, no matter where we traveled. The stuffed Steiff teddy bears were always neatly arranged, and on the bedside table was the little Black Book of Books. I was five years old the day I became aware of the power of that book.

"Frank Sinatra can't get into this book," my mother boasted while pointing at the little black book with the gold title. It was the New York Social Register and it had arrived in the morning's mail.

"They say he has Mafia connections," she whispered, even though there was no one else in the room to hear us. "But look, Marcy, your name is right there in fine print," she tapped her finger right on the line that spelled out my name and announced me as the daughter of Winthrop and Frances Neilson. She continued to leaf eagerly through the book, stopping every once in a while to show me the name of someone we knew.

"We paid an enormous amount of money to get you legally made our daughter," Mother said. I looked up at her.

"Did you know that?"

"Yes," I said, nodding.

She smiled at me and adjusted my bangs and the barrette that held "my god-awful cowlick" (as she put it), the cowlick that she was always trying to control. To this day, I laugh and think that my cowlick was the one outward thing my new mother could not control or change about me. Once, out of frustration, she grabbed some scissors and cut my cowlick so short that it stuck straight up, and for weeks I looked like I had a mini palm tree on the top of my head.

"Now that we have legalized your name, you can reap all the benefits of a good family," she continued.

"Like what?" I asked.

"Like having your name in here," she answered as she closed the book and carefully placed it on the bedside table.

I had no idea what she was talking about, but it didn't matter at that moment because everything felt good. I had been cuddling on the chaise lounge with her, basking in the sun and the warmth of her motherly love. My mother was happy at that moment and all was perfect. Moments like these became my fondest memories of our time together.

***

I was raised in the company of the glamorous and creative. For example, there were cocktails with Robert Frost, a quiet man, and Igor Stravinsky, who was dramatic and who loved me as a little girl. He even asked my parents if he could take me away for a year to his home to live. I think he lived in California. I remember his heavy accent. "She's a natural!" he said. This all came about because I liked to make up music on the piano, and when he would visit I would dress up, playact, and sing for him. One day after dinner I sang a tune at the top of my lungs that came from the film *Gigi*. Of course I had no idea who he was, or I might have been intimidated by his importance in the music world. I just loved to sing in those days.

And then there was the artist Willem De Kooning and his wife. My father had a show in Rome, and I had my photo taken with him for a matchbook.

While we were there, of course the Neilsons had a private visit with Pope Pius XII. They were to have their book—*Letter to Philemon*—blessed. He was a gentle, kind man. It was very quiet in the high-ceilinged room as we waited for our visit. Everyone was whispering. When the Pope reached out his hand for me to kneel and kiss his ring, he smiled. I smiled back, looked him straight in the eye, and then, unbeknownst to him, I pretended to kiss it—but I did not kiss the Pope's hand. Even in those days I was a rebel in a frilly dress.

My parents lived on a trust from my adoptive father's family connection to Alcoa, and gained additional income from the books they wrote: the Bruce Benson series, historical novels, Christian tales, UNICEF pamphlets, and more. They loved to take short visits to Europe to do research for their writing. Consequently, the excruciating hours spent on planes traveling back and forth across the ocean left a greater impression on me than the actual visits to Rome, Paris, Lisbon, Madrid, Casablanca, and other places.

In the beginning, we lived in Manhattan where I attended the most proper schools; after all, I was being groomed to be a debutante. My afternoons were spent at cotillion, at the Junior League, drama school, and at piano lessons. Saturday afternoons were filled with ballets, theater, the opera, and, oh yes, we had weekly dinners at the Russian Tea Room to practice proper etiquette. I was raised by nannies and presented at cocktail parties, where I sometimes felt like another object in my parents' collection. I was their token worthy cause and a conversational piece.

When I was about five or six, Boris Karloff came to a party in our Manhattan apartment. I felt an immediate attachment to him. Why, I do not know. Perhaps because he was a very kind man, soft-spoken and not at all like the monsters he had played in the movies. I monopolized his attention and threw myself on his lap, tossing up my dress and asking him to tickle my back. Everyone laughed out loud and thought this was cute, except for my mother, who was mortified. She had this uncanny ability to stare across the room and move her forehead in a way that conveyed her disgust. No matter what age you were, if you were the target of that cold stare, you never forgot it. Needless to say, as soon as she could grab me without making a scene, she escorted me out of the room and sent me to bed without dinner for my so-called seductive behavior toward Boris.

Mother favored and flattered her sons and trained me and my adoptive sister Kaleen, who came along later, to be wives of wealthy men. We were to have style, class, and dignity. Her many pearls of motherly wisdom, directed at her daughters, went something like this: "Never embarrass yourself. It is better to be underdressed at a party than overdressed. People with class wash their elbows. Smile, and don't be too forward. No one likes a pushy woman." The list of instructions went on and on.

She also had many truths and many rules. I can hear Mother's stern voice saying, "Always make your bed, Marcy. Never let anyone make it for you." It was one of those Mother-Truth statements. Why you had to make your own bed, I have no idea. It was just one of those things taken for truth.

There was one terrible incident involving Mother and me that could be titled *What Went Wrong*. It illuminates for me a bigger picture composed of many nightmare moments, the horrors of which still live on. I was about four years old. The night before, we had arrived home from Captiva, Florida. Mother was in the bathroom. I was sitting on a chair at the mahogany dining table, propped up on a phone book in order to reach the table. I see myself with big brown bean eyes, a little freckled nose, large round cheeks, and neatly clipped bangs. I was wearing a red barrette and a plaid jumper. I was stirring my soggy cereal. I could hear Mother busily clattering around the sink. Then she called out to me. "Have you finished your cereal yet?"

"Almost," I answered, and quickly scooped up a spoonful of sugar, milk, and flakes. It tasted horrible! I held it in my cheeks and thought I would gag if I swallowed any more of the slimy mess, but I knew that I would not be allowed to leave the table until the bowl was empty. I found myself daydreaming about Captiva breakfasts, which were so different from this one. I loved the pink grapefruits sprinkled with a little sugar, the powdered-sugar donuts, and the sound of the breeze in the palms, the smell of salt water, the sun, and the anticipation of adventures in the upcoming day.

The Neilsons flew with me to Captiva shortly after I was adopted. It was described as "a vacation for us to get to know each other." We lived in a small waterfront cottage where I played on the beach every day collecting beautiful shells and silver driftwood. I liked to play alone and sometimes, when no one could see me, I imagined that my real mother was the sun. I would stand on the beach with my arms wide open and my eyes closed and I could feel the warmth of her presence right there with me.

At sunset the residents of Captiva would go to the beach to watch the special green flash that occurred as the sun slipped into the sea. Not everyone could see it. The residents said that you had to be special and have a quick eye. I was one of the lucky ones because I could see the flash every time. I would run to the edge of the water and stand alone watching. During one particular sunset, I was overwhelmed with sadness. I suddenly knew what I had to do to survive in my new family, and so, with no one's knowledge and with a broken heart, I let my birth mother go. I watched her slip, like the bright red sun, into the water. There was a green flash and she was gone–my Mommy memory gone forever. The faint hues began to fade and I closed my eyes, holding back the tears, while the sound of the waves' gentle lapping comforted me. And soon after that evening, Robin too, followed her.

"Marcy, come here," my mother called from the bathroom, interrupting my thoughts. Her voice sounded different. It had an unfamiliar tone to it. For a minute I thought she was playing: acting, or something. I climbed down from my chair and approached the bathroom. The door was ajar. I took slow little steps. I could smell the Dutch Cleanser that she had just used on the sink. Although the tone of her voice was different, it had a ring to it that warned me that something was wrong and I stopped in the doorway and looked up at her. I was no taller than the doorknob because I was resting my head next to it. I really did not want to go into the bathroom alone with her. My four short years had taught me what adults can do when crazed.

"Come here," she repeated.

She was standing next to the sink with a sponge in her hand. I could feel her impatience.

"You need to be cleaned."

My little lip quivered and my eyes filled up as I asked, "Why?"

"Because you are a dirty little girl; you are dirty, just like this sink."

She looked at me. Her face was half an inch from my nose. It seemed large and distorted. Her breath smelled of the Dr. Lyon's tooth powder that sat on the sink. She had a very high widow's peak and a deep creased wrinkle over the bridge of her nose from frowning. Her eyes, though actually hazel, were black at that moment and she stared directly at me. She went back to the sink and heaped the abrasive powder on the sponge.

"We are going to have to give you a good scrubbing," she said. She pulled my pants down and began to scrub, mumbling over and over, "Dirty girl, dirty girl, you are just a dirty girl." She continued until I became raw and sore. It was an unbearable moment in my life, and the memory of the stinging still horrifies me.

In later years I never could guess what would shock her back into reality. That day it was the doorbell ringing. The depilatorist had arrived to wax my mother's legs. That became my ongoing challenge: to avoid the moments when she became utterly irrational.

Who was Mother aside from these horrible episodes? From what I know, she was of English and Russian descent. Her mother was an eccentric, beautiful concert pianist. Her father had been a handsome Russian soldier.

I can still see Mother walking down Manhattan's Fifth Avenue in her leopard-skin coat, carrying a shiny black purse and wearing matching heels. It is a crisp fall day filled with tall skyscrapers and lavish store windows. This was her idea of absolute perfection.

She loved the social life, loved to entertain, and threw great parties. People of all ages came. But her own age was another mystery to all of us. No one really knew. Once, on her birthday, I asked, "Weren't you forty-two last year?" I got a "How could you" glare from the whole family. I quickly learned that this was the way we did Mother's birthdays and the following year I did not ask the same question.

Mother believed that the man ran the show, and I think that deep inside she resented this fact, which explained many of her manipulative and seductive behaviors. Mother flirted with every man she ever met. She hated women and instilled in her children the idea that women were not to be trusted. Consequently, she never had a close female friend.

When I was in my teens and had started to take myself seriously as an artist, I noticed a small watercolor she had painted that had once hung in a discreet place in our Long Island house.

"Mother, this is a beautiful painting and far better than any of Father's big oils," I told her once.

"I know."

"Why don't you paint more?"

She smiled, lighting up like a naughty little girl with a secret. "I know, dear, but it would ruin your father if I took up painting and was better than he is," she answered. I think she really believed that, and maybe it was true, but Mother never did another painting. Perhaps it was her dream unrealized.

Mother loved elaborate stories, such as the time Winnie Churchill chaperoned her on the boat across the ocean and was the man who presented her to the Queen of England, or how she confronted Charles Lindbergh, whom she referred to as a wicked, stoic man, who threw his oldest child in deep water just to teach him to swim.

There was also the story of her conniving sister, Aunt Bunny, who lived in a mansion in California and had once deliberately broken a strand of pearls at a ball, to get all the men down on their knees to gather them for her. There was a story about her best friend from Holland, whom none of us ever met, who barely escaped the Nazis by hiding in a hay wagon in order to cross the border to freedom. The greater the number of martinis, the larger and brighter the stories became. The tales went on and on and new ones were created daily. It was clear to all of us that she had an aversion to what was plain or simple.

"The ordinary people," as she put it, "were a dreadful bore."

"Don't ever be a bore" was another rule she had for her children.

She never raised her voice, but she had complete command over her children. She had a way of saying things that made them come across as non-negotiable. She was unpredictable and one never knew what she would say next.

I remember one day in particular, when she announced to me with all sincerity, "Marcy, you are not from blue blood, and that is your problem."

I didn't know I had a problem, and to tell the truth, I had no idea what blue blood was. For a long time, I thought it was the blue ink stamped on the skin of roast beef at the market. So my four-year-old self concluded that cows had blue blood and I didn't.

Some of her statements went much deeper and cut sharply into my sense of self-worth. "Do you know how much we paid for you?" was one. Another was, "I know why you are crazy. Your mother was a lunatic and she is now locked up in an institution. That's why she gave you away." She could always find the zinger, and I . . . over time, I completely withdrew from her, afraid of what she would say next.

One night, Mother tucked me into bed. I was sitting up straight under the covers, hands together in prayer fashion, reciting the "Now I Lay Me Down to Sleep" prayer for her. She was staring at me, teary-eyed.

"You know, Marcy, the reason you don't love your Mommy is because of what the agency told us," she said as she paused and stroked my hair. "They said that you will never be able to love me, or anyone else–probably never!" she continued. "They said you were broken. That's the word they used, Marcy, 'broken'. "

I didn't respond. Instead, I began to recite my prayers again: "Now I lay me down to sleep. . . ."

"And that's why we took you home," she interrupted.

I continued, "I pray the Lord my soul to keep. . . ."

"You were just a little, broken girl." She sighed and then hugged me.

After she closed the door, I lay in the dark and I thought about what she had said. I did not know whether she had been actually trying to love me at that moment or was just telling me what was wrong with me. That was Mother's style–one never quite knew.

But I know that I went to sleep that night feeling broken.

***

After that night, I prayed to the fairies, or angels, or anyone, to please take me away. One night, not long after that incident, I was staring at the soft moonlight on the lawn outside my window when the room began to light up. I saw the fairies, the ones the Irish speak about. They were just little silent lights and I didn't feel alone or misunderstood anymore.

I loved the fairies and found joy in the woods, where I played for hours, alone and content, pretending that I was a fairy priestess. An old beech tree became my new home and, like the Druid Merlin in the old myths, I prayed to my beech tree as the Father Tree. I would press my cheek up against the trunk as I wrapped my arms around it. "I love you," I would whisper. I could feel the cold dark bark scraping me and I could smell the green wood and the moist leaves from the forest floor. I felt so alive. I danced circles around large stones like the Fey queen in the picture books. I built homes out of branches, and pretended I was a character from one of my favorite books, *The Wind in the Willows*. Over and over again, I schemed of ways to run away to the forest. I was happy.

***

We had a back porch that overlooked my favorite section of the woods, which I called the fairyland. In the summer we often had breakfast out there. We sat at a white, wrought iron glass-topped table, which was always meticulously set with pastel linen napkins and fine china. Our day often began with the smell of fresh-squeezed orange juice and buckwheat pancakes along with the sound of morning birds. It was simple joy.

One particular morning we ate our breakfast inside in the formal dining room, because the cushions on the porch were wet from a huge thunderstorm the night before. Right after breakfast I ran out to the porch to play. As I was kneeling on the floor, playing with a small set of cowboys and Indians, I spied a dead bird under a chair. For whatever reason, this dead bird made me feel a deep dread. I cannot explain why I had this visceral response to the bird, but I quickly ran inside. I didn't tell anyone what I had just seen. Hours went by and I kept hoping that an adult in the house would discover it. But no one did and my guilt grew into shame, until I could not bear my feelings anymore. I grabbed a napkin and tiptoed over to the bird and carefully picked up its limp body and carried it inside to my mother's bedroom. It was a robin.

My mother was startled when she looked down at my hands.

"It must have hit the screen during the storm and broken its neck," she said.

I looked down at it and began to feel sad.

45

"We will have to bury it in the woods."

"Can I choose where we bury it?"

"Yes, let's get a trowel."

We went to the garage and then out toward the back woods. I followed quietly behind Mother, carrying the bird in my hands. I could hear the wet leaves and twigs breaking under our feet as we walked deeper into the woods. We came to one of my fairy houses in a large oak tree.

"Here?" I asked, pointing to a soft mossy patch near the tree. She knelt down and began to dig a small, deep hole. I placed the bird on the ground in a sunny spot and went to look for a stone. I noticed that it was very quiet, as if all the creatures of the woods were watching us. When my mother finished digging, she stood up and turned to me, dusting the dirt from her hands.

"Ready?"

"Yes," I said, nodding, and carefully picked up the bird.

As I took one last look at the feathered body, I began to pat the bird with long, loving strokes. Like a column of light, the warmth of the sun coming through the trees landed on my hands. It was a beautiful moment. It was uncannily quiet. Then I suddenly felt the body flutter and wiggle in my hands. It frightened me and I jumped back and before I knew it, the robin had escaped from my hands and had flown away as if nothing were wrong.

My mother and I just looked at each other, dumbfounded. We stood there saying nothing for what seemed a long time. Then she simply picked up the trowel, and without saying a word to each other, we walked back home, lost in our own thoughts. We never again spoke about that incident, nor did we ever tell anyone what had happened.

It was moments like those that kept me attached to Mother. It was our secret. But another, darker secret—her sinister behavior—was just as real, and she never changed over the years. Life with her was never simple because there would be the unexplainable magical moments and then my fear would dissolve—until the next bad moment.

***

By the time I was a teenager, all the Neilson children, especially Kaleen, my younger sister, and I knew there was something wrong in our family. No one could say exactly what it was but we suspected the problem was Mother's unpredictable behavior and dramatic responses. She was skilled at keeping secrets and could switch personae easily. She was also good at putting on a pleasant front, which made it hard to prove anything about her was wrong. Most of all, I believe we wanted to maintain the status quo, stay in denial, and pretend that we had a normal family.

Although Mother's fixation on sex—hers and everyone else's—was clearly obsessive, we pretended it was normal. But it was an illness. Mother, with her matriarchal rule and her Bette Davis glare, had her way with everyone. Kaleen and I resented her behavior but said nothing. She had a strange arrangement with my father about these sexual matters. He knew about them because there were times, after too many martinis, when Mother read her love letters from her many suitors out loud. "Look, Win," she would say, "listen to this one from Antonio," or, "Look, Georgio sent me this little figurine," or, "What do you think of this poem Richard wrote?" It went on and on: the love poems, the desires, and the claims of undying love from strange men. Father would grimace in disapproval and light his pipe. But say nothing. Mother even bribed me once to go on a double date (as she put it) with Roberto, the son of her newest fling—a cadet from an Italian military school. I hated Roberto and I hated Mother for making me a part of her betrayal.

When bored, Kaleen and I would break into Mother's desk and read the love notes out loud, each taking a turn to imitate Mother's dramatics. We called Father a wimp and laughed it off. Neither of us could decide who was really at fault. What I do know is that we never talked about how upset we were.

My last straw around Mother's sexual escapades occurred when I was sixteen and Mother had made a pass at my boyfriend, Jim.

"Never again! How could you have done that!" I said, shaking my head and crying alone in my room while pounding my pillow.

Mother entered the room at that moment, lipstick in hand, and said haughtily, "Marcy, I don't know what you are talking about." This irritated me even more. Her voice always took on a "better than thou" tone when she wanted to take control.

"You know exactly what I am talking about!" I snapped back.

"Oh?"

"Jim! You know what you did to him."

"Jim? What I did to him?"

"Yes, Jim!" I screamed.

She just looked at me as if she were thinking about whether I was worth answering.

"You are a bitch," I muttered loudly.

"What did you say?"

I ignored her question. I already felt better with my defiance and my bad language. It was a sort of "There! Take that!" stand.

Mother gave me one of those "how could you swear in front of

47

me" looks. I stared back. She said nothing. I said nothing. It was the kind of silence that tells one more than one really wants to know. It was a message with no words. And then I saw the shadow come over her face, letting me know that something bad had happened between her and Jim.

When she saw that I had read her thoughts, she ignored my rage and ignored me, and simply went to the mirror over my bureau and began putting on her lipstick. When finished, she smacked her lips as if it was a period in a sentence and turned toward me.

"Don't forget to change for dinner," she said as she exited the room. I followed her out the door and halfway down the hallway. I was fuming.

"You can't tell me what to do!"

She kept walking away.

"You're not my mother," I yelled down the hall to her. "You are not my fucking mother!" And then I went back to my room feeling broken and angry.

"I want my real mother," I whimpered. And then, suddenly, I broke down sobbing.

***

The last time I saw Mother, she was in one of those homes for the elderly where everything she owned was neatly arranged in one small room. It was a stark contrast to her early Manhattan life. Although she had aged, she still looked like Bette Davis as she hobbled over to her bed and grabbed Chubbins.

"Here, Marcy, you deserve Chubbins. I want you to have him."

"Are you sure? Why?" I was completely thrown off guard by the gift.

"Because Chubbins is about honor and honesty, and you, as a little child, were always . . . well, you were . . ." she hesitated.

"Mother, I was what?" I asked, trying to get her to finish her sentence.

"Oh, I don't know. The most truthful? . . . and . . . I guess . . ." she hesitated, drifting off again.

"And what?" I asked again.

"I don't know, Marcy," she said, beginning to get annoyed.

No matter how I tried to get her to elaborate and finish the conversation, I never heard the end of it. She refused to continue the topic. I don't even know if she was capable of retrieving her thoughts anymore, because she was in the later stages of dementia. But it didn't matter because I was holding Chubbins!

Several years later, I stood at her grave and was able to find some words of kindness to share about her with family and friends, including some family I had not seen for decades. I looked at the coffin and I felt her stillness. She was lying dead in a white, shiny box, only a few feet away. I had always thought that I would be afraid of that moment, afraid to be too near her dead body. But to my surprise it didn't happen that way; it was quite the opposite. Instead, I finally felt that it was over. Mother and I were over. Our struggle was over. I was free now and I could choose to keep my good memories of her and know that no new horrors or Mother-Truths would come barreling down at me ever again.

CHAPTER 7
A Childhood Friend
Motherless Children

Nancy and I were the treasure hunters of Riverside Drive. It was the thrill of the hunt, the turning over of every rock, the opening of every box, the looking in and out, over and under every corner and crack that kept us searching for the grand prize of gold.

We dug with our spoons for rocks with speckles of gold and mica in them. One day Nancy came running to me. She was grinning and shouting. Her cat-shaped eyes were wide with excitement. "Look what I found," she said as she pulled a rock with real gold nuggets out of her blue coat pocket. I was speechless.

"They are real nuggets!" I exclaimed.

"I know!" she grinned.

"How did you do that?"

"I dug it up."

"You didn't." I looked closer.

"Yes, I did," she said, grinning.

"Where?" I wasn't convinced.

"Over there." She pointed to a tree.

"Wow, we are going to be rich!"

I got up and started to dance. Nancy joined me. We spun around and around until we both became dizzy and collapsed onto the ground. We laughed so hard that we almost wet our pants. We were absolutely sure that there were huge piles of gold waiting for us in the park. All that we had to do was dig it up. That afternoon our lives seemed perfect.

***

I met Nancy in second grade. My parents sent me to Chapin—a prestigious school for girls. Chapin was part of my adoptive mother's long-term plan to groom me for the glamour and the demands of the upper class. I was to fulfill her ultimate dream to have a daughter come out as a New York City debutante.

I became friends with Nancy during my grade school years at Chapin. We bonded because we were different from the other girls. I like to think of her as my first true friend. She made me laugh, with her high energy and wild ideas. I can still hear the city traffic and the sound of our roller skates against the pavement. Nancy lived on Sutton Place, which was only a few blocks away from me. And so every afternoon, if we weren't learning piano, drama, or ballet, we were heading down First Avenue to the UN Park with our nannies running behind us.

***

A Halloween experience that occurred years later, when I became a mother, reminded me of my days with Nancy, and of how much my young son matched my own determination to forge a different path. That day, my son came home from nursery school announcing that he wanted to be Dorothy from *The Wizard of Oz*.

"What?" I said.

"Dorothy, I want a Dorothy costume."

"What happened to Scarecrow, Tin Man, the Cowardly Lion, or even Toto?" I asked, an edge of hysteria in my voice.

"I want to be Dorothy," he said calmly.

Why me? I thought. Why my son? Why today? He will be teased miserably.

"Mommy, I want to be Dorothy."

"Charlie doesn't want to be Dorothy."

Charlie, his best friend, a tiny little guy with knock knees and skinny arms, wanted to be the Hulk. My son the rebel already had enough muscles in his little round body to pass as any superhero that he chose. But no, my son wanted to be Dorothy.

As I stood there, looking down at him with his fierce determination, I couldn't help but hear echoes of myself, from a day when I was about his age. I was in FAO Schwartz with my Neilson mother, who was trying to convince me that a beautiful pink satin gown with a tiara would be a perfect Halloween costume for that year.

"Here, wouldn't you like this princess dress?" she asked, holding it up to me.

I looked at it and made a face. "No. I want that one," I said, pointing to the all-black Hopalong Cassidy outfit.

"No, dear. That's for a little boy," she said as she pulled out another frilly costume.

"Please, Mommy, I want it.

She ignored me.

["I love Hopalong."

There was a bright red and orange dress hanging next to the princess one. "How about that Calypso Dancer?" she said, trying to divert me.

"No, Mommy. Please," I whined.

Nothing she said made me want anything but the Hopalong costume.

She finally resigned herself to the fact that there would be no frill or frolic for her daughter that year.

I was a tomboy and so was Nancy; it was part of our bond. I know that both our parents worried a bit about it, but I am sure that my mother thought my tomboy phase would run its course by next year's Halloween. I don't think it did.

I wore the costume for weeks. I showed it to Nancy, who soon ran home and convinced her parents to buy her a Davy Crockett outfit. I didn't really like her Davy Crockett costume. It was the dead raccoon on her head that I couldn't get past, but I knew she relished her outfit in the same way I did mine. So we sang, day after day, "Davy–Davy Crockett–king of the wild frontier." And the next year she was into Indians and so was I and the raccoon was replaced with headbands and feathers.

I know that our costumes made us heroes, and in some ways we knew that we had scored a victory over our parents. We had saved our free spirits from the doom of becoming young princesses-in-waiting. I also know that neither Chapin School, nor the cotillion at the Junior League, nor the ballet classes on Wednesdays, nor any therapist's chair, ever came close to shaping me or my character as much as that single all-black outfit and that special look I would give myself in the front hall mirror, when I tipped my oversized hat and said in a low, deep voice, "Howdy."

I loved my four short years at Chapin. And, like all the other little girls, I paraded around in a pale green pinafore, bloomers, and a dark green blazer. I competed in the appropriate, ladylike fashion with our rival school, enthusiastically sang the school song at the morning assemblies, and each afternoon proudly rolled out my little floor mat for our half-hour rest.

I remember the agony of memorizing the passages from the Bible that we were all required to learn. There were horrid arguments, and many afternoons of stamping my feet in refusal. The number of times I said, "I don't want to" and "Do I have to?" seemed endless. But I did learn the lines. And now, the passage that begins with the words, *"Though I speak with the tongues of men and angels,"* from I Corinthians, chapter 13, verse 1, is permanently engraved on my brain for all eternity. And to this day I still ponder the deeper and perhaps ancient origins of the meaning of verse 12, *"For now we see through a glass, darkly; but then face to face: now I know in part; but then shall I know even as also I am known."*

The truth is that I had to work hard at Chapin. Before that time no one had pushed me to use my intelligence the way that school did. I loved it and I hated it. I whined a good deal of the time. And I was heartbroken the day we moved away.

Nancy Beckaert and I sat together in the back of our history class and shared a childhood crush on Miss Crocker, who broke our hearts and left at the end of the year to get married. Miss Crocker taught us about the ancient Egyptians. To this day, I don't know if it was Miss Crocker's beauty or some past life of mine that captivated me and made me listen to every word about the Egyptian pharaohs.

In Miss Crocker's second-grade class I learned everything I could about the lifestyles of the ancient Egyptians. I loved spreading my crayons out on the floor and sketching drawings of Egyptian images. I even handed out little hand-folded booklets with made-up hieroglyphics. I was obsessed with ancient Egypt–I daydreamed that I was Akhenaten.

One afternoon I saw an article about the reconstruction of the Aswan Dam. The article showed the towering statues along the river that were predicted to sink into the water. My visceral reaction was an unusual response for a second grader, but my heart sank as I looked at the black and white photos of the gods aligned along the water's edge. I wanted to protest, do something–anything! I felt helpless. It was my first taste of wanting to take political action.

The next morning after history class, I asked Miss Crocker what I could do. She had no answer but I saw her pride in my question. Her smiling approval kept me loving ancient history for a long time.

The day before Miss Crocker was to leave, our parents let Nancy and me walk to the corner gift shop to buy a going-away present for her. We both felt very grown up as we marched down the street without our nannies. We took forever to choose the perfect gift. We carefully looked over each object and piece of jewelry in the store. Then we saw it in the display case. It was perfect and we both knew it. We had found a scarab bracelet with multicolored stones! But it was more than we could afford.

"I've only got five dollars," I said.

"This is so perfect. What are we going to do?" Nancy asked. We both stared at each other and then at the bracelet. Then, all of a sudden, Nancy lit up and gave that big grin of hers.

"Wait! I've got it."

"What?" I asked.

"I have my emergency ten-dollar bill with me," Nancy answered, digging into her pocket and pulling out a little worn red leather change purse. It wasn't at all in Nancy's character to have a dainty purse. She carefully snapped it open in a ladylike fashion. For a moment I panicked. Perhaps after all our rebellion as tomboys, Nancy was going to give in and become a Chapin princess.

"Where did you get that purse?" I asked in disgust.

"It's my mom's. Why?"

"Phew! I thought you were becoming a princess," I giggled. We both laughed out loud at that thought. She looked inside it and then gave that wide, elfin grin of hers. "We have enough!" she announced as she pulled out a crisp ten-dollar bill. "Look," she said as she waved the money in my face. It was as if she had just struck gold again.

"You are my very best friend forever!" I announced.

Nancy chose the silver-colored, flowered paper, and I chose the blue ribbon. We couldn't wait until the next day when we would present our gift to Miss Crocker.

We handed Miss Crocker the small oblong box, almost as embarrassed as we were proud. "Here, this is from Nancy and me," I said. Our hearts pounded as we both watched her open it carefully. She smiled sweetly at us and we blushed even more. We swore that we both wanted to grow up to be just like her. Oh please don't go away! I thought. Then she lifted the lid off the box and tears came to her eyes. She gave both of us a kiss, saying thank you and how sweet and thoughtful we were. Bingo! We smiled at each other. Just like the Egyptians we had made magic happen! We had touched Miss Crocker's heart for all eternity.

***

One afternoon in the playground, as we squatted near our collection of stone treasures, Nancy asked me a question that would change our friendship forever.

"You're my best friend, right?"

"Yep," I said, as I neatly stacked the pile of stones one by one. "Why?"

"Well, I've got a secret to tell you," she said shyly.

"Ya, what?"

"You promise to never tell anyone? Cross your heart, hope to die?"

I laughed. "Stick a needle in my eye if I do."

"Well, have you ever wondered why I never invite you upstairs to my home?"

"Ya, sort of, why?"

"It's my parents," she answered. Her voice grew sad. I thought she was going to cry, right there in front of everyone. I had never seen her cry.

"What about them?"

Was Nancy going to reveal some truth that might be too weird? I wondered if it was going to be a confession, something like, her parents were really spacemen or aliens. Or even worse, was she going to tell me that they were Communists or spies? After all, we were in the midst of the McCarthy era, and my father had instilled fear in me by making me swear never to use the word "Communist." He had told me, "If people ask you about your parents, you say nothing–absolutely nothing. Even if your teachers ask." He added, "Because they could put us in jail." Consequently, I never used that word or even let it cross my mind. But now my best friend was going to tell me a secret about her parents. Was she going to tell me this? Use the dreaded word? Was I going to hear a truth that would get me put in jail?

"Are you sure you want to tell me?" I asked, hoping she would drop the whole subject. Nancy looked straight at me, right in the eyes, as if to see if she could trust me. I am sure that by that time, my face was a bit pale and twitching. But actually, as I stared back at her, I saw a shame in her eyes that I recognized as akin to something in myself. It was as if her eyes were saying, "Please like me if I tell you this." She paused, looked around, and then bent closer to me.

"Well, they are not my parents," she confessed.

"They are not?"

"No, I am adopted," she whispered, wincing as she told me. "They had polio and couldn't have children, so they adopted me and my sister as babies."

"They did?"

"Ya." She sighed out of relief that I had not judged her. Like me, she had been told to never tell anyone that she was adopted.

"That's why they hardly ever go out of the house and they . . ."

"Nancy," I interrupted. But she had not heard me and was on a roll and could not stop talking. She was not looking at me as she rambled on or she would have seen that I was smiling at her and bursting to tell her something.

"Nancy!" I yelled.

"What?" she replied, annoyed that I was interrupting her.

"I am, too."

"You are what?"

"I am adopted."

She just looked at me, dumbfounded. It was like we were two lost friends who had just found each other. A silence fell between us. Not a bad silence–just a silence. If we had known how to cry with joy, we would have. But we had both been emotionally wounded, stunted in subtle ways by our early childhood experiences. Instead we kept the tears at bay. Not knowing how to express the feelings that were bubbling inside, we just went on with our playing. We did not say a word. We needed our space to process the immensity of what had just happened. Both of us, like live wires, at the exact same moment, jumped up and ran off to find more treasures in City Park.

I came up with the idea that Nancy and I should become secret Blood Sisters. I have no idea where I had learned about this ritual, but I think there was a fad going around at that time. Neither one of us liked needles, nor really knew what to do, but we both knew it would magically seal our friendship.

"We have got to sterilize it," I said, acting all grown up.

"Sterilize what?"

"The needle."

"How do you do that?"

"Doesn't your mother do that, when she takes out a splinter?" I asked.

"No," she answered, as if I had said something very weird.

"We have to do it or we will get the plague."

Nancy's eyes widened. "Well, what do we do?"

"You put it in a match and let it get real hot."

"Do we burn ourselves?"

"No. We wait till it gets cool," I said, laughing.

"Oh." She settled back in her chair, her worried look gone.

It took a few days for us to coordinate the needle and the matches. We kept forgetting one or the other. But we finally got it together. Sitting in the backseat of the van on the way to school one February morning in 1957, as the other children gazed out the window at the commotion of the city and the slush on the streets, Nancy and I quietly performed our ritual. I lit the match, she held the needle and we drew blood. Then we were sisters.

Little did we know that our first sister problem would occur on our arrival at school. We were promptly escorted to the headmistress's office to explain the matches. They accused us of smoking in the back of the van. We knew that we were in trouble, but we had sworn ourselves to secrecy. It took our parents coming to school to make us finally confess why we had used the matches. I don't know what our parents really thought, but it was clear that the school was unhappy with us, and at the same time relieved that they had avoided a second-grade scandal. Maybe they thought the New York headlines, on the society page of course, would read "*Second Graders from Prestigious Chapin School Caught Smoking.*" I didn't care, nor did Nancy. But she didn't get to come to my birthday party the next day, and that was hard for her.

As blood sisters, what we did discover was that the two of us never quite fit into the Chapin image. That fact alone was the power of our secret bond. We knew that we were different and, deep inside, we were proud of that. It was like an eternal sister bond—a secret mission. After all, we were rebels for a different cause.

CHAPTER 8
Mr. Aunt Nan Woods
The Fairy Godmother and Her Prince

We spent our summers on Long Island in an area called Lloyd Neck. All the land in that area had once been owned by a very wealthy family, the Woods. They lived in the Fort Hill manor, a huge brick mansion with a courtyard and gardens that overlooked Long Island Sound. In the thirties they sold parcels of land to different families. The Neilsons bought two parcels of land and owned two houses. One of them was a wooden slat cottage, which they had built by hand when they were a young married couple. That house was called Melody Woods. The other house, which they purchased later, was a huge country home, with rolling lawns and tall ancient oaks. That house was called Wood Magic. I loved it there.

We all called Mrs. Woods Aunt Nan Woods. She was the fairy godmother of our little community in Lloyd Neck and everyone admired her. She was a short woman born in the late eighteen hundreds and her impeccable taste in clothes reflected her wealthy upbringing. She had curly white hair, a very round, kind face, and very pale blue eyes. She resembled England's Queen Mother.

From my five-year old view, Aunt Nan Woods' husband was very tall and skinny, and he was a very, very old man. And he never spoke to anyone. We called him Mr. Aunt Nan Woods and none of the children in the community really knew him or particularly liked him. But everyone loved Aunt Nan Woods. I do not remember her ever speaking to us, but I loved her gentle smile and sweet giggle. She lived to be a hundred and one.

Every year there was a celebration in our neighborhood involving the old weeping beech tree, which stood on the corner of the lawn of the Woods mansion. The tree was so large that it had four iron benches hidden underneath its swooping branches. On the day of the celebration there was always a beautifully set table covered with a soft pink cloth and a perfect bouquet of flowers. There were cookies, cakes, tea, and fresh lemonade for everyone. Everything was served on silver platters, bone china, and sparkling crystal. And I don't remember anyone ever breaking a glass or a cup.

We children were always excited about what came after the tea and cookies because the treasure hunt would begin. Each of us was handed a string with a brightly colored ribbon tied to it. When the time was just right, the dinner bell would ring and we would follow our strings through the branches into the center of the tree. We would roll our string balls around corners and over branches until, somewhere in the copper-colored leaves, we'd find a hidden, tiny wrapped gift. What a storybook tea party it was, and what a magical game it was as everyone listened to the chattering, gleeful children's voices coming from beneath the branches.

It seemed to take forever to find the end of the string, but that was part of the fun. Aunt Nan Woods and Mr. Aunt Nan Woods and the families would sit on the veranda and clap each time someone came back out from underneath the tree with a gift in hand and an ear-to-ear smile.

The Woods had gorgeous old English gardens with tall brick walls that I loved to play in. One day I was sitting next to a fountain eating a warm, sun-baked tomato that I had picked, when all of a sudden, a sparrow came over to me and landed on my hand. I was so thrilled that I jumped up and actually scared the bird away. Who would ever believe that a live bird had landed on my hand? Maybe I am like St. Frances, I thought. Just then, as I looked around to see if anyone else had witnessed the miracle, I saw Mr. Aunt Nan Woods in the distance, walking past a brick archway. He was walking slowly, using a cane. I ran up to him to tell him my story, tugging at his pants.

"A bird landed on my hand!" I said, staring up at him.

He looked down at me and smiled but said nothing.

I added more animatedly, "It was a real bird!"

He nodded and this time reached out with his shaky hand and patted my head, as if to say, "That's nice." He gave a polite little wave and kept on walking.

***

As a child I harbored a fear of being lost. And so when I played alone I was very careful not to get lost in the woods. Each time I went into the woods, I would mark a tree with an arrow point from my bow and arrow set. Very carefully, I marked the trees day after day, until one day almost all the trees were marked and I became lost. I had wandered a distance that seemed to be very far away from the house. Disoriented and in a panic, I began to cry. But I remembered the rule to not keep going if you get lost. "Just stay in one spot," my Neilson father had said. So I sat down and waited and called for help. No one heard me. I waited and waited.

Lunchtime passed and no one seemed to be looking for me. I sat on a stump, alone and afraid. I was ready to give up. But then in the near distance I saw a man with a cane slowly walking up an incline. That was strange, I thought, what is a man doing in the middle of the woods? But when I ran up to him, I discovered to my relief that it was Mr. Aunt Nan Woods! He was walking very slowly up our winding driveway. The gravel driveway ran through the woods and was well hidden. Standing only a few feet tall in those days, it was very easy for me to lose sight of it.

I am not sure if I was more surprised by seeing the driveway only a few feet away or by seeing Mr. Aunt Nan Woods. I had never seen him this far from his property, and even more surprising was that he was alone, without Aunt Nan Woods. Was he lost, too? I wondered. What was he doing at our house? I thought. But I didn't care, I was just so happy to see him and I think he knew it. I saw it when he smiled down at me. I ran to him and slipped my little hand into his, even though in many ways we were strangers to each other. We weren't then. He said nothing. I said nothing. He just kept walking–slowly, step by step. I hugged him when we got to my house but still said nothing. I think we were both really shy. There was this very strange bond we had that day, as if we knew each other well.

That was the last time I ever saw him. The truth was that Mr. Aunt Nan Woods had escaped from his house and his caretakers and from Aunt Nan Woods. He had taken a very long stroll over the land to my parents' house. In his younger years he had been an avid walker. That night I overheard my parents talking about his escape and the uproar it had caused.

"They were going to call the police! Thank God we found him," they said.

Maybe he was a bit lost too, I thought. But no, his walk had a purpose. It turned out to be the last walk that he ever took, and I think he knew that inside. It was a special silence we shared as we walked up the hill. I now know that, and I think he was saying goodbye to me.

A short time later his heart gave out.

CHAPTER 9
My Adoptive Father Winthrop
The Grandmother's Silence

Father and I loved the Adirondacks, where we spent the month of August every summer. We both loved the nighttime, when we went outside to call the owls in the dark. One night I looked up at my father's tall silhouette against the starlit sky. He was waiting for an owl to answer his call. The only sound was a lone frog down by the pond. I can still smell the balsam and the fungus on the trees. Father grinned, motioning with his finger for me to be quiet. I giggled under my breath. He began an owl call, "*Tooo–Hooot, Tooo–Hooot.*"

After a few more hoots, we waited for a response. Our anticipation heightened as we shifted our positions and listened, turning our heads toward the dark woods. We waited and then waited some more. And then an owl picked up the call; a distant "*Tooo–Hooot*" came back at us.

"Did you hear that?" he asked.

"Yes!" I answered, thrilled.

My father tried the call again: "*Tooo–Hooot, Tooo–Hooot.*"

Once more, quicker this time, a new "*Tooo–Hooot, Tooo–Hooot*" came from the dark.

Father lit his pipe, as if our joy together was too much for him. His pipe was his way of detaching himself in order to gain his composure. He paused and turned toward the open field, pipe in hand, drawing repetitive, silent puffs. It was as if I were no longer there. Almost afraid to interrupt his silence, I watched as he quietly stared off into the distance. I could see that he was taking in the natural beauty: the night landscape, the full moon over the dark mountain, the pine trees, the stars, and the smells. All of it, for that moment, was my father's glorious landscape. I went over to him and slipped my hand into his warm palm. We said nothing. We didn't need to. The beauty of the night was ours.

Father loved birds and the moments we shared with birds are my favorite memories of him. I remember him saying things like, "Look over there at the sheer elegance of that Golden Slipper!" Or he would ask, "Do you hear that? It's a Towhee!" . . . or "a wood thrush" . . . or "a robin" . . . or "a wren."

To please him, I learned all the names and songs of the native birds. Then I could be the one to say, tugging at his sleeve as we walked in the woods, "Look! Look over there, it's a cedar waxwing!"

He would respond by turning toward the tree I was pointing to, his hand shading his eyes. He would smile approvingly when he spied the fluttering creature among the leaves. These special moments with the birds made us feel as if we had a soul-level connection.

Who was this man who stood in the dark and called the owls? He was a man who was like the dark night — a mystery to all of us children. He was reserved, quiet, and in some ways very simple. But who was he? I know that he was the man I called Father for most of my life, and he was the man who gave me the gift of the birds.

Others saw him as Winthrop Cunningham Neilson II, a man who could impress anyone with the way he could flag down a waiter with just the slightest nod of his head. He was a tall, handsome man with a distinguished air about him. I always thought he looked like Clark Gable with white hair and a well-trimmed mustache. In public, his Englishman's flair often overrode his down-to-earth reserved Quaker background. He came from a successful Philadelphian family who had ties to an aluminum company, where he worked for a short time as an administrator. But it became clear that this was not the direction in which he wanted to go. It was not his style or anywhere close to his dream. He quit the job and fled to Southern France, where he happily biked across the countryside as a bohemian, paint box and canvas on his back.

"My summer in France was the only time that I ever remember being truly happy," he confessed one evening after a few brandies. Did Father really say it was the only time he had ever been happy? No, he must have had another time, at least a moment, I thought. But, in all the years I knew him, I never heard him use the word "happy" again.

He was a private man and would work in his studio for hours, drinking espresso, listening to opera, and painting large canvases. I loved spending time with him when I was young. He would set up a little easel in the corner of his studio, where for hours we silently worked side by side.

"Father, do you ever cry?" I asked him one day as we painted.

He looked at me, perplexed by my question. He paused and re-lit his pipe and then turned away, as if ashamed of his response. "Only once."

"When?"

"When my father died," he said, continuing to paint. There was no more conversation for the day, only the sound of the afternoon opera coming from the radio in the background, and the soft sound the brushes made against the canvas.

"How about your mother?" I asked, breaking the silence. He did not answer me, as if I had not asked the question.

That was the one and only intimate conversation we ever had. And even though he betrayed me years later, I loved him the best out of all the family.

A few weeks after that conversation, I asked him about his mother again but he became very uncomfortable. "Your Uncle Jimmy makes a lot of money," he mumbled. "And he was her favorite son."

Winthrop also had another side: he was a dreamer. His schemes and dreams always fell short of full success, however. One year he started a tree nursery at our country home. I drove home from the Adirondacks that summer with the smell of rich mountain soil and the sweet scent of the hundreds of little fir saplings, which my father had gathered, neatly crammed into the back of the station wagon. It was a bad investment because he soon found out that it cost money to bulldoze the land and to hire workers to care for the trees. All of us in the family just nodded, thinking, "Oh, well." We agreed that the tree nursery was a nice dream, but a bad investment.

Father's next scheme was a chicken farm where he imported and raised exotic chickens from around the world. There were three large tan ones with red beaks. Father said they came all the way from Africa. Since he was an avid bird watcher, raising chickens was a perfect endeavor. During the chicken phase, I had a pet black and white chicken named Molly. Religiously, every morning, I would gather her eggs for breakfast. What we were to do with these chickens I have no idea, but his chicken collection also failed financially. No one ever said a word. We just nodded again and said it was a bad investment.

The last project Father launched was plastic paperweights. He envisioned them as small sculptures with seashells strategically placed inside each one. We flew to Captiva and began collecting shells on the beach. I ran along the seashore with the ibis and sandpipers bobbing next to me as I collected rare and beautiful shells for my father's plastic forms. But, once again, my father's business scheme failed, and soon there was a plastic paperweight in every corner of our house.

***

Most people saw Winthrop as a withdrawn, meek man who let my mother–who was spoiled, domineering, and cunning–run the show. He probably wanted to be left alone to dream of better times.

He loved the outdoors. He came alive in the crisp pine air of the Adirondacks and he often dreamed that someday he would retire to our summer house outside of St. Huberts, New York. He loved to chop wood, listen to the birds, hike, paint, write, and just exist, undisturbed.

Sadly, he died at the age of seventy, a penniless alcoholic who lived alone with my mother. Their lives together ended in a cluttered, stuffy, two-room New York apartment that overlooked Gramercy Park, far from the towering pines and granite slopes of the Adirondacks range.

***

My father was a man of many morning rituals. In my teens, when we lived in Rome, one of his rituals was walking the dogs each morning up the street to a corner flower stall, where he religiously bought a flower or two for my mother. This routine was as predictable as his choice of flowers. One morning he surprised us all. There were no flowers in his hand when he arrived home. Instead, he opened the front door carrying a rusty old birdcage. Perched inside the cage on a swing was the most pathetic, small, feather-plucked, naked little parrot I had ever seen. Its name was Yippo. Right before our eyes, my father transformed from the distinguished, stoic Winthrop Cunningham Neilson II into a little boy holding a new pet. We all laughed at the unusual sight. He mumbled and grinned sheepishly at my mother, who was aghast.

"Sweetheart, what is that?" she asked.

While cooing over Yippo, he explained that he had been compelled to rescue this poor little bird from the nasty flower man.

"The old drunk threatened to kill the bird," Father said. Just at that moment, my father put his finger too near the cage and, sure enough, Yippo leapt off the swing and nipped aggressively at the metal bars. Yippo, like his past owner, had a nasty streak, and had a bad reputation of biting everyone who stuck his or her fingers in his cage. However, this fact did not seem to discourage my father. My father cooed even more loudly, saying, "Dear, look at him. Look at what poor Yippo has done. He has plucked out all of his feathers out of frustration!"

My mother, my sister, and I all shook our heads and *tsk-tsked* in unison.

"Yes, dear, Yippo is quite the tragedy," she said.

There was no changing Father's mind and so Yippo—the featherless mutt—had found his new home and Father had found a friend.

He was determined to tame this biting little monster and, surprisingly, within a few months, he had done exactly that. Soon, Yippo, clucking with love, was eating morsels of toast dripping with honey out of Father's hand. For forty years my father brought my mother breakfast in bed, and for ten of those forty years, Yippo joined them for honey and toast.

One night, about a year after Yippo's arrival, I missed my curfew. As I tiptoed very carefully by my father's office, I saw that he was still up, working on a manuscript. And there was little Yippo, as cute as he could be, asleep snuggling on Father's shoulder. No one could argue that they had found true love.

One evening, years later, long after I had left home, Kaleen telephoned me. "Marcy! You'll never believe what Dad did," she whispered.

"What?" I whispered back.

"Well, he came home and found Yippo dead at the bottom of the cage."

"Oh no," I gasped.

"He didn't say anything. It was strange. He just went into the kitchen and told everyone to stay out." She paused for what seemed like an eternity.

"Then what?"

"He dissected the bird!" she said. "Can you believe it?" she continued in disgust. "He did it right there on the kitchen counter!"

"Oh my God," I said.

"He said that he had to know it wasn't his fault that Yippo died."

I gasped and was silent. I couldn't think of anything to say.

"And, that's not all of it," she added. "It was horrible. I think Dad is losing his marbles."

"What happened?" I asked, becoming worried.

"Marcy, we could hear him sobbing behind the door. He wouldn't even let Mom in the kitchen to comfort him."

The information caught me off guard. I could feel his pain hit me like a gust of icy wind. After our conversation ended, I hung up the phone, speechless, and sat in the dark for a long time. Then suddenly, like a convulsion, I was weeping uncontrollably.

***

That was a long time ago. Years later I returned for a visit to Captiva. I waited once again for the green flash of the sunset. It had been so long since I had been there in that peaceful place. The sun was about to set, and the pink hues, so prevalent in Captiva, were filling the sky. If this beauty could only last forever, I thought. Then, all of a sudden, a large white bird took flight. It flapped silently upward into the pink sky. I recognized the bird and my heart jumped with the same excitement as it had years ago. I heard myself call out, "Father, look! Look over there. It is a Golden Slipper!" As I watched it fly off into the distance, I felt Father's presence next to me. I looked over at him. He seemed younger than when I had last seen him. We didn't need words at that moment. We never really did. As we stood together in silence, I could feel something different about him. All of a sudden I knew what it was–he was truly happy.

CHAPTER 10
Kaleen, My Adoptive Sister
A Mother's Last Hope

Kaleen was the answer to my pleas for a baby sister. About a year after my arrival at the Neilsons' home, a plump six-month-old baby girl arrived. She was sucking a pacifier and had short, silky blonde hair and huge blue eyes. And I swear she knew at birth just how to bat those baby blues. To make matters worse, she also had a Mae West smile that got her everywhere and everything she wanted. In short, I had not thought out the long-term effects of a little sister.

Kaleen was different from me in every possible way. I was quiet most of the time and she was loud. People said that she could be an opera singer with her powerful lungs, but I thought that her baby yells were out of tune. They said it was most likely colic because she screamed all the time. I thought she was spoiled.

We shared a room in the beginning and every night Kaleen would toss her milk bottle out of the crib. And every night a loud thump of the bottle or an occasional shattering of glass would startle me out of a deep sleep.

Crashing milk bottles were not my only problem at night. As a toddler, Kaleen learned how to climb out of her crib and steal my blankets. It was not that she was cold or deprived of anything. Kaleen simply wanted everything I had.

The blanket stealing became a problem and I complained to our nannies. No one knew what to do and for a long time everyone thought it was cute and even funny—except me. So they gave Kaleen a training bed, with lots of blankets, and told her that she was a big girl and needed to stay in bed. But the problem continued. Then one night Kaleen's nanny decided to tie her into the bed with some strips of cloth. This worked and for a few days all went well. I got to sleep through the night and Kaleen didn't seem to mind the ties. Then my parents found out that their child was being tied to the bed. The nanny was immediately fired and I was moved out of my room into the unoccupied cook's room. Aside from feeling a bit displaced, I was happy to have a room of my own.

Growing up, Kaleen knew how to get whatever she desired, whether it was a blanket, a room, or that extra allowance. She learned quickly that a loud scream worked better than a sweet smile. She had no problem asking for what she wanted. As a teenager, if she didn't get what she wanted, her philosophy became: Don't ask, just take it.

She was precocious when it came to the ways of the world. She was skilled at explaining the unexplainable, and when her answers made no sense, she simply got louder and more demanding. It worked every time.

***

As I said, we were opposites. For example, when we were living in Florida and I was still climbing trees and frolicking in fairyland, at the age of seven Kaleen was trying out cigarettes.

One morning Mother discovered her in the bathroom smoking. Only a year earlier, while we were living in Portugal, we found out the hard way that Kaleen had a fondness for matches. She lit her mattress on fire and caused quite the stir. So it only made sense that cigarettes would be next. And of course Mother, with the first smell of smoke, jumped out of bed and ran to see where it was coming from. It was the bathroom.

"What are you doing?" I could hear Mother's horrified voice from down the hall.

"Nothing," Kaleen said calmly.

I am sure Kaleen's mouth was hanging open at that moment. Her mouth always hung open whenever she was about to lie or when she got caught doing something bad. I think that when she was very young she had decided that the open-mouth look conveyed innocence–or at least total ignorance.

"Are you smoking?"

"Nope."

By then I had walked down the hall to the bathroom. Classically, Mother was standing by the doorjamb in her hand-on-hip, foot-tapping, I-have-caught-you! mother pose. Kaleen, with her long, blonde silky hair, was sitting on the toilet, looking up at her, and she was smiling sweetly.

"Well, then what are you doing with my cigarettes?" Mother asked.

"I was just lighting them."

"I am not stupid, Kaleen," Mother said as she turned around and bumped into me.

"I am going to put an end to this right here and now."

"Mom, what are you going to do?" Kaleen had just a bit of a worried look on her face.

By then I was smirking behind Mother's back.

"Marcy, you too," she said.

"What?" I said, stepping away. "Why me?"

"Both of you follow me right now," she said as she grabbed the pack of cigarettes. We followed Mother to the living room.

"Kaleen, look what you've done now," I said, sneering.

"Shut up," Kaleen said. It was clear she was getting a bit concerned. She had an amazing knack for getting out of trouble and I don't remember her often being punished. So this was a new approach of Mother's and we had no way of knowing how it would play out.

"Sit down!" Mother said, pointing to the chairs. We sat.

"What are you going to do, Mom?"

Mother said nothing.

"I was only lighting them," Kaleen said.

Mother walked over to her, took a cigarette out, and handed it to her. "Here," she said. And then she handed me one.

We looked at each other.

"You two girls are going to smoke these all the way to the end," she said, smiling at us triumphantly.

"What do you mean?" I said, dumbfounded.

"Smoke them," she repeated.

"Mother, I wasn't smoking," I whined as I glared at Kaleen, who began to giggle.

"Mom, are you joking?" she said.

Mother said nothing, struck the match and went over and lit Kaleen's cigarette. Kaleen slowly drew in the smoke and exhaled in her Greta Garbo fashion.

"Smoke it! All the way to the end," Mother said. And then she turned to me and did the same.

I coughed and gagged on the bitter, burnt taste. My feeble attempt to inhale the way Kaleen did had failed. It was the longest cigarette I've ever had. But finally it was over. We finished our cigarettes. Kaleen pushed the butt into the ashtray and turned to Mother, smiling.

"Can I have another one?" she asked.

***

Kaleen and I often went into Mother's room and borrowed things from her—such as perfume, clothes, and sometimes her jewelry. Frustrated, Mother announced that she was putting a lock on the bedroom door. The locksmith came and soon a bright golden deadbolt was in place. Mother hung the key on a hook near the front door of the apartment. Whenever my parents left, they locked their room and took the key. While I was indignant about the whole thing, Kaleen shrugged it off—somehow she had found a way to get an extra key.

Our bedrooms reflected our differences. Kaleen's room was plain— no poster, no décor, nothing—with white walls and one overhead light. Mine was elaborate, with all kinds of objects, candles, and art hanging everywhere. I loved classical music and jazz. Kaleen listened to the radio. My bookshelves were lined with books of poetry and philosophy. Kaleen had the largest comic book collection in the world. Once in a while I would read one of her romance comics.

***

In one visit to my parents in my early twenties, after I had moved out, I arrived to find Kaleen, Mother, and Father in the middle of an argument. It seems that Kaleen had come home late at night after a party and in a drunken stupor, and had decided that she wanted to redecorate her bedroom. She needed a side table and spied the perfect one in Father's studio. She dumped Father's things on the floor and attempted to carry the table up the stairs. But her plan did not go smoothly. The table became wedged in the stairwell. She pushed and shoved, but couldn't move it. Finally, she had given up–too tired, and too drunk–and went to bed.

I arrived at the point where Kaleen was indignantly yelling at Mother and Father for accusing her of moving the table.

"I didn't touch that damn table!" she screamed.

"Well, Kaleen, just who do you think did?" Mother said sarcastically.

Kaleen looked at me, to see if she could push it off on me.

"Look, I don't live here anymore–you can't blame me," I said, backing away.

"It was Uncle Erin's ghost!" Kaleen proclaimed.

We turned to each other and shrugged our shoulders. There was always a slight chance that this could be true.

"He must have moved it," Kaleen said, pleased with her answer as she walked away.

That answer worked and the table was moved back to Father's studio without anything else being said. To this day, Kaleen denies that she had anything to do with the table in the stairwell. My parents' solution to tables that moved in the night was to send Kaleen to a "good Catholic" boarding school the next year.

***

Kaleen was tall, but for all her height she was ungainly. She wasn't any clumsier than I was, but because she was so tall and a presence to be reckoned with, her slips and slides were magnified and her booms seemed louder. This was clearly evident late one night when we were coming home from a bar in Kaleen's teeny-tiny, bright red sports coupe. We had stopped at a red light. Kaleen was tapping her finger as she sang along to some jingle on the radio—off-key, of course. Suddenly, out of the corner of her left eye, she spied a dark, crawly shape sliding down her door window. Even with all her loud, brazen ways and tall Amazon stature, Kaleen, like me, was petrified of spiders. A medium-size spider in a small Fiat is perceived as a giant tarantula in a matchbox. No matter what state you are in—drunk or sober—the reaction will be the same. Kaleen screamed and pushed me out my side of the car. She was all legs as she climbed over the stick shift, and yelled, as she shoved, "Get out! Get out, it's a spider!" That was all I needed to hear to move quickly. We abandoned the car in the middle of the street. Kaleen didn't care that her car was slowly rolling toward a lamppost, because as we watched, we both agreed that we'd rather pay for a new fender than shake hands with a spider.

***

One night, years after Kaleen had moved out of state and we were no longer talking to each other, I went with a friend for a drink at a bar where Kaleen and I used to hang out. As I looked around the smoke-filled room, I was struck by its familiar look: even though it had been over ten years since I had been in the bar, it was pretty much the same grungy place it had been in the early seventies—the loud jukebox and the dreadful smell of stale beer and cigarettes were all there. I am sure that if I had looked hard enough, I might even have seen the same bedraggled regulars hanging out at the bar, perhaps only looking older and a bit more forlorn.

"God, it's been a long time since I've been here," I said to my friend, who sat across from me, sipping her drink. We had decided to do something different. What was strange about that particular place that evening was that my friend and I were sitting at the same table that I had sat at years ago with Kaleen, to have one of our very few heart-to-heart sister talks.

That night we both had had way too much to drink and in a rare moment, we had spilled our guts to each other. In those days Kaleen was a very striking young woman who looked a lot like a tall, blonde-haired Cher with a prominent nose. She was a party girl, a wild woman, and, to people who didn't know her well, she came across as confident—a "don't mess with me" woman, and a "give them hell" type of gal. She gave the impression that she was going somewhere in life. She wanted to be cool, interesting, elegant, and glamorous. She wanted the whole bit, but dainty and graceful were not traits of hers, and this bothered her. Her demeanor was that of an Amazon, a great white Goddess, and there was nothing delicate about her moves or presence. In those days men would often jokingly call her The Great White

Goddess. She loved the nickname and played it to the hilt, tossing her blonde, silky mane at them and strutting away onto the dance floor. Kaleen had the art of flirting down to a science and men adored her for it. I thought she was bossy with her men and I cringed at times.

"What are you cringing for? I am just having strong opinions!" she would snap at me. Wherever we went, Kaleen would run the show and I would watch from the sidelines.

After her high school graduation, Kaleen came to live with me. I had tried to rescue her from drugs and booze, but I was naïve and ill-equipped to save her. Soon after she moved in with me, I realized I was failing miserably as a big sister. For a long time I ignored the fact that I couldn't help her. It simply wasn't in my nature to give up on someone. But I was only twenty-one and barely navigating the dramatic highs and lows of my own life.

That night at the bar, when we had our heart-to-heart talk, she was more serious than I had ever seen her. She sat for a long time just drinking and watching the crowd.

"What's the matter?" I asked.

"Nothing."

"Nothing? It sure seems like it is something that is going on."

"Oh, I don't know. It's that I am nothing. I have no goals, Marcy, not like you."

"Me? What do you mean?"

"No talent. Nothing," she said dispiritedly.

"Yeah, but that's not everything."

"I disagree. You are an artist and you've got something inside."

"Do you mean talent?"

"No, Marcy, it's more than that. You've got something—spirit. Ugh! That sounds weird, but it's like you see something I can't see," she explained.

"Yes, but you can, too." I was surprised by her perceptiveness, since we had never talked about that side of myself before.

"You are somebody and you know where you are going," she said, and laughed.

"I do? I don't know about that." I shook my head and took a big gulp of my drink.

"All I can be is one hell of a party girl," she said, taking another sip of her whisky on the rocks and looking around. "Where's the damn waiter anyway?"

Then, at that very moment, as if the universe had perfectly staged it, "I Am Woman" came blasting on the jukebox. Kaleen began singing along, slurring her words: "I am woman hear me roar. . . ."

Her voice was annoying to me. It had always been annoying to me,

71

and it was always loud. And, to top it off, she always sang off-key, especially when she was drunk. It drove me crazy. How can she embarrass herself like that? I thought. She stopped and got a serious pout on her face again, rattling the ice in her glass, as if she were searching for something.

"I just want to be a mother and have money, that's all," she said.

"That's all?" I teased.

"It's that simple," she sighed. "I don't want to be anybody," she said as she stared straight at me. "I am not you," she added.

I didn't say anything.

"So, tell me, Sis, is there anything wrong with my plan?" she asked as she tossed her hair back over her shoulder and leaned back on her chair, her index finger tapping her drink.

"No," I answered.

There was an uncomfortable tension growing between us and I saw the tears in her eyes. Perhaps it was one of the few times I ever saw the haunted look that I knew reflected what she hid inside. It was the kind of look that said, "This pain ain't going away–ever!" She sipped more of her drink and continued, "You know, you were always something growing up."

"Well, not always," I interrupted.

"Yes you were, Marcy, you were my big sister and damn, you left me alone to cope with them!" she exclaimed.

"With whom?" I asked, sipping my rum and tonic.

"Them–the parents, those fucking parents," she sneered, and then laughed. "I ain't forgiven you for it, ya know," she teased as she crunched on the ice.

It was clear she was getting drunker.

"You know, Marcy," she waved her finger in a sort of mocking manner. "You know what . . ." she drifted off for a moment.

"What?" I prompted.

"I just figured it out," she replied.

"Figured out what?"

"Why I stayed drunk the whole time I lived with them. You left me there and I couldn't handle it. Mother, that is. You betrayed me. We were supposed to leave together someday. You promised me," she said accusingly.

"Yes, but I had no choice the night that I ran, Kaleen. I hadn't planned to leave then," I tried to explain.

"It is all your fault that I am a drunk now." She laughed again.

It was a vulgar laugh this time, and it got to me. She motioned to the waiter, showing her empty glass and saying, "Jack, honey, another one, make it a double shot this time."

He smiled and went to get it.

"Kaleen, do you think you should?"

"Leave me alone."

What she said hurt me and made me feel angry but I looked at her and said nothing. What would be the point? She was drunk and I was drunk. It would only become a fight. I wanted to fix her, be a big sister, hold her and tell her it was going to be all right, tell her that I forgave her for all the times she had gotten me in trouble, coo over her–love her. But my head was throbbing and I knew it wasn't going to be all right. She was heading downhill fast. The other truth was that I had stepped onto the same slippery slope that she had and we were both going down.

***

Years later, after a bitter misunderstanding had separated us and we were no longer speaking, I heard from the family that she had married an evangelist preacher. She was still loud, my family said, but now she proselytized loudly. From what they said, Kaleen had found a cause: it was Jesus, and she was hanging on for dear life. She had gone from having no spiritual beliefs to saving every sinner she met and was telling everyone, "Get down on your knees and pray for your sins–Alleluia!"

I met her husband once when Kaleen, Wink, and I came to empty Mother's apartment after she had been moved to a nursing home. All I can say is that I felt very uncomfortable around this man, who gave me no eye contact, stood with arms folded in the center of the room, and said nothing. What I found surprising was the extraordinary contrast from the past in Kaleen's demeanor–she had become very quiet–almost meek.

As I look back, I believe that Kaleen, like a wild tornado on an open Midwest field, spun through her early years, out of control, until one day she stumbled and lost herself. But it was only after she had gone through the other side of her personal storm that she was able to find her grace, with God's help. Sadly though, from what I hear, the sister I knew, the woman with a fierce character, a magical strut–a Goddess fighting her demons–has vanished.

***

Kaleen still has a place in my heart. I miss her humor and the times we had. But she still refuses to talk to me, I think because she sincerely believes that I am not good enough for her. I wish I could have been the sister she wanted, but I couldn't. When I think of her now, I imagine her trying to rescue the world and everyone in it: herself, my mother, my brothers, her children, and any lost soul—except people like me, of course. I can hear her saying, "Just get down on your knees and pray to the Lord and see the light" as she arranges her many children and now grandchildren around her. I see her picking up the youngest, a dead ringer for herself, and exclaiming, "See the light! Just see the light!"

CHAPTER 11
Wink, My Adoptive Brother
A Mother's Good Son

Wink, my eldest brother, is without a doubt the kindest of all the Neilsons. His actions are considerate, moral, and, above all, responsible. He doesn't have the flair or bad-boy charm that my older brother Jock had growing up. Instead, he has a quiet steadiness that grows on you the more you get to know him.

He is a tall man and has inherited Mother's Russian cheekbones, wide grin, and her pronounced widow's peak. As he has aged, his looks and mannerisms have begun to reflect Father's in an uncanny way. There is the same tap on the pipe, the same little-boy twinkle in his eyes, and the same grumbling mutter that Father always used when displeased. But Wink's laugh is distinct and belongs to him alone. His laugh is a big guffaw that rises above the noise of a crowd. I have noticed, though, that he carefully restrains the second guffaw, as if one is enough. He then quietly sits back in his chair and returns to biting his pipe.

Wink also has a distinct boyish quality that only a mother who has raised a son would recognize. It is a side of him that appears when he is overtaxed or physically ailing. It is the way he talks in those moments, his tone of voice, that lets you know he is being brave and suffering quietly. Wink is an intense man with high blood pressure. He is high-strung and nervous and comes across like a racehorse waiting for the gun to go off.

I wish I knew more about Wink, but life did not turn out that way. Our time together has always been in passing, or in a quick visit, here or there, a conversation on the phone, a promise to get together. But somehow we never do.

So, what I know has come from our short time together and a bit of hearsay. By the time I arrived at the Neilsons', he had already moved away from home and was in college. After college he joined the Army and was shipped to Germany, where he met and married a lovely woman named Ilse.

Frances raised Wink. He was conservative, a mother's son, and a success. I think he tried harder than any of us to take the high road and choose the ethical way. And he was a good son all the way to the end. He stepped in, took charge, and cared about our parents near the end of their lives, while the rest of us stayed on the sidelines, too busy to care, to forgive, or to tolerate.

Wink never got into real trouble. He rebelled in small ways, carving out an identity that ran counter to Mother's expectations. Some of his habits triggered a disgruntled stare from her or a whisper behind his back, like the day he brought a full glass of water to the dinner table. Drinking a glass of water at the dinner table was a no-no—Neilsons drank wine with dinner or nothing at all. Even Kaleen and I were served diluted wine with our meals. Another rebellious trait that displeased Mother was his love of sports, especially basketball. A golf game here and there was the extent of our parents' sports experience. And last, but not least of his rebellions, was undershirts. After the Army, Wink started wearing white undershirts. Mother told me that this was what men of a different class did and she disapproved. As she put it, "Men like that, they sit around in their undershirts and drink beer and watch sports and get fat."

During most of my young years, I was too wrapped up in myself to notice how kind he was, but I have grown wiser and I have come to see who the heroes were and who the villains were in my life. Wink was the best of what the Neilsons could become.

All of the Neilson children have an underlying drive to obtain some invisible and often unattainable goal. Wink is no exception. We show this competitiveness in different ways, by being hard on ourselves and everyone else around us. But when I look at Wink, I would say that he tried harder to gain Mother's approval and respect than any of the rest of us did. He was a good son, dodging Mother's nasty moments and being very, very patient.

Why is Wink different from my other siblings? Why does he refuse to have the "better than thou" attitude with me that I see in Kaleen and saw in Jock? Why has Wink valued intimate moments over social and monetary victories? I think the nature of his relationship with Mother goes a long way toward explaining why Wink became the kind one.

Wink didn't get what he deserved on the day he was born. There were no hurrahs or cheers. Rather, there was a quiet, undeniable dread on my mother's part. Nowadays, we might say that her behavior was due to a postpartum psychosis. But in those days it was ignored. His arrival quickly fell into the background of Mother's personal tragedy. Two days before Wink's birth her mother died, and she became deeply mired in her grief and anger. I think he felt that Mother didn't know how to truly love him as a child, because whenever she looked at him she was reminded of the sad days after her mother's death. Consequently, I think he tried all his life to be seen for the loving man—the good child—that he truly was.

The eldest-child syndrome also played a part and ate at him for years to come. He took responsibility for Mother in very practical and often difficult ways. For example, he found the retirement homes and had her over for holidays. This is something none of the other children can claim, not even me, except for the one gesture I made the day she was placed in a group home, when I took her beloved, cranky old cat home with me.

76

I was about six years old when I had my first insight into how it must have been for Wink to grow up in the Neilson household. It was the day Mother was beginning the dreaded ritual of reading the "last letter" from her dying mother to me.

"Marcy, go grab that little chair and pull it up to my bed," Mother said.

Dutifully, I went to find the little ladder-back chair, the one with a straw seat and painted flowers on it. I pulled it up close to the large mahogany bed and sat down.

"Good. Now listen carefully," she said as she ceremoniously walked over to the little red leather jewelry box on the bureau. I can still hear the snap of the lock as she opened the lid. Carefully, as if it were a crown of jewels, she used both hands to lift a faded pale envelope lying on top of the diamond and emerald rings and gold jewelry.

"This is what my mother wrote to me on the day she died," she said, carrying the letter back to the bed and sitting down on its edge. She always acted as if we had never sat down together and read this letter before, but we had. I had heard it many times and I knew to expect to hear the same sad, loving words of a dying mother to her daughter many times more.

"*Dear Babbie*," she would begin. This time, she peered over her glasses down at me, to make sure I was listening. "That's what my mother called me–Babbie–it means baby in Scottish."

I nodded. I always made sure my back was straight up against the chair and that my hands were folded on my knees in a ladylike manner. I was expected to say nothing. She continued, "*Dear Babbie, by the time you get this letter, I will be gone. . . .*" Mother grabbed her hanky at that moment and I gripped the seat of my chair. I was holding back the emotions that were slowly welling up inside me. I hated sad stories about loss. I hated the letter and I hated the ritual. She read on and she began crying. This always happened at the exact same point where her mother said something like, "Babbie, you are my favorite." The reading of the letter always ended with Mother weeping hysterically.

"Come over here, Marcy. Give your Mommy a hug," she would say, motioning for me to climb up on the bed with her. Reluctantly, I would walk over, climb up on the bed and put my little arms around her to comfort her loss.

On the day that I remember concerning Wink, the letter reading went differently. She stopped at the "You were always my favorite" part, and looked up from her glasses and paused, deep in thought.

"Marcy, you know that I was pregnant at that time. Right?"

I nodded yes.

"Your brother, Wink, was born just a few days later."

"Yes," I said. I kept staring up at her.

"How horrible that was. Sometimes I think I hated him," she said, her face crumpling.

I said nothing but began to twitch a little in my seat.

"I resented him for that."

I could feel my anger at her welling up inside me, and I wanted to protest. Scream. Say that I loved my big brother. I realize now that Wink and I were connected by Mother's ambiguous feelings toward both of us. I had replaced her stillborn baby and Wink had replaced her dead mother.

"Oh, how I loathed that little baby, with those demanding, beady eyes! There he was, Marcy, lying in bed looking up at me, with his chubby, fat little arms trying to snuggle with me. It was horrible," she said.

"But, Mommy, I like Wink," I protested.

"Shush," she said, putting her finger to her mouth.

"I couldn't get away, you know," she continued as she bit her lip and stared off into the distance. It was like she was on stage, giving the performance of her life.

"All I wanted to do was cry and be left alone." She leaned over to me and whispered, like a naughty little girl telling a secret to another little girl.

"I've never forgiven him for that."

I said nothing.

I think Wink intuitively knew that Mother had rejected him as a child. But I also think that he tucked the knowledge neatly away and never gave it another thought. In truth, I believe Mother resented all her children for needing attention, especially in the moments when they cast a shadow across her limelight–her show.

Wink had wanted to be a writer–a great writer. It was his passion and his dream. He studied journalism at Harvard, and even worked one summer for the *Albany Times*. One afternoon, when I was ten and visiting Wink and his wife, Ilse, where they lived in a tiny apartment in Flushing, New York, he came out of his office with some papers in his hand. He was animated–something you didn't get to see very often with him. He wanted to share a short story that he had been working on. It was a story about a man who struggled through tumultuous relationships and secretly wanted to be a minister. I don't even remember what happened in the story. But I knew he was writing about himself. I saw his spirit striving to stay alive. And I never forgot who I believed he was and who he really wanted to be.

He was a good husband to his perfect wife, and he was a good father to his two beautiful daughters. And he put aside his writing and became a good provider–a businessman working on Wall Street. But his love was writing and his passion for spirit-filled and heart-touching stories never left him. Quietly, at home in the evenings, he typed away–it was his lifeline.

***

A dog has always been a part of my life, helping me when I feel alone or when I just need to feel the free spirit that I feel with animals. Babbette was the first of many dogs whom I have regarded as my spirit guardians. The story of Babbette's arrival goes back to when I was eleven and in a terrible mess. I called Wink for help.

It began when Father received a grant to work in Spain at the Alhambra for the summer. The only problem was that no children were permitted to live on the premises. Consequently, the plan was to have Kaleen and I live down in the village with a strange family who spoke very little English. I balked at the idea.

"I don't want to go," I said to my parents one night at dinner.

"But why not?" Mother asked.

"I don't want to. That's why," I said.

"But, dear, you and Kaleen will learn Spanish."

Kaleen nodded and stared at me, as if to say, don't you dare not come with me!

"How fun that will be!" she said.

"No, it won't be fun," I said, ignoring Kaleen's glare.

"We have already arranged it with the family in the village."

"I don't want to stay with strangers," I said.

They could save money if I didn't go and they liked that idea. By the next day it was arranged that I would spend the summer at my mother's sister's home. Aunt Catherine had a beautiful home outside of Philadelphia. She was an always-trying-to-be-good, overwrought, overfed, pie-baking woman who was relentlessly cheerful. Her husband, on the other hand, was an insurance man who sat alone in his room in a straight-backed chair every night and drank himself to sleep. My very strange and very spoiled cousin, Bartram, also lived in the house. He was fifteen and lived on the third floor.

Every evening they would huddle around the TV and watch *The Rocky and Bullwinkle Show*. That was the only thing they ever did together as a family. Why I do not know, but when they watched they would laugh together and be a happy, normal family. And then when the show was over, each would retreat to his or her respective corner of the house.

Within a week of my stay, my aunt fell down and broke her leg. She

79

was stuck downstairs for most of the summer, sitting in a chair with a large cast on her leg. I was glad she was stuck downstairs, because we had been sharing a room for the summer, and she snored and kept me up all night. Now she was sleeping on a cot made up for her in the TV room. But crutches did not stop Catherine from getting up every morning to roast some lamb or beef or chicken for Bartram, who hated breakfast food and refused to eat any leftovers whatsoever. At noon he would come downstairs, and every day a roast and a new chocolate cake would be waiting for him on the kitchen counter.

Bartram was the strangest guy I have ever met. He could have been the prototype for every black-raincoat-wearing horror-film character. He was a tall, skinny guy who wore black-rimmed glasses and sixties-style greasy hair neatly parted on the side. And then there was the tie that he always wore. The tie pleased my Aunt Catherine, who was convinced her son was going places in the world. What nobody knew was that he belonged to a Nazi organization, and he told me more about the group than I wanted to know as an eleven-year-old.

"Do you know that the Nazis know everything?" he asked.

"No."

"Well, they do. Best files and record keeping in the United States," he boasted.

"Really?"

"Yes, even the FBI gets information from them."

"Where do they come from?"

"There is a meeting place on Long Island."

"Really? That's where I live! Where on Long Island?"

"Never mind that. I can't tell you that unless you are a member."

"Are you a member?"

"Yes, I am working for them."

"You are? What are you doing?"

"I can't tell you that either."

"Oh."

"Did you know the Jews own everything in the media? All the TV stations and the radio?"

"No, do they? So what does that mean?"

"It's their plan to take over. It means we got to get rid of them," he said, smiling.

I didn't like what he was saying. I didn't know a lot, but I knew it was wrong and that it was scary.

Bartram was a genius in a nightmarish way. He was crazy, but just sane enough to keep his madness a secret. He was a straight-A student, a mama's boy who hated his father and the world at large. He made horror films as a hobby and had a darkroom and a film projector where he religiously watched grade-D films with lots of blood and girls screaming. He lived a very seedy, secret life that no one knew about and died—or was murdered, as most people think—years later. And no one ever found his body.

One night in the darkroom when Bartram and I were developing a set of photos, Bartram molested me. I ran out of the room and down the winding stairs to my aunt, who had fallen asleep in front of the TV. I was too ashamed and too scared to tell anyone, then or later.

But I was in tears when I called Wink the next morning.

"I want my family," I said.

"Are you missing them?"

"Yes." I started to cry.

"Would you like to come visit me and Ilse for the Fourth of July?"

"Yes!"

By the next day I was on the train to New York where my big brother was waiting for me. I was being rescued, although no one knew that but me. I still could not tell Wink the truth. I was too ashamed.

"I think you need a dog," he said, smiling at me.

"A dog?"

"Yes, one that is yours. Mother and Father have only given you pet turtles and they don't last very long."

"Yes, my poor pet turtles. Do you remember when Jock came home drunk and threw up in the turtle bowl?"

"No, I don't." Wink was way too conservative to be having this conversation, but I went on.

"Well. Of course he did not know that it was my pet turtle bowl. He was going to flush the contents down the toilet, but he said that in his drunken stupor, he saw this little green thing floating around and for a moment he thought that he was really sick and throwing up a tumor or something. But it was just the turtle, so he reached in and got it." I laughed out loud, envisioning Jock's drunken dilemma.

"Back to the dog," Wink said. Looking at his expression, I realized that I had given him a bit more detail than he was comfortable with hearing.

"Yes, the dog," I said, moving on.

"I think a dog would help you."

"Really?" I began to get excited and I started to daydream about my very own dog. Even though there were lots of dogs in the house, they were all Mother's and I had not had a dog of my own since High. It would be like having a best friend all the time.

"Would you like a whippet?"

"Oh, I would love to have one." I hugged him and I knew at that moment that I loved him.

The next morning we went to a breeder and Wink bought me my first dog. She was a dog whose spirit would return as a guardian dog for me, lifetime after lifetime. A dog who began her first life's journey with me as a whippet, who then returned as a mutt, and then as a part wolf and then a malamute. And now, as I look deep into the eyes of my little perky Jack Russell, Harvest, I can see all the doggie lifetimes, going way back to this whippet.

I named her Babbette, short for Elisabeth—George Washington's wife—because it was the day before the Fourth of July. I took her back to Aunt Catherine's.

For the rest of the summer, from dawn until sunset, I lived outside. I pretended I was a dog and got a terrible case of poison ivy from chasing rabbits under bushes, but that didn't keep me from the outdoors. Babbette was my best friend, and we ran in the fields together, lay by the running brook, and took long walks through the back woods. I found my spirit again, thanks to Wink's gift. And Bartram was never able to lay his hands on me again. Babbette and I were free.

***

Wink and I lost touch after that summer, but when I became a wild and out-of-control teenager, he was the only Neilson who did not openly reject me and make me feel worthless. As I look back, I see that when my life as a child seemed to become a swirling maelstrom, he was always there in the background, offering a helping hand. Whether it was a small gift sent from Germany, his mention of me in a radio interview, a smile, or a sincere question, his little gestures helped let me know that I was real and not just an object whose purpose was to please others.

***

Years later, at the end of my teens, I realized that the Neilson family had always treated me as if I were a ticking time bomb, ready to explode. No one ever really said anything, but I could sense it. No one talked about feelings or what was wrong. No one tried to find a solution. Problems were simply ignored. And consequently, as I saw it, I was ignored and it made me feel crazy.

My brothers' and their families' rejection of me increased when I was in college in Connecticut. One weekend, a confusion as to whether I was going to be invited to a get-together with them increased my frustration to the exploding point. I had been looking forward to it all week. Wink had called me a few days before and told me he would get back to me. When the day came I began waiting for the phone call. I was hoping that time had healed our differences. But life never went that way—at least not for me. I had thought that they would call me, as planned. But as time went on and I waited for them to call, I began to realize that it wasn't going to happen. I began to drink.

I was torn with my need to keep my dignity, to stay away from them, to be above their rejections. But suddenly the pain of all the rejection, which I had buried deep inside, the memories of all the times that had caused me to experience a deep self-loathing, rose out of me like the dead rising from the grave. It was a force to be reckoned with. It grabbed me and, before I knew it, I broke the rules of common etiquette that I had been raised with and I called them. Within a few minutes, slurring and yelling, I pulled all the skeletons out of the closet. I was angry and I was talking. I talked about our dysfunctional family. I screamed into the phone about the abuse, the sexual exploitation, the lies, the cheating, and, above all, I spoke about how much they made me feel as if I were a blatant disgrace to the family. At the other end of the phone they maintained a cool, calculated silence and then, when I was finished, without a word they simply hung up the phone.

Wink called early the next morning and came over to see me. I think he felt sorry for me. It was one of those fragile moments that remain forever carved in my heart. It was the kind of moment when no one can say the right words to fill the empty spaces. I could only say thank you with my humble silence. And that is what I did. We did not talk about the night before nor what I had said. Instead he tried to be kind and take an interest in my life. He stuck to safe topics, asking questions about my art, my plans, and my education.

It was the right thing to come see me. Little did he know how important his warm, conservative heart was in saving my fragile, broken self that day. Little did he know that I was hanging on to a lonely edge carved out by the rest of the Neilsons.

***

Years later, when Wink's children were grown, one day something happened to Wink. I think we all expected it. How could it not happen? Wink couldn't be the "good guy" anymore. One afternoon he came home and asked for a divorce and announced he was moving in with a younger woman. I think he thought that the world around him was shaking and looked like it would crumble. I heard all of this through the grapevine. It did not mean for one moment that the life he led before he broke away was wrong. It was quite the opposite. Ilse was a perfect wife and Wink was a perfect husband. They continue to respect and care for each other and they stay in contact. But Wink chose to be himself that day. He courageously chose to make a change–to be the man living his dream. He followed his passion and his deep, rich spirit. Wink followed his heart and lived the story that he had always wanted to write.

CHAPTER 12
Switzerland
A Gift from the Mother of the Mountains

When I was thirteen I was sent to a boarding school in Switzerland. Boarding school had been Mother's ultimate threat of a punishment for me. Many times I would hear, "If you are not careful Marcy, it's off to boarding school."

"I don't care," I would snap back.

"You know what happens at boarding school—don't you?" she'd add.

"No, Mother, I don't know what happens," I'd reply.

"Well, you might find out someday," she'd say threateningly. Of course after living with the Neilsons I had become accustomed to imagining the worst, and boarding school was no exception.

Then one day, after a dramatic fight with Mother, I yelled, "I want to go to boarding school." Mother stopped arguing and looked at me, dumbfounded.

"You what?"

"I want to go to boarding school."

"You do?"

'Yes, I want to go where Nancie Smith's parents are sending her."

"But you barely know Nancie!"

"I don't care."

***

After taking care of the details of registration and payments, Nancie Smith and I were on a plane to Geneva, Switzerland. Although it was architecturally interesting, Geneva was just another European city to me. But when the school van left the city and began to climb the winding mountain road into the mist toward Villars-sur-Ollon, I saw the beauty of Switzerland. Even though I had never been there, the green hills and the breathtaking, snow-covered mountains seemed so familiar. I gasped at the sight and my mood lightened considerably.

After unpacking and settling into our room, I went to dinner. There, as I listened to the conversations around me and watched everyone mingle, I discovered that the common language for the school was French. No one had warned me that we were going to be speaking French. My knowledge of French was minimal. All I knew came from a blue book that Chapin School used to teach the French version of "see Spot run," a reader of the fifties. Also as I looked around, I saw that I was the youngest student there.

I could identify the few Americans in the room because their attire seemed flashier and their manners were a bit more abrasive than the obviously well-bred English girls who were quietly chatting at the end of a long wooden table in the corner. Although battling my shyness at that moment, I was glad Mother had taught me proper etiquette. But I was also furious with her because I was sure that she had purposely left out the French-speaking part of the boarding school. Yes, I knew she was having the last laugh.

After a few months I adjusted to the different lifestyle and the quaint ways of Maison de la Harpe. Even in the restricted environment of the school's rules, and the days that often seemed more like the 1930s, I felt free. On a very deep level, I knew I would have the space and time to discover myself in new ways, without anyone telling me who I was supposed to be.

I was a very serious thirteen-year-old. I read a lot, especially poetry. I thought about philosophy a lot. I was excited the day I came across Kahlil Gibran's book, *The Prophet*. I want to be a prophet! I thought. But how does one do that? I asked myself. How do prophets become prophets? And are there girl prophets? I had no answers. I decided to write an epic poem—a book just like Kahlil Gibran's. But my Prophet was a great wise oak tree that lived in the center of a forest, where all the animals came to listen to his wisdom. In the end a terrible storm came and uprooted the tree. The animals grieved, but one day in spring they saw a new sapling growing from the heart of the old tree. I was pleased with my epic poem.

Of course I was not living in a permanent state of angst while I tried to figure out how to become a prophet. Just the opposite. Like every teenager, I also wanted to be popular, make friends, have fun, and most of all just do what teenagers do. It took awhile to be accepted, but my bad-girl, rebellious streak, my depth of understanding of human nature, and my sense of humor helped me win friends and gain respect. I shared my book with some of them. Soon word got out that I was the one to go to for advice. I was always surprised that older students came to me with their questions. Mmmm, I mused, maybe this prophet idea is working. So I played the prophet.

That was one of the most inspirational periods of my young life. The great mother mountains, the valleys, the vast sky, and the sound of cowbells and silent snow of Switzerland all fed my soul. Many years later, in a meditation I discovered that I had had a past life in Switzerland, where I had lived as a milkmaid. I also found out it had been my happiest lifetime.

In that little finishing school in the Alps, I had my first taste of political organizing. It began with a rule: the school wanted students to speak French all day. For over fifty years its administrators had enforced this rule by secretly giving two students a small piece of cardboard called the *papier*. Those students were to look for the students who were not speaking French.

If a student was caught speaking her own language to someone else before 6 p.m., the *papier* was passed to her. The students who were left holding the *papier* at the end of the day were made to memorize a French passage and recite it after dinner. I hated public speaking. I also hated the whole idea because it created distrust and made students betray each other.

One day while eating lunch I realized that this practice could be overthrown! We could unite. We could each volunteer to take the *papier* for the day—thus liberating ourselves from the oppression of the spies assigned by the headmistress. About half the students thought it was brilliant and followed the plan. But then of course there were always the goody two-shoes . . . the ones who obeyed rules.

The school's teachers came in all shapes and sizes, each with a distinct style. Miss Smee, the English teacher, always wore her dark brown hair in a hair net. Her prewar-era wardrobe consisted of below-the-knee-length skirts, plain white cotton blouses, and a variety of tan cashmere cardigans. She always, always wore short red ankle socks with her walking shoes, and when she clucked, she reminded me of a well-bred English hen. Madame Amigue, the headmistress, was a tall, thin, middle-aged woman who smiled a lot, said nothing, and was always ahead of a student's pranks. The students instinctively knew not to trust her silent smiles. The school also had a ski teacher on staff, who looked like a rosy-cheeked Amazon. And the American students had a math teacher who lived in the village. She was a very old woman whose father had taught her Algebra orally on their hikes through the mountains. We went to her house for our math classes. She smoked too much and her house smelled of cat urine. It was hard to concentrate.

But one teacher at the school left a profound spark in my heart. Unlooked for, she became one of the most important people in my young life. Her name was Mademoiselle Ponchon. She was about twenty-three, was the French teacher, and was the opposite of Miss Smee in style and presentation. She had free-flowing blonde hair, was a beautiful Jane Fonda look-alike, and had very French mannerisms. Mademoiselle Ponchon was very serious about teaching French, though. She was fiercely passionate about having her students do a good job. I can't count the times she slammed her hand down on my desk and yelled, "*Non! Non! Non! Qu'est-ce que c'est?*" as she pointed to my messy homework. I cringed every time I heard "No! No! What is this?" in French. Before long, I decided she hated me. It seemed to me it was always my desk she was slamming her hand on and it was always me she was correcting. It all seemed unfair.

One afternoon Mademoiselle Ponchon sent a student downstairs to my room to tell me to come upstairs to her study. She usually did this when she had a question or a correction about our homework. Uh oh, I thought, I must have done something wrong. I slowly walked up the stairs. I was almost in tears, dreading the scolding that I was about to get. I knocked on the door.

"*Entrez*," she answered. I went in and stood there. She stared at me and said nothing. I stared back. She smiled. I tried to smile in return. I noticed that she was holding something behind her back. Oh God, what is it? I thought, expecting to see my homework papers tossed on the floor. Instead she walked over to me and placed her hand gently on my shoulder as she handed me a wrapped gift.

"*Pour toi.*"

"*Moi?*" I said, not quite believing it was for me.

"Yes, for you," she continued in English. Then she looked at me and said in a more serious tone, "*Ma petite* Marcy, you are special. You need to remember that." She added, "You are the most intelligent in your own way." I was speechless, and I am sure my face showed my surprise. She laughed. "I always wanted a little sister when I was young. You know, I lost my father when I was young and I lived alone with my mother." Still speechless, I mumbled a thank you.

"You are exactly the sister I dreamed of having," she said.

"Really?" Her kind words made me want to cry.

"*Oui.* Yes. *Maintenant, ouvrez il!*" Now, open it!

I unwrapped the gift and smiled. It was a little black and gray stuffed dog. That gift made me so happy. With that act of kindness, Mademoiselle Ponchon allowed me to glimpse the truth of my own self-worth. It has remained with me throughout my life.

***

As the months went by, Mademoiselle Ponchon continued to be extra hard on me with my homework, as if now she had even more right to expect only the best from me. After all, I was her little sister. She did not stop slamming her hand on my desk, but now I knew she cared and it did not bother me quite as much. She treated me like a little sister and rescued me from getting in trouble. We spent time together chattering into the late hours of the night. She introduced me to her boyfriend, a passionate poet who wrote a beautiful poem about me. It was the first and probably the only time I have ever had a poem written about me.

The other students liked Ponchon; after all, she was the youngest on staff and so in many ways was one of us. Of course, the rest of the faculty adhered to old-school thinking and disapproved of her. You could see it in the way they held themselves and the tone in their voices when they spoke to her. To me she was one of the single most caring persons that I have ever encountered in my life. She gave me the gift of love. One evening she gave me another gift: a beautiful silver necklace in the shape of a heart, with an anchor and cross on it. She wore it all the time.

"This represents Hope, Love, and Faith. You will need this in your life as you grow up," she said softly as she put it over my head. "It comes from Southern France," she added. I wore that necklace proudly every day. But one hot spring day, as we climbed to the top of the ski mountain where a beautiful lake lay hidden in the hills, I lost it during a swim in its icy clear water. My silver talisman of hope, faith, and love slipped off my neck and settled to the bottom of the lake. My heart broke.

Under a full moon that night, I went out on the balcony and wept, in despair over my lost necklace. I prayed that I might find it the next time we climbed the mountain. "Please God, let me have it back," I begged. In the last few months of school, in some ways I had neglected Ponchon as I moved on to a popular group of students. I felt guilty about that and asked God for forgiveness. I was heartbroken. "I am sorry. I hurt Ponchon," and continued to pray, thinking perhaps this was my punishment. I felt that losing the necklace was a very bad omen. Would I lose Ponchon, too?

As I sat wrapped up in a blanket, watching the moon move in and out of clouds and then across the face of the Matterhorn, for some reason I decided I would try smoking a cigarette. Between my tears and sniffling I inhaled by mistake. I immediately started coughing and gasping for air, lungs and body totally shocked. Soon everything was swirling around me; the moon grew bigger and sent a light across my chest. And then I saw the light grow all around me. Like massive mother arms, the mountains embraced me. I felt as though I had been blessed by a cosmic visitation–a confirmation. I did not say or do anything. But a feeling of extraordinary wonderment and extreme knowing blossomed in my inner being. At that very moment, I saw a glimpse of my future. I saw that my path would be profound–sometimes painfully heartfelt, but deeply meaningful.

Was the loss of the necklace a premonition? To this day I do not know if it was the cigarette, the broken heart, Mademoiselle Ponchon's love for me, or all of it, but at that young age I embraced myself. I accepted my life's path. It felt to me like a perfect alignment of the heavens.

***

When school ended I returned to the Neilsons, who were living in Rome at the time. As I had feared, I lost contact with Mademoiselle Ponchon. To this day, a string of Venetian glass beads that she gave me and a hollowed-out piece of bark from the mountains of Villars still sit on my bureau. For over forty years I searched for her. I sent letters to people who I thought were she, only to have them returned with an "I am sorry" letter. To no avail, I made overseas calls and spoke in broken French to people who could tell me nothing. I gave up, only to try again years later. It had been an ongoing hope of mine to find her some day to say thank you.

Over the years, whenever I tried to find her, I found myself asking a familiar question. It is the heart question that I have lived with my whole life: How could someone who meant so much to me just disappear?

***

Then one day, after all the years of giving up hope of ever finding her, I unexpectedly came across a new phone number. Once again I left a message on a stranger's phone somewhere in France, hoping this would be the one. That afternoon I came home to a message on my phone.

My tears caught me by surprise as I listened to the message and heard her voice once again, saying, "Hello, Marcy? It's your big sister, calling from France. . . ." As I listened, something inside me softened. Ever so gently, I began to feel a timid reopening of a place in my heart. A sweet clarity came to me as I basked in the familiar presence of a beautiful, beautiful soul.

Ever has it been that love knows not
its own depth until the hour of separation.

–Kahlil Gibran, *The Prophet*

CHAPTER 13
Rome
Reaching Across Time to God the Mother

In my teens I had an insatiable need to understand the meaning of life—Rome became the perfect platform for me to embark on my mystical quest. While other teenagers thought about their next date, I was thinking about the next planet in the universe. I went to a lot of strange places and had many visions while I searched for answers to mystical questions. I was searching for spiritual answers and even though I did not find the Goddess until I was an adult, she was always there in subtle ways. I realize now that she was hidden in the poetry and art that surrounded me while I lived in Rome. She was everywhere—she was Minerva, Diana, Ceres, Venus, or Turan. Sometimes I saw her in the statues of Mary holding her child, found in corners of cathedrals and of churches, built upon ancient temple sites.

I was easily bored as a young teen. As a pastime, I practiced trying to grasp the concepts of infinity, of God, Death, and Rebirth. As I fell asleep, I often envisioned traveling through the vast universe. I even tried to make up my own mystical symbols. The closest I ever came to visualizing what infinity might look like was the day Kaleen and I were playing with the dogs. One of the whippets dropped a chewed golf ball into my lap. I looked at its surface, which had been ripped apart, and saw that it was constructed of hundreds of rubber bands crisscrossing each other.

"Aha! That's what the universe looks like," I said out loud. Kaleen looked at me as if I were a space alien. "What are you talking about?" she asked as she snapped her bubble gum in my face.

"This is what the universe looks like!" I said, showing her the torn golf ball.

Kaleen gave me one of those "what planet do you come from" looks. "Just give me the ball," she said as she grabbed it from me. "I don't know what you are talking about, Marcy." She turned the golf ball around in her hand, trying to see whatever it was I was seeing. It baffled her.

"Forget it," I answered, feeling defensive. I took the ball back and threw it for the dogs. That was the only attempt at an intellectual conversation I ever had with any Neilson. I never told them about my brilliant mirror metaphor for God or the donut-shaped symbol for omnificent power. Nope, they couldn't understand. And I also knew that they wouldn't care.

When I lived in Rome, the famous landmarks were accessible to everyone. In the sixties, it was much simpler to go to many of the ancient sites. Tourists did not fill every room of every museum or ruin. There was a sense of space and peace—a dignity to the past. There were no fences or gates to pass through, no need for tickets or reservations to enter a museum, no guards with guns. In those days, there were open doors and at times friendly faces. I was free to go where I pleased without bumping into crowds.

One day, I found some steps that went through a wooded area to a corner of the Borghese gardens. I came upon a building with a sign that read *Museo Etrusco*. I learned later that this building had been a sixteenth-century palace and the main artifacts had been excavated from a tomb in Cerveteri. In those days, it did not seem to be a huge landmark and it felt quite welcoming to a young, curious teenager like me. The moment I stepped inside the front door of the place, I knew something profound was happening. It was eerie. All of a sudden, I felt disoriented. Intense, ancient energy vibrated around me and drew me further into the building. When I came upon a sarcophagus of a reclining bride and groom from the sixth century BC, I stopped and gazed at it for a long time. As I stared at the faces of the two Etruscans, I was overwhelmed with emotion. Their hand gestures and eyes called to a place inside of me that I didn't understand. But I never forgot the feeling, and I returned to the quiet museum room with the reclining figures as often as I could. I loved being with them and feeling the strange sensations. Whenever I looked into their almond-shaped eyes and stared at their serene smiles, so common to the Etruscan art, I felt something special happening inside me. I felt as if I were psychically plugged into them. I felt connected on a cellular level. I understood their mysterious gaze. In those days I imagined that there was a secret code embedded in the funerary sculptures.

I found that the more I spent time with them, the more I was able to understand the ancient mysteries and questions about the meaning of life. I'd close my eyes and feel a swirling sensation that often turned into an unexplainable joy. At other times, I felt tranquil, as if I were remembering a past life where I saw myself gliding in a canoe on a smooth lake in the mountains. I did notice that each time I psychically connected with these two figures, a gentle breeze would sweep through the building and a strong scent of Roman pine needles would fill the space. I do not remember if there were any open windows, but I noticed that whenever I went to that corner of the room where the coffin stood and closed my eyes, the same breeze and the same sweet, musty smell always wafted through the room. Strangely, I never saw a guard or another human being in that museum—no matter what time I was there. I was always completely alone in the room. In those days, it was Rome's and my secret treasure.

***

Something special happened to me one morning in my school in Rome. I was in detention for having done something or other and my punishment was to dust the shelves in the old library, every Saturday, for a month. It was a beautiful mahogany room in an eighteenth-century Roman villa, filled with old books on shelves that went all the way up to the high ceilings. I was standing on a rickety ladder, cleaning with one of those ostrich feather dusters. I was standing next to a huge, open window that overlooked an enclosed garden. It was a perfect spring day and the wisteria was in full bloom. The scent mingled with the musty wood of the room. I sighed, longing to be in the garden instead of trapped inside. Frustrated, I looked at my watch and saw that I had one more hour to go. As I turned back toward the shelves, I heard a thump. I turned around to see what it was. Across the room a small, maroon-colored book lay open on the floor. I wondered how it had fallen, since there was no one else in the room. I climbed down the ladder and went over and picked up the book. The open page contained a poem. As I touched the yellow, stained paper of the opened page, I felt a magical tingle. It read,

Who are you, reader, reading my poems a hundred years hence?
I cannot send you one single flower from this wealth of the spring, one single streak of gold from yonder clouds. Open your doors and look abroad.

It was a straightforward poem about the beautiful day, and I felt that Tagore had magically crossed time to reach out to me. It was as if his hand came out through the pages and invited me to step into his sweet-scented garden. His hundred-year-old poem, a simple testimony to beauty, had reached out from the past to touch me in the future as I stared out the window at the garden. It was a perfect alignment: a spring day, a beautiful garden, and two romantics. "Open your doors," he wrote, and I opened my heart. I was enraptured by his words, as if we were lovers.

I stole the book. It is one of the few things I have ever stolen. But after I leafed through the other pages, I knew that I had to have this book—not a copy. Rabrindranath Tagore was going to be mine forever.

***

I was a romantic and a seeker of truth, and as a teenager I read a lot of books. I felt the writers understood what I was struggling to become. But I lived in a sometimes-hostile world, where people did not dare to dream big dreams or challenge established spiritual dogma. I did not find a female philosopher or a single strong female figure to follow. With the exception of Emily Dickinson, who retreated from society, Jo, in Louisa May Alcott's

Little Women, Grace Metalious's *Peyton Place*, or Margaret Mitchel's *Gone with the Wind*, which made me cry and whose heroine did not get much credit for her inner strength, there were no female figures to help guide me as a young woman growing up.

Imagine if there had been books available about powerful women who were thinkers and leaders; women who wrote about the philosophy and traditions of the Goddess. What would growing up have been like for me and other girls then? Would it have made a difference? I like to dream about the differences it would have made if a strong, independent mother figure, a female protector, nurturer, brave woman, emotional being, wild and ecstatic, had been in place for me to honor—would my life have taken a different course? How would it have felt to have turned to her in prayer and said, "Our Mother, who art in heaven"? What power could have been inspired in me if the Mother of God had become God the Mother?

I loved the bustle of Rome, and especially the rush of sensations that came at me from every corner. I loved knowing that this ancient city's vibrant energy and art had flourished for centuries and that some things never change—the clamor of voices from the vendors bickering, the women sashaying by the young men, the old women sitting on stoops gossiping, the Parthenon cats, the pink glow of sunset on marble, the sun-baked cobblestones, the smell of cool moss on terra-cotta walls, and the sound of trickling fountains. They all became vehicles ready to transport me into the past.

The beauty was astounding. I used to gaze up at the ceilings of the great Roman Cathedrals and daydream about the old masters, such as da Vinci and Michelangelo, or Bernini, Raphael, and Titian. In those days I felt that I was in the right place—but in the wrong century.

When I was fifteen, I took my paintings and hung out at the Spanish Steps. With many other artists, I sold my work for pennies to the thousands of tourists who crowded Rome during the summer. In those days I painted two types of pictures. One was commercial in style and influenced by Cubism. The others were more dramatic and of otherworldly images, which were profoundly connected to my spirit. Every morning I would neatly arrange my small watercolor portraits on the steps in a row, making sure to put one or two of my mystical ones alongside them.

One day as I sat talking to a few curious onlookers, two American women came over to my spot. The larger of the two was a middle-aged, somewhat loud-voiced woman. The other was younger, more quiet and placating. I noticed that the older woman had a commanding air about her as she pointed to one particular fanciful watercolor of mine.

"How much?" she asked. She had a strong American accent. I told her the price and she bought it. As I wrapped it in brown paper she looked around at my other work and then watched me wrap the painting. "Do you know who I am?" she asked, towering over me.

I looked up at her, shading the bright Roman sun from my eyes. "No," I said, shaking my head.

"I am Mrs. Rockefeller," she announced. The younger woman looked at her strangely, as if to correct her.

"That is, Mrs. Ex Rockefeller," she said, turning to the younger woman, as if to say, "there, are you happy now?"

That must be her daughter, I thought, as I smiled politely. "Nice to meet you."

"I am an art collector," she said as she looked over my work. "I don't think those over there are very good," she said as she pointed to the few mystical oils.

"But this watercolor is good," she added, smiling, and then she left. The younger woman followed behind her. I did not know whether to feel complimented or insulted. But I brushed off the doubt and comforted myself with the fact that I could boast, with a bit of pride and humor, that my art had gone to the Rockefeller collection.

One of the best moments in my art career came a few days after the Rockefeller incident. It was in the afternoon and I was heading home after a day on the steps. It had been a good day financially. It was a hot day and I was thirsty and tired, and stopped to get a soda at a sidewalk café on the Via Veneto. I leaned my oils up against a chair and sipped my drink. As I watched people stroll by, a very handsome, blue-eyed, blond-haired man in his late twenties–or maybe early thirties–came over to me. He smiled, and I was taken by his sophisticated air and simple manners. In those days I loved the look of men in ascots and expensive white shirts–which this man was wearing.

"Do you mind if I take a look?" he asked as he pointed to my oils. He had a soft voice and he clearly had an Italian accent. He began speaking to me in Italian, and I responded in Italian, but then we switched to English. I put my oils down and he squatted on the sidewalk and looked carefully at each one. He put about five of them to one side. He didn't say anything at first. Then he looked up and stared right at me. I got lost in his blue eyes and I sighed, already smitten.

"These are very good," he said, smiling.

"Thank you."

"How much is this one?" He pulled out a yellow oil painting of a nude man crouched on a desert, with his face hidden in his hands. In the distance was an eclipse setting on the horizon. I gave him a price and he pulled out the money and handed it to me. I thanked him.

"You are going to be famous," he said, smiling gently at me. I was excited by his comment. He is so handsome, I thought. If only I wasn't fifteen.

"I would like to offer you a show," he said.

"A show?"

"Yes, I have connections. I know many owners."

"Really?" I said, trying to be collected and more professional. I did not want to show too much excitement or let this stranger know that I had a crush on him.

"Yes, really." He pulled out a piece of paper and wrote a name and a number on it.

"Here, call me and we can talk." And then he left with my painting under his arm.

I gathered my paintings as quickly as I could and took the first bus home. I ran up the stairs, not even waiting for the elevator. I burst into the apartment and ran directly to my father's studio, where he was working on a large oil of a bird of paradise. "Father, guess what happened!" I said. I told him about the incident. I thought he would be proud of me. He listened and I could see that he was proud, but he was also concerned. He looked at the name on the paper and gave it some thought, then said, "No. You cannot have a show."

"No?" I said, getting angry.

"You are only fifteen years old."

"So what!"

"Fame at too early an age can destroy the spirit of a young artist," he answered as he turned back to his painting.

There was no show. I never called him back. I was disappointed and angry with my father for weeks. But maybe my father was right. I'll never know.

Who was this handsome man? This stranger who validated me as an artist and who recognized the spirit in my work and liked it? Told me not to give up? Who said I would be famous? He is a man of controversy in Italy, and perhaps he wasn't even supposed to be in the country that day in the sixties—who knows. He was a prince of the royal family of Italy, and he sparked the dreamer in me.

Would my life have been different if I had had that show? Would the art world in the sixties have recognized the spirit in my work? I will never know. But I will be forever grateful for the handsome man who noticed my potential, and who, out of nowhere, popped into my life for a moment to tell me not to give up.

CHAPTER 14
Running Away
The Motherghost Beckons

By the time I was sixteen, my life felt overwhelming. I began to think about running away from home on a daily basis. From the outside, everything looked okay. But I was miserable most of the time. There was no one thing that sparked me to leave. There was no angry outburst or visible abuse or drastic miscommunication. No, instead there was a slow erosion of my happiness. There was a voice inside me that grew with each day, a voice that told me, "You do not belong here with them."

It is not easy for a teenager to run away and leave everything behind. It takes courage. Nowadays when I see homeless teenagers in a documentary, I understand their plight. They might seem tough, but they are simply frightened children, lost in a senseless world. Notice how many times runaway children reach out to each other and form small communities of clinging spirits. See how they push away their sorrow with cigarettes, drugs, booze, and indifference. Look into their eyes and see their truth. Even within their fragile moments, laden with fear and despair, they somehow remain resilient. They are the lost ones skateboarding down the sidewalks of their lives, as if the finish line were just a curve away.

I was a raging teenager in the sixties. The horrors of the Vietnam War paralleled my angry confusion. Every night on the news I saw despair. I was horrified by the images of burning monks, war casualties, political unrest, and desperate protesters being beaten by cops. I watched my parents ignore everything unpleasant; their eyes would glaze over as the news blared from the TV. Like true alcoholics, they denied any truth that they had no control over. I watched them sip their martinis night after night and exchange pleasantries. I began to believe that nothing would change.

We were waiting to move into our new home and were living outside of Philadelphia in an apartment complex. The sterile skyscrapers, dark brick buildings, and Tudor homes neatly lined up in a row were a jolting contrast to Roman architecture. Where once piazzas and cafés had been my escape, billboards and brightly colored plastic shopping centers now took their place.

I was homesick for my friends and I especially missed my French boyfriend, Jim, with his sophistication and manners. I longed for our endless conversations about poetry, philosophy, and theater. In contrast, I was now hanging out with a bunch of lonely, angry high school kids who spent their time in pot-filled rooms gazing at psychedelic posters. I was miserable.

Too many rum and cokes one summer night helped change the direction of my life forever. That night, my new friends took me to a college party and I stayed out so late that I missed my curfew. When I stumbled into the apartment that dreadful night, my father looked tired and forlorn, older than his age. He had lost control over me years before. As we stared at each other, I felt that our souls had reached an impasse, and I don't know who was more lost at that moment–him or me. But as I stood, swaying, reeking of booze, and acting like a typical, defiant teenager, I saw that there was nothing either one of us could have done to make anything better. What we needed was bigger than simple words or apologies. We were trapped within a psychic schism, another realm where two hearts must say goodbye before they are prepared to let go. I knew this intuitively and I wasn't quite sure whether the spinning in my head was from the booze that I had guzzled earlier or my overwhelming feelings of defeat.

I was slurring my words, swaying from side to side, as I explained to my father just why I had ignored my curfew. "But, Father! I was, ya know . . . I was just with . . . ah, my friends . . ." I started to laugh at myself. I was hopeless–it was hopeless trying to make up an excuse. It took too much effort.

"Go brush your teeth and go to bed," he said mildly. He then lit his pipe and waited for me to follow his orders.

"Make me," I said defiantly.

He looked at me with disgust, bit down harder on his pipe, and walked away. He was too dignified to confront me.

Just once, show me a feeling, I wanted to scream. Just once. I laughed as he turned away. "I am sixteen years old, Father. I am not your little girl anymore."

He said nothing.

"You can't make me *do* anything."

He continued to ignore me and began to pace. I started following him around, tripping over the coffee table, slurring my words.

"You are just a damn weak man, you know."

He went to his desk and fumbled with some papers. I followed.

"Father is a weak man, weak man," I repeated in a singsong voice as I turned toward the bedroom. And then I began to giggle, and over my left shoulder I said, "And that is why Mother . . ."

Then it happened. He spun around so quickly that I heard a book drop. Maybe he threw it. I don't know, but it startled me, and I turned back around. It was like a thunderbolt had struck him. I had never seen him that angry. His gray eyes were black, and the vein in his right temple was pulsating. He came toward me, self-control gone. He grabbed my hair, spun me around, and dragged me into the bathroom headfirst. Father was not prone to violence and I was stunned. Suddenly he was raging at me. The man who was too scared to say "boo" was now ready to beat me. Then he stopped.

"Brush them," he ordered.

"You can't make me."

I spat into the sink. Flustered, he let go of my hair and stood there, regaining his composure. I glanced in the mirror and saw that my eyeliner was running down my cheeks. I looked like a whore and in some ways I felt like one. How did this happen? How did we come to this ending?

I stared in the mirror and saw nothing but a messed-up adolescent staring back at me.

It was clear that the explosion inside me had been coming for a long time. A psychiatrist back in Italy had seen the danger signs and had prescribed tranquilizers. Father, who maybe had taken two aspirins in his life, had protested at the time. But the bottle was there. I grabbed it off the shelf. I wanted to numb the pain swelling inside me.

"What do you think you are doing?" he asked as he grabbed them from me.

"They are mine."

"You shouldn't have these. I don't care what the doctor thinks," he said as he emptied them into the toilet. I gasped.

"Wait!" I screamed.

But it was too late. Father flushed the toilet. We both watched the little blue and white pills swirl around and around. Then there was a dreadful gurgle and they were gone.

We were both silent.

Father, still flustered, grabbed my hair once again and led me out of the bathroom to the living room, where he threw me onto the sofa.

"Sit there," he said. And he returned to his desk and began writing.

I was disgraced. I sat for a long time, my arms tightly folded, whimpering with rage.

"You can hurt me physically," I said, breaking the silence.

He ignored me. I waited.

"But you will never really get me," I muttered. "You'll never get me to think like you and Mother." I was crying now. "I won't let you take my thoughts. They are mine and you can't take them!" I yelled.

No answer.

The room was silent except for a dog barking outside. I sat on the sofa, my heart racing. I stewed in my drunken rage for what seemed an eternity. I began to sob. My thoughts went everywhere, from early childhood moments of my adoption, to playing in the woods, to Kaleen, to Mother in her good moments, Father in his, and then my thoughts came right back to then and there, to that very moment in time.

In that moment, at the very impasse, as I went over my life and felt my inner wounds most keenly, I crashed into my self. I felt as if I had hit a wall or a gateway, but I didn't know which one it was. But I did know that a challenge was being laid at my feet. I stopped crying. I ceased feeling.

I don't quite know what happened to cause this shift, but with the utmost dignity that I could muster, I stood up, straightened my shirt, wiped my tears, and walked over to the picture window. The sky was dark and I couldn't find the beauty of a starry night. Give me something, I whispered to the universe. Give me just one star—something to hold on to. There was nothing. The city sky hid the faint lights of the stars. I looked down at the parking lot and watched the moths fluttering around the globe of the streetlight. They reminded me of the fairies dancing around, around and around. . . . I kept staring at them, mesmerized, until I felt something turn inside me, and I knew it was time. I turned back toward the room and quietly walked to the front door. I walked like a well-bred lady—just what the Neilsons had taught me to be. I walked past my father without a word.

"Where are you going?" he asked without looking up from his writing.

I didn't answer.

He looked up. "Get back here. I am ordering you," he said.

I ignored him.

"I am telling you to get back here! Marcy, do you hear me? I am your father."

That did it. It was the trigger, and for a moment, out of nowhere, an image of a tall, thin, very blond man smoking a cigarette appeared. It was a flash. Was it a deeply buried memory, coded in my genes, that told me to leave it all behind? His voice, which had an English accent, whispered to me, "Go for it, Robin. Go for it, baby. Leave!"

I turned around and looked back at Winthrop, my father. I stared straight into his eyes. I didn't want to feel anything for him. But I did. I didn't want him to know that I would miss him when I was gone and I didn't want him to know that he was my favorite Neilson. I paused for a moment. I felt very centered but very alone in the world. I answered with the best control that I could muster under the circumstances, and said in a calm, detached, somewhat austere voice, "No, you're not my father," believing for a moment that there had been another father. I slammed the door behind me and ran. I ran down the corridor and turned the corner. By the time he opened the front door to yell after me, I was gone.

I jumped into the elevator. As it went down, an uncanny, surreal feeling came over me. Like a Salvador Dali painting, my life was melting away floor by floor.

In truth, I was free—a barefoot teenage runaway—with no money, no home, and no idea where I was going.

All I could think was, Oh, Mother, help me.

My heart my mother. My heart.
My heart is the living heart of earth.
My heart is the blinking eye of night.

I am earth covered with earth
one with earth, returned to earth.
Left in the mountain,
I live under the mountain;
I am the heart of the mountain.
I am rising up the stirring of bees.

I am my moments in time.

–Adaptation of Normandi Ellis translation,
from *Awakening Osiris: The Egyptian Book of the Dead*

CHAPTER 15
Jock, My Adoptive Brother
A Mother's Dream Boy

The morning after I ran away, when the train pulled into Grand Central Station during rush hour, was the single most horrible, shameful, embarrassing moment of my life. The filth of the city and the stench of the station were overwhelming. I was tortured by a raging, clanging hangover as I tried to tiptoe my way through the mass of pushing, shoving people trying to get somewhere quickly.

I looked pretty bad. My long hair was tangled and flowed over my very wrinkled clothes. To top it off, I had no shoes. I looked as bad as I felt, and even New Yorkers, who have seen it all, turned around to stare at me as I walked by them.

New York City, where I was born and where my mother abandoned me, was the place where every neurotic trigger that was imprinted in my psyche came blaring at me one at a time, as I began to push my way through the crowd to the landing. Nothing changes, I thought. I'm still looking for a home. Still lost, still confused, still hurt, still no answers. I am just a fucked-up, sorry excuse for a person, I thought.

When I got to the top of the stairs, the crowd miraculously split, like the parting of the waters, and ahead of me on the floor I saw a small, delicate figure crouched up against a post. She looked homeless, a runaway like me. I could see from the tracks on her arms and the dark circles under her eyes that heroin had taken the better part of her life. It was weird; I was curiously drawn to her and I couldn't move away. I just stood staring. She looked up at me with forlorn blue eyes. They were deep and asked questions that I had no answers to. Was she a sign from the cosmos? I don't know, but it felt like she was saying to me, "Go home. Turn around. Go back!" I said nothing. She said nothing. We didn't need to. Then I walked away.

"Forty-Five West Eighty-First Street, Excelsior Hotel," I said as I jumped quickly into the cab, slamming the door behind me. I was hoping the cab driver hadn't seen my bare feet.

I had called Prudy in my drunken frenzy the night before. Prudy was the only true remnant of a caring mother figure that I had in my life as Marcy. She was my sister-in-law, but she had always been pivotal in my emotional journey. She was someone who had behaved in a loving way toward me and had been very protective of me since I was seven years old. It was logical for me to ask if I could come stay with her and my brother the day I ran away. She had told me that Jock was in New York for a business meeting and said that I could meet him at the hotel. So I knew he was expecting me. That was good, because I was spending the last bit of borrowed money that I had on the cab ride.

Even though I had two older brothers, and Wink had been kind to me, I had bonded with Jock, who was the black sheep of the family. "You are never going to be any good," I had heard Mother yell at Jock one day. "Look at your grades—what kind of college do you think you're going to go to? What? You want to be a fisherman?" It went on and on and soon I knew Jock and I had something in common—we were never going to live up to Mother's expectations. I think Jock cared more than I did about that fact.

Jock, who was thirteen years older than me, became my big-brother hero one afternoon when I was six years old. Mother and Father had bought me a special wristwatch.

"Here, Marcy, you are old enough to have a grown-up watch now," my mother said. I couldn't believe it. My eyes widened as my mother handed me a beautiful, gold-rimmed wristwatch with a leather band. I was so proud of the gift and felt so grown up. I paraded around for days flashing my watch to everyone I bumped into.

Then one day during naptime, wanting to see how it worked, I took the watch apart. Soon all the tiny parts were neatly spread on my bed and, within minutes, I was panicking. I couldn't put it back together. Where does that piece go? And that? And that? I asked myself as I tried different parts in different positions. Nothing was fitting. It was not ticking anymore. I was in trouble and I was scared.

I tried and tried for a long time to put the watch back together. My naptime hour was over, but I did not call down the hallway for permission to get up. No, I was being very quiet as I hid in my room.

Suddenly there was a knock on the door. I jumped. Jock popped his head in. "Want to go for a walk?" he asked. I said nothing and hid the watch under the blanket. I must have looked pretty pathetic and probably pretty guilty. "What's the matter?" he asked. Tears poured down my cheeks as I showed him the broken pieces of my watch. He smiled and walked over to my bed and gathered all the pieces. He very carefully and methodically put it all back together. I was in awe as I peered over his shoulder. That was the day he became my big brother.

***

The cab pulled up to the curb and as I looked at the hotel entrance, I knew getting through the door and walking by everyone looking the way I did was going to be a challenge. Do not make eye contact, I told myself, and walk with dignity. Just act normal, as if you know exactly where you are going. I paid the driver and walked directly past the doorman. I don't need to say how hard it was to walk into one of the fancier hotels in New York City barefoot. It was a humiliating nightmare. But I did it. I went directly to the elevator. "Room 216," I said to the elevator man, who was staring down at my feet. Thank God Jock's room was on the second floor.

"To your left," the man said as he opened the door.

I found my brother's room and knocked.

"Come in. It's unlocked," he called.

I opened the door and slowly walked in. He was lying on the bed and, from the looks of the mess in the room, the half-empty glasses of booze on the bedside table, and the overall seedy miasma that filled the place, I was sure that he had had quite a night. I had been around long enough to know that he had not slept alone that night and I wanted to yell at him, but my head hurt too much and I was in no position to preach. What about Prudy, your wife? I thought. What about Prudy? But I said nothing.

"Hi," he said.

"Hi," I answered.

And then we exchanged glances that somehow spoke of mystery, of karma perhaps, that may have warned that we were standing at a crossroads in our lives, and somehow our lives reflected each other's. Tragedy was inevitable and we both knew it on some level without saying anything. His would be the end of a marriage and mine would be the end of a family.

"It's been a long time."

"Yes, it has."

We stared awkwardly at each other from across the room, absorbing all that was in that moment. And then Jock broke the silence.

"We are quite a pair, aren't we?"

"Yes, we are," I said, nodding.

His eyes began to well up. Mine too.

"I remember when you were a little girl and Mother and Father arrived home with you. Those big brown eyes . . . Do you remember?"

"Yes, I do remember that day."

"You were such a little girl–such sad eyes."

"Yes, and I remember when you punched me in the stomach for changing your TV show. It really hurt but you said it would toughen me up." I laughed.

"I did?"

"Yes, it was Paladin, you know, *Have Gun–Will Travel?* You were watching it."

"Oh," he said as he searched his memory.

". . . and I wanted to watch Mickey Mouse," I said.

"Mickey Mouse?" he asked, making the same face he had years ago. We both laughed.

"And now look at us both. You're all grown up and, I might add, looking like a wreck, and me . . ." he paused, looking straight at me. "I used to carry you on my shoulders through the woods," he continued.

We both remembered the exact moment that he was talking about. We both loved our home in Long Island. At that moment, our silent tears for each other were all that we needed. The distinct sound of the city traffic below had a haunting, familiar feeling to it as it drifted through the hotel window.

"Go get cleaned up. We need to get you some clothes for the plane," he said as he jumped out of the bed and looked for his tie. "We are flying to Rhode Island. That's going to be your new home."

I cried.

***

Soon we were on the plane. The roar of the engines began to build as we headed down the runway. "Ready?" Jock asked, turning to me with a big grin. It was the same grin I had seen so many times when I was a child and he was teenager. Jock had always loved the thrills of life. He was a risk taker, which later as an adult became his lifestyle in the world of high finance.

Sitting next to him reminded me of an afternoon in New Jersey at an amusement park, when we sat side by side in a roller coaster. He had bullied me into getting on this horrible, spinning, out-of-control amusement ride.

"Come on, Marcy, have some guts."

"But I don't want to have guts," I said, dreading what was about to take place.

He ignored me and before I knew it I was strapped into a seat next to him, holding on to the bar across our waists as the car rose swirling in the air. I hated every moment of the ride.

"Wasn't that great?" he asked when it was over.

"Nope," I said, furious with him.

He laughed at my overwrought expression and teased me about going again. I refused and that became the one and only amusement park ride I have ever taken.

Plane rides were different for me. They were exciting, but not out-of-control frightening, like roller coasters. Jock and I both loved the thrill of the takeoff. So as the plane began to lift off the ground, we closed our eyes and felt the power gently push us back into the seat. We felt free.

It was a short trip but I had time to reminisce with Jock about when

I was kid and he was a teenager. In those days we were always running around teasing and chasing each other. Of course he was much bigger than me, and so he let me win most of the time. It made me smile as I sat on the plane next to him, remembering our childhood.

***

Jock was always getting into trouble, but in those days, he seemed unafraid of the consequences. "Aw, come on, Mom," he would say with his little-boy look. Sometimes he used his charm and would give Mother a gentle peck on her cheek. This charm worked when he was still young, but in later years his relationship with Mother became twisted. She took control of his life–especially his marriage–until there was nothing but a big mess. Then without any explanation, he walked away from both–his marriage and Mother.

One evening when Mother and Father were out at a cocktail party, Jock borrowed Mother's new black and yellow convertible. She had just bought it. When Jock walked into the front living room, I was watching an episode of *Sky King* on television. I was so engrossed in the show that I didn't notice him leaning up against the doorjamb, grinning and jingling the keys to Mother's new car.

"Want to go for a ride?" he asked coaxingly.

"Ride?"

"Yes, in Mom's new car."

"But *Sky King* is on."

"Who cares about *Sky King*? You can watch it tomorrow."

"No, I can't."

"Yes, you can."

"No, I can't," I said as I turned back to the television. "Does she know you are borrowing her car?"

"No. She'll never know."

"I don't want to go," I said. Sometimes Jock's driving was a bit scary.

"Marcy, stop being a sissy!"

Just then, Mary, our summertime cook, walked in to tell us dinner was ready. Mary was babysitting and in charge of me. She overheard our conversation and firmly told Jock no. I was relieved.

"Oh well, see you later," he said, and walked out to the garage.

The next morning I heard Mother calling upstairs to his room. "John Fullerton Neilson, get downstairs. Right now!" she yelled.

Uh oh, I thought, that is the voice she uses when we are about to get in trouble. I was right. Jock must have had a few beers the night before because he had dented Mother's brand-new car! He got into big trouble, but he was too old to be grounded. I went out to the garage where Mother and Jock were inspecting the damage. I did not expect what happened next. I became deeply triggered by the image of the torn, bent metal. I ran into my room and slammed the door behind me. Surprised at my dramatic reaction, Jock and Mother stopped arguing and came after me. By that time I was on the floor, weeping hysterically. I don't know why I was crying so hard or whether I was furious or scared.

"Marcy, what's the matter?" Jock asked as he knelt down next to me and began gently to stroke my back. I couldn't stop crying. Jock picked me up and carried me out to the garage. "Let's go see the car again," he said. I screamed louder and buried my face in his shoulder.

"Marcy, it's okay. I am all right!" he said reassuringly, trying to comfort me. I stopped crying and looked down at the car's fender. "I am not hurt, Marcy, I am not hurt," he said, looking directly at me. I looked at him and then at the car and then back at him. "I am not hurt, Marcy—don't worry," he repeated over and over while giving me a gentle kiss on my cheek.

I sighed and wiped my nose on my sleeve. "But you could have died," I said.

***

The plane began to descend to Providence airport. The captain's voice telling us to fasten our seat belts brought me back from the past and into the challenges ahead. I was getting excited to see Prudy, whom I loved deeply. We would be in Jamestown soon and maybe it would all be okay, I thought. But I didn't know what my future would be like and for a moment I became afraid. I turned to Jock for reassurance and he smiled. I smiled back. It was a brother-sister moment.

Unfortunately, the brother-sister moments were exactly that—just moments. In the years that followed Jock and I had many confrontations and hurtful episodes. As I wrestled with who I was through my teenage years and tried to find where I belonged in the world, our relationship deteriorated. We were no longer young and resilient and able to repair the wounds we inflicted on each other. With his cunning maneuvers and his need for control as he also tried to find the answers to his life and failures, Jock became more and more like Mother. He became so much like her in so many subtle ways that after awhile I felt crazy around him. One day, without either one of us ever saying we had ended it, our relationship was gone. But every few years he would telephone me to check in. He couldn't let go.

***

Late one afternoon years later, he telephoned me. "I need to talk to you," he said. I could detect an undercurrent of sadness in his voice. But I said nothing. I had always been able to recognize that gloomy side that he hid so well when he was young. He told me that he was just checking in to see if I was okay. But I knew the phone call wasn't *really* about me. I could sense an urgency and tightness in his voice. He kept the conversation light, however, with polite questions and family gossip. He never got to tell me what was so pressing, because his wife came home unexpectedly. She did not like me and he was afraid she would find out that he was talking to me. "Gotta go—Eve's home," he said as he quickly hung up without even saying goodbye. That was the last time I talked to him. What he did not get to tell me that day was that he had just found out that he was dying of cancer. And he had no mother to call.

CHAPTER 16
Prudy, The Winged Isis
The Mother's Heart

As I stepped out of the car after the long trip, the horrendous day and the stress from running away started to fall away. A peaceful sensation greeted me. I stopped and watched the last faint hues of the setting sun. I smelled the sweet scent of honeysuckle and tasted the salty, sea marsh breeze. It felt gentle and healing. It was a stark contrast to the dark brick homes I had left behind in Philadelphia and to the harsh sounds of Manhattan. Except for the lone chirp of a cricket, the island felt very still. Having returned from living in Rome, where I had wandered for hours among the ancient ruins and felt the spirits from every stone and corner, it was clear that the energy of this little island held ancient power too, but it was a very different type.

There was something else present on the land–something that felt more ancient, more beautiful. The energy was beyond human and the feeling I sensed that night felt like open wings embracing me. That feeling has never gone away. Whenever I return to Jamestown, with the sea and the same sweet scents of honeysuckle and salt, I feel those same ancient spirits calming my nerves–watching me–and I feel safe.

Prudy opened the door and let out Luis, an enthusiastic, large English setter, and Bertie, a small, overweight, yapping Dachshund. Both charged down the path toward me. I bent down to pat them and looked up at the house. I laughed as I patted Luis's smooth soft head because I knew that even though Prudy had many friends and often was the star of any party, her heart belonged to the dogs. As I looked into Luis's rich brown eyes, I knew this handsome dog was most likely her true love.

With a martini in one hand and a wooden spoon in the other, Prudy waved and waited by the doorjamb with her three children giggling and clinging to her legs. I looked at her as I walked toward the cottage. It had been a long time, but even time did not stop Prudy and me from reading each other's state of mind. We reflected each other in a strange way. We each tried simultaneously to put on a good face for the other. But something felt askew with Prudy that evening; I couldn't pinpoint it but I knew it was there. As I stepped through the doorway into a quaint and beautiful little room, filled with antiques and knickknacks, I could smell the familiar tuna casserole that I had loved as a child.

"Welcome," she said, smiling and giving me a big hug. It was all that I needed and I sank into the radiance of her strength. Quietly, I felt her take me into her heart and under her wing. For me she was like the ancient winged Isis, who in many ancient images is shown with spread wings, shielding the

111

heart place of the soul.

With a Katharine Hepburn manner and a golden light around her, Prudy is one of those people you notice when she walks into a room. She doesn't have to say anything to make her presence known. She is a gentle woman—not loud or crass. She has dignity and at the same time she has fierceness, a line you do not want to cross with her. She is the remnant of a mother figure for me. And even to this day, with all of the confidence and sense of self-worth I've gained, when Prudy says jump—I jump.

At dinner that first night, she announced: "You can stay here. We'll send you to a private school and get you a good education—straighten out your life." She listed what I needed.

I breathed a sigh of relief.

"Tomorrow we will get you some clothes." I laughed at the thought of Prudy going clothes shopping. She hated to do that. She often mismatched her prints. In those days, in the sixties, the two of us did not make the same fashion choices.

Prudy got up and dialed the phone and handed it to Jock, who looked at her and grimaced.

"No. Not now," he whined. As he took another sip of wine, his dread of confronting Mother was written all over his face. The phone was ringing.

"Hello?" Mother said.

"Hi, Mother. John here," he said, gathering himself and using his formal name.

"Hello, dear."

Prudy and I looked at each other and rolled our eyes at the sound of Mother's sickeningly sweet voice.

"Mother, we need to talk about Marcy."

His attempts went nowhere and, just like he had done all his life, he backed off in the face of Mother's demands. Prudy, disgusted with his spineless approach, grabbed the phone.

"Mother, you must help her. It's unconscionable that you would do anything else," she said.

"Well, Prudy dear, we wouldn't be in this awful mess if you hadn't filled Marcy's head with silly ideas years ago."

Furious with what Mother had just said, she hung up the phone and walked over to the side bar and poured herself another drink. Jock was beside himself. I had never seen anyone do that before. No one had ever hung up on Mother before! Prudy was outraged and, starting that evening, took on my cause and battled all the Neilsons whenever they said no to helping me. I knew that they didn't really want to help me. I saw that, the night I ran away, when I hid under their apartment window to see what they would do if I were gone. Would they care? Would they miss me? The answer was no. It was clear that the Neilsons simply wanted to wash their hands of me. Within half an hour after I walked out the door, Father, as usual, ignored what had transpired, had a night toddy, turned off the lights, and went to bed. So when they wanted to repeat this type of "let's wash our hands of her" behavior by saying, "Let's check into the Caring Times Children's Service and see if she can go back to a foster home," Prudy stepped in and said, "Oh, no you don't." With a strong sense of ethics and fierce determination, she demanded that they break into the financial trust left for all the grandchildren.

"You will send her to a good school until she graduates, and you will help us feed and clothe her, too. You will take responsibility for your child—adopted or not!" she said. They could do nothing else but listen.

***

I never went back home to the Neilsons. To be more accurate, I was never invited back. I did humble myself and ask to come back once, a few months after I had arrived at Jock and Prudy's. I had begun my downhill slide into more teenage trouble and failure. The idea of being a failure in Prudy's eyes was unbearable for me. It always has been. I wanted to shine for her.

I called the Neilsons and asked to come home.

"Hello."

"Mother, it's me."

"Who?"

"It's Marcy."

"Marcy? Oh."

"Mother . . . I am sorry."

She said nothing.

"Can I come home?"

"Win, pick up. It's Marcy."

"Hello, Marcy?" my father asked, clearing his throat.

"Father, can I come home?"

"Uh." I could hear him tapping his pipe on the table. It was something he often did before he filled and lit it. The stuffing of the pipe was his signature pause, something he would do just before he would say something difficult.

"Mother? Father? Can I?"

"No . . . you cannot come home," Mother said.

"But, Mother, why? Father?"

"You can't come home until you have proven yourself to us."

113

"What?"

". . . and then maybe we will think about whether you are good enough—for us," she added.

"Good enough for you? Fuck you all!" I yelled.

And then Father, like punctuating a sentence in one of his manuscripts, did it. He edited my life. Something no one else had been able to do. His carefully chosen words cut through all the innuendos within the Neilson family's silence.

"No, Marcy, you cannot come home. And let me tell you, I will do whatever, I repeat, whatever, it takes to keep you away from my family," he said.

Had he said "his" family? Could he make it any clearer? I didn't think so. I had become the enemy.

Father, the man whom I saw as a victim of Frances, was implying that I was evil. This hurt more than the physical abuse, the emotional slaps, the abandonment, the betrayals in my life. More than all of it put together. In one shot, Father had killed the remaining fragile, vulnerable place within me, where my sense of self-worth lived, as if it were a bird falling off a branch.

The Neilsons' response to my plea to go home stung like winter ice on my already fragile self. After that day, I never tried again to go home.

Prudy just kept caring about me. With that same sense of integrity and control, she guided me like a mother would a child or she would a younger sister. She taught me about the good and the bad and the rules of society and life. Sometimes I listened and sometimes I didn't, because the truth was that sometimes she was right—and sometimes she was wrong.

When I arrived in Jamestown as a troubled sixteen-year-old, Prudy was only thirty years old. But life has its own twists and turns. I arrived at what turned out to be the wrong time, just when Prudy's perfect-looking marriage, and the family I had hoped to make mine, were in trouble. Her life was crumbling around her. I saw it in her eyes and in my brother's behavior. I became the overload.

That year Prudy tried to protect me from the harshness of the world and from my own self-destructive behavior. Our life journeys reflect each other in very strange ways. I have finally come to realize now, as an adult, that sometimes we look at each other and see choices we didn't make and, ultimately, like in Robert Frost's poem "The Road Not Taken," we experience the other's life as that road not taken.

Although I was only seven when I first met her, even then I saw her amazing spirit. I knew deep inside me that she had seen my spirit too. And knowing that fact, that we valued each other's preciousness, has kept our relationship intact even in the awkward times. Years later, one night over

114

dinner in a restaurant, she said to me, with tears in her eyes, "The day I first met you, I looked at this skinny little knock-kneed girl staring up at me with big, brown, and very sad eyes, and I wanted to just hug you. I wanted to whisk you away from the Neilsons. I wanted to take you home."

"In some ways you did." I wanted her to know how important she had been to me. How happy my childhood summer visits to her had been. How she helped me feel visible.

"You made me feel wanted."

"Good," she said.

"And then I had to go and let you down." I could feel a dark mood, old and familiar, welling up inside me. It was as if we were moving through a time tunnel together. And we were heading toward a period in our lives we had both tried to bury.

"It was not a good time for any of us." I could see by her expression that she had also moved back through time and into those difficult days.

"I can't tell you how bad I felt that day," I said. I could feel the pain in my chest as I thought about the day that I lost the only family and home that I ever really felt I had had. "I am sorry." I was getting teary eyed.

I had never really apologized to Prudy for my past behavior and hurtful actions toward her. I had wanted to say I was sorry for years, and that evening as I sat facing her in the restaurant I realized that I had, instead, punished myself about it for years and that I had been carrying a great deal of remorse and terrible feelings of failure throughout those times. The dreaded feelings that I had buried were suddenly out there in front of us. She grabbed my hand across the table. Tears were in her eyes too. I am shy and less openly expressive than she is and I felt my inner teenager recoil as I tried to pull my hand away from her. It was such a strange knee-jerk response. It was too much intimacy. And it was too important for me. That moment felt like a turning point in the wheel of time of our souls' journey.

"Don't pull your hand away from me," she said, surprised by my reaction. "Don't pull away from me," she said again in that very familiar, commanding voice.

Like I said, when Prudy says jump, I jump, and so I kept my hand in hers, hoping it would all be over soon, this moment when she openly showed her motherly, big-sisterly love for me.

"Look at you now."

I said nothing and attempted a shy smile but still looked away from her.

"Look at me," she said.

I looked at her.

"I am so proud of you." She cupped my hand in both of hers and then gently let it go. "I am so proud," she repeated.

There are times in your life when you know that you've waited a long time for something. This was one of those moments. I had waited to hear those words from someone my whole life. And when it finally happened, I took her words into my heart and knew that I would hold on tight to them forever.

***

Prudy has her own story. I believe that her upbringing broke parts of her naturally free spirit. Prudy's mother was a scary woman with absolutely no tolerance for someone saying no to her. Mrs. Coleman was a woman of order, high society, and temper. She reined in Prudy's wild escapades. Like me, Prudy found an escape in nature when she was a child. She, too, had a special tree to climb and hide within. A tree whose branches embraced her and who she talked to and told her sorrows to. Maybe that was why Prudy helped me, because she saw in me something precious that was similar to something in herself that she had lost. I don't know.

Prudy channeled her powerful spirit into becoming a good athlete, a well-read woman, a wonderful gardener, a bird watcher, a mom, a lover of nature, and a woman of society. For the most part, Prudy obeyed the rules set forth by her upbringing. But she was far from being a stoic, goody two-shoes.

That's because in irresistible moments of free-spiritedness, her wild, passionate, rebellious nature would arise. And so a good-girl bad-girl struggle still plays out in her life in small ways. I remember one of those times when I was young. My nieces and nephew and I would be in the backseat of the car while Prudy drove home too fast on a backcountry road. We knew the spot on the road–the bump on the hill. We knew it was coming. It added to the excitement.

"Get ready, kids," she'd call out. We would grab the armrest, hold our breath, and then, for a split second, the station wagon would fly through the air.

"Wheeee!" she would say, giggling. She always turned to see our reaction. "That was fun!" she'd exclaim.

"Don't be too good. Break a few rules. Live a little," she would often say with her bad-girl laugh. We'd all nod in unison, our eyes sparkling with excitement and trepidation.

Then there were the nights when we would go skinny-dipping right off the busy road, or the time when we stood in the eye of a hurricane until the winds came back and we ran for shelter.

Sometimes we could hear her devilish giggle everywhere, which was in stark contrast to the well-bred woman Mrs. Coleman had shaped. Whether it was an outrageous statement, a belch, a twinkle in her eye, her swinging from trees on Main Street, or the one more martini, it was all a thumbed-nose response to Mrs. Coleman's upbringing.

To this day, Prudy's spirit still peeks out in fleeting moments, free and happy, as she tap dances on the table of life. Prudy didn't give up and, thanks to her, I did not give up either.

***

Prudy is the only person in my life who goes back to my childhood with whom I still have a loving relationship. That says it all in a nutshell. Prudy had a hard time with me and couldn't handle the fierce storm inside of my wild teenager self. In all fairness, I don't think anyone could have. It triggered something in her and I think it frightened her. And I just couldn't stop behaving in self-destructive ways. Between getting kicked out of school, drinking too much, and sleeping around, my stay was doomed. Every time I messed up, I saw Prudy's disappointment and I loathed myself even more.

I was a teenager who was heading for a wall. Actually, I didn't hit a wall. Instead, one drunken evening, I fell off the top of a second-floor landing and hit a radiator.

"Oh my God, I think I have really hurt myself," I said as I stumbled out to the car holding my head.

My friends turned on the light and from their looks I could see it was bad.

"What is it?" I asked.

"Yuk, it's gross. There's a gash in your head."

Blood was pouring down the side of my face.

"Quick, get that towel," I said.

"Marcy, we have to go to the hospital," they told me.

"Not the hospital, I can't do that. My brother will kill me."

We drove around for a while, but I ended up in the hospital with a concussion and stitches crisscrossing the back of my head.

"Marcy, you have totally embarrassed this family," Jock said on the phone the next morning.

"I am sorry," I said. Blood was caked in my hair and my head was pounding, making me nauseous.

"There are no more sorrys. Get yourself out of the hospital. Take a bus to my office and I will drive you home to Jamestown," he said.

"But Jock, the doctor said I needed to rest. Not move too much."

"It will toughen you up," he said.

117

"But . . . Jock, can't you come get me? I'm really feeling sick."

"No buts, Marcy, it's over. You are out of here," he answered, ignoring my pleas.

By the time I arrived home in Jamestown, Prudy had packed my bags. It was over.

That was a bleak day in my life–the day Prudy gave up on me. She couldn't fight the Neilsons. She couldn't fight the schools. She couldn't fight my brother, and she couldn't fight me. She just let me go. I wanted to say goodbye, but my heart was broken. As I walked to the car, she did not look me in the eye, nor did I look in hers. I did not look back. My pain and my shame for having failed her ate away at me for a long time. In some ways, I think she felt the same.

What is even stranger, that very night, when I fell off the steps and my life began to fall apart, my birth mother was dying in a Manhattan apartment far away with her family nearby. As Prudy painfully let go of me and sent me out into the world alone, my mother from long ago silently stepped back into my life–but this time as a ghost.

***

When Prudy returned to Providence for the winter, she made an effort to rekindle and hold on to our relationship by inviting me for dinner on Tuesdays. She and Jock had called it quits and he had moved out and was living in New York City. She was alone with her children.

Prudy and I kept up our dinners for one more year. I went off to college and she moved away to get a quick divorce. We lost each other for over thirty years, with only sporadic moments of hellos and goodbyes in between. Prudy went through two more marriages and I through many more crashes of the heart. But we never completely let go of each other.

***

One Christmas day, years later, I was in Jamestown at my friend Sylvia's house.

"Prudy wants to see you."

"Prudy? Why?" I asked.

"I don't know."

It had been years since we had talked and I wasn't quite sure why she was asking for me. I was so different now: I called myself Eclipse; I was older, poorer, wiser, and very mystical in everything I did. My life was such a contrast to hers, filled as it was with friends, tennis, golf, and travel. Would I have anything to say? I worried about this as we drove over to her new house.

We parked in front of the most perfect little shingled cottage with a front porch and a big yard. It reminded me of the childhood days I had spent with her in all the summer cottages she had rented. She greeted us at the door. A huge fire was roaring as we walked in. My hair was graying and hers was still the same, with a beautiful blondish tint. I noticed that she was extremely thin. As I looked at her, I wondered if she was okay. Her face was drawn and pained. The pain in the room was palpable as we sat there. It was a strained visit and we talked about nothing. She didn't say anything, but I noticed that when she hugged me, it felt as though she was afraid of losing me. I felt deep inside that after all these years apart, she was calling me home in some way.

"I want to see you again soon," she said.

"Okay. Next week?"

When I got home I was overtaken with an unexplainable grief. I wept all night without knowing why.

The next morning I called Sylvia.

"Is there something I don't know?" I asked, worrying that Sylvia was going to tell me that Prudy was dying.

"You don't know?"

"Know what? How would I know anything? Remember, I don't see Prudy or hang with anyone who knows her."

"It's her son."

"Her son? Johnny? Or the other one?

"Yes, Johnny. He died. Didn't you know?"

***

Prudy grieved fiercely in those first few years. She walked until her body ached; she drank herself to sleep; and when alone in the wee hours of the morning she would cry, hurt by an unbearable loss. Her perfect life had shattered–her heart was broken. And as I looked into her blue, blue eyes–so deep and so frightened–I saw our karmic tie–our lifetimes together. I saw how she had reflected love to me and how she had taught me about mother love. I knew it was my turn to help her–to silently take her under my wing now. To mother her in a quiet way. And, with the irony of life, it was only then, so many years later, through feeling Prudy's loss of her own child, that I began to understand and relate to the pain my own mother had most likely experienced the day she gave me up forever. In a visceral way, I understood the pain that all mothers feel when they lose a child.

119

Mother III

THE GROWING-UP YEARS

1967-1977

CHAPTER 17
My Education
Housemothers

My life changed drastically after I left Jock and Prudy's comfortable home. That summer I worked as a mother's helper for a family, who gave me a room on their third floor. I cleaned house, ironed shirts, cooked, and took care of three high-spirited children, who were all under the age of seven. I was exhausted at the end of the day.

I spent a lot of evenings collapsed in my favorite overstuffed armchair, which faced a small eave window. I spent hours in the dark, staring out over the rooftops of the nearby houses. I sat so still and erect, I could have been mistaken for an ancient Egyptian statue. I discovered that at certain times of the month, the full moon's light would move across my chest. In those moments, I imagined a Goddess from some childhood Greek myth Frances had read to me reaching out from the moon to place her hand on my heart, healing my grief.

In direct contrast to the calming moonlight experiences, at other times I could feel a ghost's presence. It seemed to be struggling to get my attention as I lay in the dark. "Remember who you are," I heard over and over in my thoughts. I never saw a face, but I often wondered why the energy was so familiar and why it made me feel melancholy.

***

In time, self-preservation took over and I began to set goals for myself. I was forced to address what I was going to do when September came. I was afraid of becoming homeless. I knew two things about myself: I wanted to graduate from high school and I wanted to be a great artist.

The winter before I was kicked out of Jock and Prudy's home, I was suspended from Wheeler, a private boarding school that I had attended as a day student. I was told I could reapply in the fall and was placed on a waiting list. I decided a boarding school would solve my problems–it would give me a home. I sat in my big chair plotting out my life on a little piece of paper. I made a list of what I needed to do to save myself: one, I wrote, get back into school, two, get a scholarship, and three, get the Neilsons' money from the Grandmother educational trust to pay my way.

I focused on those tasks. I called Wheeler the next morning and set up an appointment with Miss Comery, who had been the head housemother for over thirty years. No one got into the boarding school without her approval. She did not officially have that power, but I didn't doubt that she held all the strings to my reacceptance into the boarding school. Miss Comery was a stern, elderly woman who frightened everyone. She was a small, stout lady with a large nineteen-thirties presence–a woman who sat erect on a wooden chair, arms folded, and looked over her nose and large bosom as students pleaded their case. But I knew her two big secrets. One, she had a sense of humor and two, she had a very big heart. I spoke to her heart. I used every smile, graceful gesture, and brilliant idea I could come up with, and I convinced her that a strong daily structure, with its rules and schedules, would reshape me into a perfect student. My use of the words "a perfect student" was stretching it. But my pleas with Miss Comery worked, and my new home became a boarding school.

It was not the happiest of times because my freedom was severely restricted. But neither was it the worst of times for me because I felt safe. I did well within the school's structure. I had no worries about how I was going to survive. My only concerns were getting to class on time and not getting kicked out. I did it, and I graduated from Mary C. Wheeler, one of the top Rhode Island schools. And I say this with a sense of accomplishment: only a few years later I even returned to become a teacher at that school. And years after that, I returned as a parent.

There's something happening here
What it is ain't exactly clear
There's a man with a gun over there
Telling me, I got to beware

I think it's time we stop, children,
what's that sound
Everybody look what's going down

—Buffalo Springfield, "For What It's Worth"

CHAPTER 18
The Message from the Future
The Mother to Become

For me, adulthood was about learning—the hard way—to take responsibility for my choices and to stop blaming everyone else for my misery. But before I learned those lessons, I got sidetracked and hung out with a wild group of artists. I created excitement, drama, and a tumultuous life filled with drugs and booze. I got involved with both men and women and learned the many heartbreaks that come with loving. It was difficult for me to see where I was going in those days and I ended up creating a terrible mess of my life.

I went to an art college in New Canaan, Connecticut, and after moving from apartment to apartment, I temporarily settled down with a group of students in a house on a lake. I was extremely poor, with only sporadic jobs to help feed me. In the spring of my first college year, I bought a cheap bamboo pole and fished for food in the lake after class and daydreamed about the years I spent in the Adirondacks with my father fishing for trout. A roommate who worked at a grocery store as a cashier came to my rescue and arranged for us to steal a roast beef or a steak once a week. But most of the time, I lived on borscht soup with whatever vegetable was on sale for the week thrown into it. That year was a far cry from my fancy childhood days when we dined at my favorite restaurant—Manhattan's Russian Tea Room—where they served the best borscht soup ever. I was skinny in those days, but I was healthy. To this day, I believe that my diet of beets and cabbage kept me healthy.

***

One glorious warm spring day, when the dogwood was in full bloom and the robins were chirping, I decided that such a day called for an adventure. I had a bad case of spring fever. "Who wants to cut class?" I asked my friends as we pulled into the parking lot.

"Come on, Tom, let's go to the city," I said.

"Can't. Got too many canvases to stretch."

"Jeff?"

"No, I've got a test tomorrow."

"Nancy?"

"Nope, I'm broke."

"Oh well, the train is coming. You are all going to miss some fun," I teased, and off I went.

In those days I did things like take off without a plan, take trains to nowhere, and on impulse hitchhike out of town. I was on my own on this adventure, but the tug inside me was strong, and within minutes I had pulled into the New Canaan station and jumped on the first train heading to New York City.

The train was packed with commuters, but I finally found a seat a few cars back. I sat down next to a middle-aged man who was reading the morning *Times*. He was a large man and inched over to make room for me. He smiled as I sat down and then returned to his paper. I relaxed into my trip and pulled out a book, which I had bought the day before, titled *How to Develop Your Psychic Skills*.

"Excuse me. What are you reading?" the man asked a few minutes later. I looked at him and moved closer to the window. I had no intention of talking to him, and I gave him a polite, closed look and went back to my reading.

"No, seriously—are you a psychic?"

"No, are you?" I said, a bit irritated by the intrusive question.

"No, I am an opera singer, but I read palms."

"Opera singer?" I said, a little less standoffishly, realizing that he was probably safe to talk to.

"Yes, but I do read palms as a hobby."

"Oh."

"Show me your palm."

"What?" Once again, I moved a little farther away.

He laughed. "Don't worry, I'm not going to do anything. I really am a palm reader," he said, as if he had read my mind and knew about the apprehension I was feeling when he persisted in striking up a conversation.

I slowly opened my palm and showed it to him.

"Ok, what's it say?" I said, challenging him.

"Hmm, I see you lived in another country?"

"Yes."

"And you lost your mother?"

"How do you know that?"

"Oh, it's right over there." He pointed to a little line on my palm.

"Yes, I'd say you were in Europe in the early sixties, and the initials of your name are, let me see, M. M. N." He smiled and looked directly at me. "But that does not feel exactly right. Do you have another name? Nickname?" he asked.

I was astonished and I quickly looked around to see if I was carrying anything that revealed my name. This is getting weird, I thought. But it was the sixties and one was bound to run into something weird in those days.

"You are right. What's my birth date?" I asked, testing him further.

"February twelfth, nineteen fifty."

That clinched it. My heart jumped, and I pulled back my hand. He had frightened me, but he had also hooked me.

"Don't worry. Everyone tests me. But most importantly, I want to tell you that you are protected."

"I am?"

"Yes, guardian angels. Two of them. They are like mothers hovering around you. Making sure you make the right choices," he said, and laughed. Then he went on, "Though at times, it's going to be hard for you."

"I know, other psychics have said that too."

"But you will be okay. Hmm, there is someone who is looking for you."

"There is?"

"Yes—a woman. Is your mother alive?"

"I don't know," I answered and slumped back in the seat.

"Do you believe in spirits?" he asked, looking straight at me.

"Well, I guess so." I wondered how he knew; in those days I didn't tell anyone that I could feel guardians around me.

"You are going to have some notoriety, too."

"I am? Is it my art?" I had wanted to be a famous artist with recognition and validation. In my mind it would have made all the struggles and loss all right.

"No, you are going to be famous for something else."

"Writing?"

"No, I see people listening to you. And you have a dog."

"I will always have dogs."

"And yes, I see money."

"Money, great! I bet you say that to everyone."

"No," he said, shaking his head.

"I am so poor. It would be great to have some money! Anyway, how do you do all that?"

Just at that moment, the train pulled into a station outside the city. The man looked up at the sign. "Oh, this is my stop. Got to go." He stood up and shook my hand and gave me a warm smile. "Nice to meet you."

"You, too."

"Oh, by the way, I am not a palm reader." He winked.

"You aren't?"

"No, I am a psychic." He pointed to my book and laughed. "I fudged a bit, because I knew you wouldn't listen to me if I told you differently." He laughed again. "But I really am an opera singer, too. That's not a lie."

"Oh, really?" I laughed.

"Good luck. Nice talking to you," he said. And then he was gone.

CHAPTER 19
Jess: A Heartbreak
Those Who Commit Matricide

The end of the sixties was a strange time for me. I listened to music all the time, as if the songs contained the answers to the questions I had about life. Music both inspired my art and comforted me in hard times. I got caught up in the free-love, anything-goes beliefs of the times, which sometimes led me astray and into big trouble. Like my love affair with Jess, whom I met in my second year of college.

When I walked into the drawing class the first day and saw him leaning over a student's drawing, a chill ran up my spine. He was attractive, but I was reacting more to the strange emotional connection I felt to him. I wasn't drawn to him because he was tall, dark, and handsome, either. No, he was just an average-sized man, slim, with a bush of beautiful dark hair. He didn't dress like the other guys in school. Instead, he had a shabby prep look about him. He was clean-shaven and wore a yellow Brooks Brothers shirt and dark brown corduroys; he provided a nice relief from most of the grungy, bearded blue jean-clad men who attended the school.

I could feel the intensity of his eyes following me as I walked by him to my easel. When I sat down I looked straight at him and I felt his very dark soul pierce mine. He smiled and I smiled back. It seemed innocent enough, but I knew in some way that I was doomed to be with him.

He stuttered as he introduced himself to the class. "Hello, mmmy name is Jess Cordan. I am yyyyour teacher this semester." I was surprised and found his stuttering strangely appealing. I wanted to jump up and wrap my arms around him, like a mother would do for her shy little boy.

All that fall, I secretly dreamed of Jess, and I went to his class religiously. I told no one about my crush, because I was in a relationship with Sedgewick, a photography student, who was quite a few years older than me. I think it was Sedgewick's red Lotus sports car and his southern accent that seduced me into becoming engaged to him. The fact that he raised horses as a hobby, dressed well, and had all the right credentials made him a perfect match for the person I was brought up to be. I can honestly say that he was my last attempt to become the Marcy that would meet the Neilsons' approval.

Sedgewick and I were going to get married, and we made plans for a summer wedding. Maybe I can pull this off, I kept saying to myself as we talked about possible places for our honeymoon and houses where we might live. I almost did pull it off, until the snowstorm on Christmas Eve.

Jess lived in Woonsocket, near Providence, and he offered to drive me to Providence, where I was staying with some friends for the holidays.

It was quite the drive in a blizzard and it took hours to get there. Jess and I talked about everything. Our conversation went from Nietzsche, to Lorca, to Jesus, to the Rolling Stones. As we pulled up to my friends' house, we began to argue about the ending in the French film, *Sundays and Cybele*, where a psychologically disturbed older man befriends a young orphan girl.

"No, Jess! He wasn't going to kill her!" I argued. I wanted to believe that the guy was innocent. Jess, on the other hand, was raised to be a hardcore realist, by a mother who believed that the checkbook should be balanced and that reality was what you saw and nothing more. He saw the opposite in the movie, and made his case. "You are a fool! Of course he was going to kill her. What about the knife? He was carrying it toward her as she slept," he said.

"He was only going to give it to her, lay it gently by her side as a gift. He had told her it was magical. Remember?" I argued. "You could see in his eyes that he loved her."

"Yeah, well, maybe, but he couldn't really love her. He had to kill her."

"Why do you think that?" I asked, getting annoyed.

"Because he loved her."

"What do you mean? That makes no sense!"

That statement alone should have been my warning, my clue that Jess was full of strong feelings and self-hatred. I should have seen that love was as hard for him as it was for me. Years later, I realized that I had never heard him speak of his mother. It was as if she did not exist in his mind. I should have run after his statement about Cybele's love, but instead I leaned over to say goodbye. I felt the warmth of his body, and we kissed. It was one of those kisses where you don't want to let go. There was no return. The kiss caught my heart like a prisoner.

"Bye," I said, as I stepped out into the blizzard. The chill of the snow embraced me as I ran up the steps.

"Thanks for the ride," I called back.

But he was already gone.

***

The phone rang the day after Christmas. "Hey, it's Jess. How are you doing?"

"Hi. Good."

"Want to go back to Connecticut early?"

I closed my eyes and prayed that I would say no. "What about Sedgewick?"

"It's up to you. Don't tell him," he said.

***

Sedgewick found out that I had gone home with Jess. And he came knocking at Jess's door, enraged. The banging on the door woke both of us up. Jess grabbed his robe and ran downstairs to see who was banging so loudly. Sedgewick stormed in and walked past Jess, straight upstairs to the bedroom, where I lay naked under the sheets.

"Come on. Get dressed," he said, looking around the room. "I am taking you home. Now," he added, looking away. He walked over, found my clothes, and threw them on the bed. "Get dressed."

Jess was still downstairs, staying out of it. He had gone outside to smoke a cigarette. I knew without a doubt that it was another one of those crossroads moments in my life. I looked up at Sedgewick and everything he represented, and I looked at Jess's simple wood-paneled room and everything that he represented. Sedgewick is a nice guy, I thought. I felt his heart. But, oh my God, he is so boring. He would make a good husband, and take good care of me—but, oh my God, I would die—my spirit would fizzle out. Doing the right thing isn't always the answer, I decided. I realized that I couldn't pull off my relationship and upcoming marriage, and that I would never pull it off. I would never be the Marcy that everybody in my past had wanted me to be.

"I'm not going, Sedgewick," I said.

"Yes, you are!"

"No, I can't."

"But we are getting married."

"No, I can't." I looked down at the bed.

"What do you mean, you can't?"

I looked up at him. "I just can't."

Sedgewick began to cry.

"I am so sorry, Sedgewick. So sorry that I've hurt you," I said. I wrapped the sheet around me and walked over to comfort him. He jerked away. He looked at me, and I saw that he was a broken man and also a furious one. Then, as quickly as he had arrived, he ran out of the house, slamming the door behind him. Within a week he had transferred.

I went back to bed and sat for a long time staring at the swirls and patterns of the wood on the wall. I wondered if I had really made a wise choice. I knew I hadn't. Just at that moment, as I began to doubt what I had done, Jess reappeared with a mug of coffee for me, and he crawled back into bed. He felt warm and welcoming. I snuggled down into his arms, knowing I had chosen passion.

Jess and I lived together for the winter semester. But our relationship soon became a disaster. There were too many drugs and too much drama, with the reek of self-destruction running through it all. I moved out, but we continued seeing each other. The dance of our souls, wherein we felt so connected or bound, would not let us say goodbye easily. It was as if we were finding our way out of a maze that we had created with our passion.

I never loved a man with as much intensity as I did Jess. But it came to an end a year later, when he slept with my housemate. I found them in bed one night when I came home from work. I didn't say anything; I just went to my room and closed the door. There in the dark I felt my life beginning to crumble.

The next morning Jess came to my room after my housemate left for spring break. I was still in bed, hurt and wanting to hide from everyone. He came in and lay down beside me. I turned away. He reached out and turned my chin toward him. Those eyes that I could not leave seemed so sad that day. I just looked at him and then suddenly he began to weep like a little boy. I think he was weeping for all the sorrow that he held in his life. God knows what pain and secrets he held inside his heart.

He wept so hard that I began to pull myself together, thinking he was having a breakdown. For hours, I was compelled to hold him in my arms, like a mother would her child. We said nothing. Evening came and the tears had stopped. We made love as if our souls were saying goodbye for the last time. We slept gently in each other's arms until midnight, when he got up to leave. We still said nothing. As he was dressing, I sat in the dark watching his silhouette against the streetlight. In the shadows, his taut, beautiful lean body reminded me of Adonis.

"How could you, Jess? How could you have slept with her?"

He didn't answer.

"Jess, I need to know."

Still nothing. He began to leave, looking annoyed. He stopped as he reached the door. He leaned up against the doorjamb and said nothing.

"Jess?" I said louder.

He suddenly spun around and looked at me. "Marcy, how could I not have slept with her?" he laughed, dismissing any guilt.

"How could you not have?" I repeated, getting angry at his sarcastic tone.

"Wake up, it's the sixties!" he interrupted as he turned away again and walked out of the room. He never looked back as he closed the door behind him. It was over. Jess was gone.

I tried to forget the pain his leaving caused me. I had lost not one but two people in my life. I couldn't find a replacement for my housemate, who moved out to live with him. I had no extra money and this added to a very fast downward spiral that had begun in my life. I lost my home and ended up on the street, sleeping in the school basement for a few weeks. It just got worse. I began popping pills to stay up all night to paint, until one day–I crashed.

One morning I was lying on the basement floor of the school, snuggled in my sleeping bag, with my hound dog, Curdie, and my cat, Sien. We stayed warm next to the boiler, which stank of burning oil. My life felt unbearable. I had no money and there would be no breakfast. I pushed my hunger pangs away. It was very early. At the tiny basement window I spied a bird pecking at the frozen ground for food. I stared at the bird for what seemed a long time. I thought about how strange a perspective it was to be looking up from an underground level. To be quietly watching this little creature go about its life. I felt as if I was in my grave.

Maybe it was the empty space that gave me room to think clearly or maybe it was a simple pause in life, but suddenly something came together and clicked like a new frame in a silent film. "God damn, Jess, I hate you for this!" I yelled. I could feel an inner fire rising. With it came the inner strength that had always been with me in the darkest moments of my life. I hate this, I thought as I looked at my surroundings. I hate being poor and homeless–a wreck. A surge of self-preservation rose inside me, becoming a strong defense against the starkness of my reality. My feelings rushed through my mind and broke loose. No way am I going to break, I thought. I started pacing in the small space. I am going to make it. I am going to make it. I am going to make it, I kept repeating. Then I flashed on what the opera singer on the train had said about my guardian angels. "Angels, I need you," I called out loud. Tears were streaming down my face. "I need you right now!" I pleaded. I was so angry at life at that moment. "Help me!" I yelled.

There were no lights, no mystical moment with soft music and angels appearing to save me. Nope, it was not at all like that. It was just a strong feeling that lay somewhere between my heart and my solar plexus. A feeling that I had a purpose in life and this purpose wasn't about lying on a basement floor or feeling sorry for myself. A calm came over me.

I looked at my watch. The school was opening and I could hear people arriving. So I quickly packed my sleeping bag and hurried up the stairs. I rushed out to the parking lot, with my cat under my arm and my sleeping bag in my hand. Curdie ran by my side, leaping and barking playfully all the way to the car. "Marcy, where are you going?" someone called. I kept going. As I got into the car and placed Sien in the backseat, I was relieved to see that I had just enough gas to get back to Providence.

"Come on, Curdie, in the car," I said. I couldn't help but laugh as I watched him saunter toward the car. Curdie was a laid-back coonhound mutt and even in moments of drastic life changes, he kept his cool. He looked at me curiously and then jumped into the front seat, wagging his tail. He was ready to go.

"We're out of here," I said as I ruffled the hair around his collar. It was that simple. I drove away, leaving college life behind forever.

CHAPTER 20
Victoria of The West
A Child of an Alcoholic Mother

I came back to Providence and found a menial job as a dishwasher and my life went along at a simple but depressing pace, until an old friend arrived and moved in with me for a short time. Victoria, who nicknamed herself Victoria of the West, talked with a Southern drawl but had never lived in the South, smoked joints like they were cigarettes, and flashed a smile that would make anyone fall in love with her. When she walked into a room with her long, strawberry blonde hair, shiny and soft like a Revlon model, men turned around. She was petite but claimed in private moments that she had a little round English maid's body. She'd smile sweetly at guys and say, "howdy fellas," wink one of her big brown eyes at them, and any favor was hers. She had the art of manipulation finely tuned.

Strangely, Victoria was one of the few people whose eyes had nothing behind them when I looked deeply into them. I saw no dormant ghost waiting to be reborn, no pain, no haunting, nothing. She truly was a "what you see is what you get" type of gal.

Victoria lived on another planet. But she had a good heart and was a seeker of utopia. Her eccentric flair mesmerized me, and we became good friends after high school. Victoria and I spent a lot of time stoned and talking about what the world needed. We were both dreamers and wanted to be part of the bigger picture.

Victoria lived with her mother, an alcoholic, and her very rich stepfather. Her mother's only dream for her daughter was marriage and the gifts of high society. Victoria's mother disliked me and saw me as a woebegone girl who was in her daughter's way.

"Some day, Marcy, we are going to have a home—a big place with lots of dogs for you and lots of cats for me," Victoria would say.

"Yes," I would answer, dreaming of the commune we would build.

"And just the right people will live there," she would add.

"Yes, and lots of children."

"And lots of flower gardens."

"A home for the poor . . ."

"The lonely . . ."

"The tired . . ."

Then inevitably one of us would jump up, strike a Statue of Liberty pose, and start the "give me your tired, your poor." speech. We had such big hopes in those days. But how were we going to do this?

One afternoon, not long after Victoria's arrival on my doorstep, she swept into the living room, carrying a glass of Chablis in one hand and a cigarette in the other.

"Marcy, I think we should check out this commune, down south in Florida."

"Down south? What commune?" My spirit perked up.

"Yup, that's what I think we should do," she said as she flopped down in the easy chair.

"How can we do that?"

"Well, tomorrow is my birthday."

"What's your birthday got to do with it?"

"Well. I've got this . . . here . . . money that my big ole daddy left me when he died. The will said I had to be twenty-one before I could have it."

"And let me guess, you are going to be twenty-one?" Victoria was almost two years older than me, even though she graduated a year behind me.

She took a sip of wine. "Yep, I think a commune is a good way to spend this money. Don't you agree?"

"Well . . . Is there enough?"

"We have enough to buy land. . . ."

Victoria came from a wealthy family and, who knows, I thought, maybe she had a good idea, and just maybe the dreams we had shared could come true.

"What's the commune called?"

"Oh, I don't know, does it matter?" She refilled her glass.

"Well, how are we going to know where we're going?" Over the years I had learned to be patient with Victoria when it came to details and facts.

"Now that's the big question. Do we ever know where we are going?" Victoria always did that—created one-line philosophical statements—catch phrases. Victoria–isms, I called them.

"Come on, Victoria, what's the name?"

"Oh, Precious something, Precious Hearts, tarts, sweets or something. I don't know. Maybe it was Precious Shells, that would make sense, wouldn't it? Since it's in Florida."

"How are we going to get there?"

"Well, I have a pretty brand-new bug–remember?" she said, smiling.

"Yeah, you are right," I said, getting up to pour myself a glass of wine.

"I think we need to do some research in the commune business," she said with a haughty expression.

"Okay, I'll start packing," I said, and went to look for a bag.

By the next day we were heading down the road toward Florida. The Young Bloods, Grateful Dead, and Joan Baez were on the radio to serenade us all the way. We were quite the sight–two happy-go-lucky hippies: me in jeans, leather vest, bandana, and of course wire-rimmed sunglasses, and Victoria in an Indian import skirt, bells galore, and a flower print shirt. And of course, no bras. After all, we were living in the sixties, just riding the wave. All was cool.

A week later, we arrived in Coconut Grove, a ritzy, old-money town where I had lived with the Neilsons in the early sixties. "Here, go this way," I said. "I remember there is a main square. . . . Oh, there's St. Stephen's, my old school. Did I ever tell you about it?"

"This sure doesn't look like a place where a commune would be," Victoria interrupted.

We asked around, looking for other hippie-type people, and we were directed to the law firm of an Allen something or other. He was a wealthy, middle-aged lawyer, a wannabe guru, who had twenty people living with him. I didn't like him from the minute I met him. But Victoria was doing her thing, and I went along.

Florida is no New England, as we found out when Allen showed us to the house. We drove down the driveway to an elegant mansion with palm trees and stucco walls surrounding the property. To add to the ambiance, lush gardens hid a kidney-shaped pool with a fountain at one end. We were speechless.

The commune was too laid back even for Victoria. Children were running around naked and it seemed like no one was sober. In the week that we stayed there, I couldn't figure out who was whose partner. Sometimes I wondered if even they knew. New Age music with a southern twang played nonstop in the background. The large, nearly empty carpeted living room had one long sofa and heavy white curtains drawn across its windows. Between the claustrophobic feeling I got from being in the air-conditioned space and the awful, twangy music, the whole thing became torture.

One evening I was sitting and watching Victoria get a massage from a man who was six foot three and who looked like he was surfing on her back. He was very skinny and had a very long, blond beard. To top it off, he was naked. Every time he dug his heel into her back he'd say, "Can you feel that?" I could see that he was getting a cheap thrill from it all.

Victoria's freckled face grew brighter with each dig, and she protested and squealed like a guinea pig. I couldn't stop giggling every time she grunted. But I was growing tired and hungry and I wanted to get out of there and never come back.

"Victoria, this sure ain't our 'give me your lonely, your tired,' " I said confusedly as I headed upstairs. There I found two very young children in a bathtub, unsupervised. One was screaming. The water was running slowly, but it had already reached their shoulders.

"Where's your mommy?" I asked.

Both looked up at me and shrugged their shoulders. The youngest began to cry again. I turned off the water faucet, grabbed a towel, and got them out of the tub. All I could see were flashes of two drowned children floating in the tub. The whole thing freaked me out. And fully triggered my mothering side. We all came down the stairs.

"Daddy, Daddy, we want dinner," the two children said as they ran over to the man on top of Victoria.

"I want to get out of here," I said to Victoria.

"Why? There is a party tonight."

"I don't care. I want to get out of here now." I was shaking.

Victoria sat up. She looked at me with one of her slow, "I am thinking" expressions.

"Now, Victoria. Remember Dylan and our dreams."

"Well, maybe later," she said.

"Victoria, remember we are going to change the world?"

"Ya?"

"Well, this isn't it. The world, that is."

"Oh," she said. Had she forgotten everything we stood for?

She looked so out of it, I thought. "Victoria!" I ran to the car and grabbed Dylan's album with "Girl of The North Country" on it. "Any of you guys listen to Dylan?" I asked as I headed to the record player.

"Can't say we do," they answered.

"Well, listen to this," I said as I took the twangy music off the record player. We waited.

If you're travelin' to the North Country fair
Where the winds hit heavy on the borderline
Remember me to one who lives there
For she once was a true love of mine

It worked. I watched as Victoria transformed. Victoria of the West reappeared. With a swagger and a sway, in her best southern drawl she said, "Boys, we gotta be going." And out the door we went.

***

We drove out of town as fast as we could and did not stop. Late that evening, as we drove through some Floridian town, I saw a cabbage patch.

"Victoria, stop! We can make coleslaw."

"I suppose we could," she said with a grin, as she pulled over to the side. I jumped out of the car in my bare feet and ran into the field.

"Ouch ooch eeech," I said as I started walking over the small rough stones used for drainage. I couldn't just pick the first cabbage that I saw; no, I was looking for the perfect cabbage. I was in the middle of the patch when a police car drove up. Have you ever tried to hide in a cabbage patch? Cabbages only grow about ankle to knee high. When the cops drove up and started to slow down, I dropped to the ground. I think it was one of the more foolish things I have done. And I think the cops thought so too and had a good laugh. They drove away, never saying anything. Then, right in front of my face, I saw the perfect one. I grabbed it and ran back to the car, ooching and eeching all the way. I threw it in the backseat and off we went with our loot—one big green cabbage.

It was a good thing I got that cabbage, because not long after that incident, we were stopped in a back town in Georgia at five-thirty in the morning for going two miles above the speed limit. Two cops, the kind you don't want to mess with, stopped us. As I saw them walking toward the car, I quickly hid the few uppers and hits of acid we had in the leaves of the cabbage.

"Howdy, women. Do you know how fast you were going?" the first cop said.

"No, officer. I do believe it was the speed limit," Victoria said with a smile.

"No, ma'am. It wasn't," the second one said.

"Oh." Victoria smiled again.

There was absolutely no sign of life anywhere around, and no danger that we would have hit someone, but there was no way we could plead for mercy. Two miles above the speed limit was two miles above the speed limit.

"Ma'am, we could throw you in jail, unless you pay the fine right now." The cop looked at his partner and smirked.

"How much will that be?" Victoria asked.

"Two hundred dollars will do—cash, that is," he said, tipping his hat.

Victoria turned to me and, in her ever-so-amused manner, said, "Want to go to jail?" as if she were asking me if I wanted to go to Tahiti or the Bahamas.

"Victoria, are you crazy?"

"Am I crazy? Let me think about that." I could see she was searching for one of her Victoria statements.

"Victoria! Fuck the deeper meaning right now. Just say we will pay."

"Well, we haven't gone to jail yet."

"No. I do not want to go to jail."

"So the answer is no?" the cop asked.

"Victoria, the cabbage will rot if we go to jail," I whispered, rolling

140

my eyes to the back of the seat where the one large cabbage sat.

"Lordy! I almost forgot the cabbage!" she said as she pulled out our last $200.

"Here you go, officer," she said, smiling.

"Why, thank you, ma'am. Have a nice day, ma'am." And the cop walked away.

"Excuse me, a receipt?" she called after him.

"Victoria, we are not getting one. Let's just get out of here," I said, shaken by the whole experience. After that we crawled at twenty-five miles per hour all the way though the back towns of Georgia until we hit the highway.

The cabbage in the backseat sat alongside a garbage bag that had been filling up as we traveled. The bag began to smell of rotting food.

"We have to get rid of that bag or I am going to throw up," I said.

"Okay. The next time I see a stop on the highway. I want to look at the map anyway," Victoria said. It was dark by the time we stopped at the beginning of the New Jersey Turnpike. Victoria pulled out a map and turned on a flashlight to look at it. Suddenly a cop came over.

"Get out of the car!" he yelled.

"Why?"

"Just get out of the car." He held a flashlight in Victoria's face. "Ya on drugs?" he asked.

"No." The truth is, Victoria on a good day looked like she was on drugs, but she wasn't at that moment.

"Then why are your eyes looking funny?"

"It's the flashlight beaming in my face," she said, and laughed.

He put the light down. By then another cop, a short, stocky man, got out of the patrol car.

"What's going on?" he asked.

"Drugs," the first cop said.

"Why aren't you girls wearing bras?" the short one asked, staring at my breasts.

"They are uncomfortable," I said.

"I bet you have drugs in the car," he said. "George, start searching the car."

Oh God, we are in trouble now, I thought, as I saw the cop pick up the cabbage. He threw it down on the ground. And then began looking through every piece of garbage.

I wanted to laugh about the garbage but I didn't. We just waited until they were finished.

"We know you have drugs," they said. Then they tore the car apart.

141

They didn't find anything. But the car was a mess.

"Pick up the garbage or we will give you a ticket for littering," the short one said. "And we don't want to see your face in this state again." And then they walked away.

After we had picked up the garbage, and I had carefully placed our prize-winning ruffled cabbage back on its seat, we left New Jersey and weren't seen in that town again.

We searched through many towns in New England, looking for the perfect place for a home. But we never did find our golden land. Then one cold rainy day in Vermont we left our beloved cabbage in a field of mud and held a cabbage funeral. The rain was pouring down our faces. Victoria and I looked at the cabbage and then at each other.

"Home?" I asked.

"I suppose so," she said.

We didn't say anything as we headed back to Providence. We didn't need to. Inside, we both knew the dream of a commune was fizzling out, and so were we. I was relieved that we didn't have to find the land or build the dream. A good night's sleep in my own bed would do.

Victoria and I looked at each other as the car pulled up to my apartment that afternoon. We were both exhausted and depressed. James Taylor's "Fire and Rain" was playing on the radio. Victoria started singing along.

"I am going home to my Mom's tonight. I need a good meal," she said.

"I suppose it isn't going to happen. The commune, that is," I said.

"I suppose not," she said, smiling.

I felt if I got out of the car, it would be the end of a dream. But somewhere on that trip I had gained some wisdom. Somehow I knew that not all dreams need to be chased and not all friends need to be kept. I would be happy to find a job and have a place to live. Simplicity–not poverty–but simplicity was what I craved that day. Something had changed, and deep inside I knew Victoria and I needed to go different ways.

"See you," I said as I grabbed my bag from the back.

"Yep."

We smiled.

"Thanks, Victoria."

"For what?"

"For the ride?" I laughed.

Just at that moment, my housemate opened the front door and let Curdie out. He saw me and came bounding over to the car, wagging his tail and barking.

"Curdie!" I said, jumping out of the car and kneeling down to give him a hug. He was ecstatic and licked my face, whimpering with joy.

"I love you, Curdie," I said, tears rolling down my cheeks as I buried my face in his collar. His love was infectious and I began to feel happy. I knew he had my heart.

"Oh, what the hell, it was just another adventure," I said. I looked around and felt the excitement in the air. Providence was just beginning to show the slightest signs of spring. That alone helped buffer the disappointment I was hiding inside. I bent down again and wrapped my arms around his back and smelled the sun-baked scent of the street on his warm, furry neck, and listened to him pant. It was pure love. His big brown eyes looked up at me with absolute acceptance, and my soul melted away into a trillion sun-baked moments. I learned what my old dog had known all along: that while some say home is where the heart is, I say home is where your dog sleeps.

After my whirlwind adventure with Victoria, I settled back into my apartment and Victoria moved back to her mother's house. I accepted that Providence was going to be my home. It was not a perfect place, but it gave me time to continue to find myself. And in a few days my sense of humor about life and about myself was rekindled.

CHAPTER 21
The Image in the Mirror
Is My Mother There?

It was the spring equinox, and to celebrate, a group of friends and I decided to drop some acid–Purple Haze, to be exact.

"Let's go to the beach," Becky said.

"We've already done the beach trip. And it's too cold," Brad said. We all laughed at the pun.

"How about my parents' house? It is really comfortable and we can all stay the night. They are in Europe for the month," Jan said.

Everyone thought that Jan's idea was great. Except for me. I was house sitting that weekend for my friends the Tuttles, who were going to the Cape for the weekend. The house would be all mine.

Even in those days I was different from most of the friends I hung out with. I considered myself to be an intellectual, someone who thought deeply about things, and I wanted to experiment with acid, to see where the little purple dot would take me. I wanted a mystical tour. The last time I had tripped with them, I spent most of it sitting in a chair watching Chas trying to eat a bowl of hot oatmeal. He had methodically prepared it just before the trip took off, but when he sat down, grinning, to eat his favorite dish, he realized he was too stoned to know whether the oatmeal was too hot and would burn his mouth. I watched him cautiously lift the spoon to his mouth and, just before he bit down on it, quickly withdraw it, commenting that he thought it might be too hot. This went on for an hour, until I relieved the poor boy of his dilemma by taking a big scoop of sticky, cold cereal. "It's cool enough," I said. And I walked away shaking my head, angry with myself for having wasted so much time on his oatmeal. So, this time I wanted to be alone.

"I want to trip alone," I said.

"Alone?" they all answered together.

"Yes, alone. The Tuttles are gone, and I have always wanted to trip in that dressing room of mirrors."

"The dressing room of mirrors?" my friends again said together.

"Yes, I think it would be cool to stare for hours at a zillion images of me."

"I think it would be scary," Jan said.

"Me, too," Carol said.

"I think it will be great," I said.

"You are crazy," they told me.

"No, I am not. I'm curious. So you all go to Jan's," I said, and off I

144

went to the Tuttles' house.

This was going to be profound, I thought, as I prepared for the acid trip in the fancy dressing room of mirrors. Hadn't I spent a lifetime looking for the little me, the child I was before I was adopted? The child who had a mother. Who had I been? What did that little girl look like? How about my mother? Would I be able to find her? Feel her? Would she be waiting in the mirror for me? Or would I see my future? Anything could happen, I thought.

The room of mirrors had been built in the twenties—by a bishop, of all people. It was a beautiful circular room with tall wall-to-wall painted mirrors. When one stood in the center and looked at a certain angle, one could see oneself in every direction, infinitely. Yes, this is going to be a trip with a message, I thought. I was both excited and afraid of what might be revealed.

I got the candles and interlaced them with a few roses in the center of the room. I then lit some sandalwood incense, started the tape player, and sat in a lotus position, dressed in a white robe. Jefferson Airplane's "White Rabbit" began playing: "One pill makes you larger. And one makes you small. . . ." I was waiting for my enlightenment—to discover who I might be. I waited and waited. Would this be like the ancient Egyptian hall of mirrors? Or would it be the fairies dancing around me as I had seen in the picture books? Or would it be something completely different? And then came the familiar roar of the drug in my head. The walls began to breathe and the floor began to rock. I held on, knowing this phase of the drug would pass. The painted flowers on the mirror began to dance and look like fairies, and I began to laugh. And then things became quiet again. I was in the part of the trip where all knowledge is revealed. I looked into the mirror, stared as hard as I could at the infinite images of myself.

"I am ready," I whispered. I stared some more.

"Come on, show me."

Nothing. Nothing happened. I couldn't even see myself. My mind was blank. And the harder I tried to see my image, the less I could.

I had forgotten something very important. I had failed to remember to wash the mirrors beforehand, and now, what would have been bypassed, overlooked, missed, on a regular day—the simple patterns of fingerprints on the glass—captivated me. I spent four hours staring at fingerprints! Nothing more. Nothing else. There were no profound "ah ha's" or inner truths revealed. No enlightenment. No mother speaking to me. Just a hard, cold piece of wisdom—that acid was not the answer to the cosmic question: Who am I? And mothers are not found in mirrors.

CHAPTER 22
The Motherghost's Question

After I came back from my adventure with Victoria, I rented an apartment with another woman for about a year. While I was alone one night, I took a good look at my life. I felt stuck in a quagmire. My room was a mess. My life was a mess and I knew that I needed to pull it together. I had no parent to tell me, "Get your shit together, Marcy." But I could see it in my more mature and caring friends' eyes. I could see their concern and I could hear it within their silence. I was getting tired of myself. I was becoming bored with life as a tragic, angry, radical artist. I wanted change.

I was feeling pretty down that night as I sat on my bare mattress in my empty room. I played with the beautiful red hues from the reflections of the candlelight in the wine. "Gotta get off this stuff," I said to the empty room. These drugs are going to kill me, I thought. I knew that. I was going nowhere. I sat alone in the dark and I thought for a long time. I thought about my life and the mess I had made of it. I began to cry quietly. "Help me," I whispered in the dark. "I'm in trouble."

Somewhere in the middle of my tears, I felt a presence come into the room. I looked up and saw a glow in the corner. It did not frighten me at all, and its energy felt comforting. As I stared at it, I noticed that it seemed angelic or even motherly.

"Find the innocence in your life," the spirit said.

"The innocence? What do you mean?"

"Find someone who is precious to you."

"There is no one in my life. I am alone," I said.

Silence.

I thought about what she had said for a very long time. It didn't make sense in the beginning. I searched through my life for what was precious. For someone who was innocent. It was not easy for me to find those things in my current life. But then the image of someone I found precious came to me. I saw Sara Tuttle, my friend's new little blonde-haired baby. I had watched her one day as she sat in her high chair splattering oatmeal on the tray and giggling with each splat. I laughed with the memory of the many splats of oatmeal and the sound of her giggles.

"It is little Sara?" I asked.

"Then make a promise to Sara," the spirit answered.

"How?"

"You know how. Remember when you were very young and innocent," she said. And then as quickly as the glow had appeared, it was gone. I thought about what had just happened. Children and animals had

146

always provided a safe place for me to be happy. And Sara was one of those children. But what did she mean, I knew how? Then I knew what to do. I grabbed the candle and went to the closet, where a full-length mirror hung on the door. I stared at my skinny body and saw how bedraggled I looked. I pointed at myself in a stern manner. And as I had done as a child, I began to pretend I was a powerful magician. My heart lightened and I raised my hand as if I could wield imaginary powers. It was the strongest I had ever felt about myself.

"You will not be able to see Sara Tuttle ever again if you do any more drugs," I commanded, speaking in a fierce voice that seemed to rise up from within me. I looked myself straight in the eye and used a gesture that seemed to come to me naturally, as if I knew how to seal a spell into the mirror. Then I was done.

It worked. Maybe I was tired of my life and the direction I was going in. Maybe it was the spirits helping me, or maybe it was my love of one infant that helped me get off drugs. Whatever it was, it worked. I slowly began to turn my life around.

First, I found a job as an art teacher. It didn't pay a lot, but it came with a free apartment in a nice area, and I began to paint again in the evenings. Somehow, my life was coming to a place of ease. I was resting for just awhile.

I knew instinctively that someday I would be okay. My life would not be an endless maze. I could see that my fierce determination to survive any challenge had always helped me. And I also saw forces greater than me were there to guide me. Most importantly, I realized that I had been blessed with a sense of humor.

In the months that followed I took the necessary steps to help myself; I got a job and stabilized my life. Not long after that, the letter that ultimately led to the reading of my father Alfred's will arrived and changed my life forever.

Let me not pray to be sheltered from dangers,
but to be fearless in facing them.
Let me not beg for the stilling of my pain,
but for the heart to conquer it.

–Rabindranath Tagore,
Collected Poems and Plays of Rabindranath Tagore

CHAPTER 23
The Stone Bird
The Fairy Godmother's Messenger

When I was twenty-three, I discovered my emotional limits the hard way. After a door-slamming exit by an angry lover one terrible night, combined with too much booze and too much sorrow, I simply gave up hope. To ease my grief, I grabbed the first pill bottle on the medicine shelf and swallowed its contents with the last bit of wine in my glass. A few minutes later I called my shrink to say goodbye. Then I passed out.

I came to in a hospital emergency room. My arms were strapped to the table and my stomach was being pumped. That was the moment I decided that drama was not the way I wanted to live my life.

I had a rough time in the days that followed. In addition to a serious case of tachycardia, the pills' aftereffects and the breakup left me more depressed than ever: I discovered that I was still me and the same questions of where I was going in life and what I was doing remained unanswered.

As I was struggling to find myself, a wounded gray pigeon, who I named Henry, came to live with me. He was a very pushy pigeon, as pigeons go. The universe probably sent him to me, I thought. Between my hound dog and the pigeon, I was not allowed to wallow in my depression for too long. Henry, with one leg tucked under his fluffed-up chest, perched on my bedpost and gave me a stern, cross-eyed look, as if to say, "So, young lady, what are you going to do with your life?"

For days I lay in bed and stared at the walls and then back at Henry. I tried to find some kind of spiritual anchor to help me and failed. An angel, an apparition, music, anything will do, I yelled at the empty walls. But nothing came—except Henry with an occasional coo and a cluck.

Then I tried to look at my predicament with humor. I thought of Wile E. Coyote, who was determined to catch the roadrunner. In one cartoon episode, Wile E. runs up a mountain, only to reach the edge of a cliff. Horrified by the near disaster, he comes to a screeching halt and scrambles in midair and makes it back to the edge. With no dignity left, he carefully crawls backward on his belly, inch by inch, to a safer place. In my mind, I was on my belly crawling backward, away from my edge—bit by bit. And yes, Henry saw it all and was laughing.

Then one morning, the sunlight spilled into my room in just the right way and I felt better inside. To top it off, Henry wanted out. He is ready to leave! I thought as I opened the window and let him go. "Bye, Henry," I called as I watched him fly out and over to a rooftop.

A side note to pigeon-lovers—they never leave you if you take them

149

in and feed them. Henry wanted freedom—not a goodbye. No matter how far away I took Henry, he found his way home to me and was waiting at the window to be let in. To this day, I don't know which event set us both free: when I actually moved or when I took Henry out of state to Cape Cod.

It was only a few days after Henry's first flight into freedom that I finally returned to my art and started carving a stone sculpture of a bird. It was a good physical workout and carving took patience. It was perfect therapy for me.

One evening, a friend took me to see the movie, *Harold and Maude*. I immediately fell in love with Ruth Gordon, who played the part of Maude, a free-spirited, wise and very eccentric older woman.

In a scene I loved, Maude sees a seagull flying across a sunset sky and refers to the bird as a glorious bird. Harold looks at her as if to say, Maude, it's only a seagull! Maude responds by telling the story of a friend who always thought a flock of birds that he watched, every evening for years, were glorious birds. That is, he thought so until the day he found out that they were only seagulls. How sad she thought this was! She said that seagulls or not, they would always be simply glorious birds to her. I understood what she meant. After all, wasn't my Henry quite the bird?

As my friend and I filed out of the theater, I said, "If only there was a real-life Maude in the world."

"Maybe there is," she said, amused.

"Maybe," I sighed.

My friend was right, there was a real-life Maude! She was a woman of spunk and adventure, with a magical twinkle in her eye. It was Ruth Gordon, who, according to people who knew her personally, said that she was a perfect fit for the eccentric, free-spirited character she had played in the film. I was beside myself when I heard this and I decided I had to meet her.

The universe was on my side, and not long after the day at the theater, I found out that an acquaintance of mine was Ruth Gordon's summer neighbor!

I decided that I wanted to give her my stone bird. With great enthusiasm I got back to work and finished the last details of the sculpture. It was a beautiful, polished alabaster bird with its head tucked under its wing. I named it Inner Peace.

The next morning I telephoned Ruth Gordon in Edgartown, Massachusetts, and asked if I could deliver my gift to her. To my surprise she simply said yes.

I took a ferry over to the island a week later. It was a perfectly beautiful day; the sky was clear and the air was vibrantly alive with ocean summer smells. I walked down the road lined with white picket fences until I came to her house. I have to admit that I was a little nervous about meeting someone so famous. Her movie was very popular, and when I think about it now, it was pretty presumptuous of me to think that she would meet with a complete stranger. But she did. She opened the door herself. At first, I was speechless. I had not expected her to be so tiny. She only came up to my shoulders. She looks just like a little fairy godmother! I thought, as she ushered me in.

She had a simple sandwich lunch set for us on the veranda. At lunch I pulled out the heavy box and placed it on the glass table.

"This is for you," I said.

When I gave her the present, she was like a little child at Christmas. Her eyes sparkled as she slowly untied the ribbon and carefully tore off the light blue wrapping paper. She looked at me and smiled and I smiled back politely. She lifted the lid of the box. Peered in. Jumped up and pulled it out. I jumped up to offer help, but she had already placed the bird on the table. She gasped and sat back down.

"I thought of you, when I carved this bird," I said nervously.

She smiled.

"It is a glorious bird," I added, hoping that she knew that I was referring to the line in the movie.

"Oh my," she whispered as she continued to stare at it. She leaned back and studied it. Turned the sculpture carefully in all directions. We said nothing. My shyness and nervousness overwhelmed me. And then I saw tears roll down her cheeks. It made me teary-eyed to watch her and to know that I had wanted all my life to do just one piece of work that would be so powerful that it brought tears to someone's eyes. And that it happened right there with Ruth Gordon.

Still teary-eyed, she turned to me and said, "I have worked hard all my life." She paused, sighing. "And sometimes I have even wondered whether it has been worth it. And then something like this happens," she said. She reached out and stroked the bird, then leaned back again. She gestured toward the bird and then turned directly to me. She stared into my eyes and I saw her soul. I was surprised to see in it the pain and doubt she had suffered.

"It is in moments like these that you know it has all been worth it," she said, and gave me a big hug. It was an important hug and it felt like she was giving me back my life.

When I left the island I was smiling inside and out. As I stood at the bow, heading toward the mainland, the sea winds were gently warm and welcoming. For the first time since that awful night of pills, I was happy and relieved that I was still alive. Ruth Gordon never knew about Henry and that the tears she shed were over a sculpture of a pigeon–but you know, I think she would have appreciated that secret. She would have understood that Henry and my sculpture had saved my life. She would have said Henry was my glorious bird.

Mother IV
Finding My Family
1977-1983

CHAPTER 24
Choices
The Rejection of Motherhood

A few years before the arrival of the money, when I was very poor and feeling that I had no future, I went to New York City with my boyfriend, Bobby, to get an abortion. It was December fourth, a date I will never forget.

"Did you remember the blanket?" Bobby asked.

"Yes," I said, throwing a little traveling bag in the backseat of the car. "What time is it?" I asked.

"Four-forty five. What time is the appointment?" he asked, looking at his watch.

"One thirty," I said, getting into the car. In his usual organized fashion, he had carefully left driving instructions, a phone number, and an address on the seat. I picked up the papers and I clutched them in my sweaty hand for the whole trip.

We said nothing to each other all the way down to the city. No radio playing. No words. I smoked a half a pack or more of cigarettes on the way. The sun rose on a bleak, rainy day. I felt myself beginning to shut down.

Why couldn't Bobby have been the right person? I thought. Why did he have to say to me, "I will think about getting married," after I told him that I was pregnant? Why did I have to feel that he judged me so harshly when he said that? The "I'll think about it" reminded me too much of all the previous rejections in my life. And all I could say was, "Fuck you, I want an abortion," in return. Even after he came back and put his arms around me and said, "I've thought about it. Let's get married," I knew that it was too late. I couldn't do it. The moment was dead.

"I want an abortion," I repeated, and looked away. It's all wrong, I thought. I can't marry him.

"Why?" he asked, startled by my answer.

"I am too broke to keep it and I am only twenty years old."

"But I thought you wanted to get married. What happened?"

"Forget it, Bobby!" The more we talked, the angrier I got.

"Anyway, I have been sick most of this pregnancy. Something is wrong. I can feel it."

My feelings were all over the place. I knew getting an abortion would trigger memories of all my losses. But I knew it was the right choice and I have never doubted my decision. It was right for me. Still, no matter how right it felt, I was really scared. I knew then, as I know now, that there are times in my life when I just shut down, don't think too much, and move forward–get through whatever it is. This was one of those times.

I have always been scared of doctors and this time was no exception. My anxiety became palpable as I stepped into the clinic office. It was a very narrow basement room with a desk at one end, where a receptionist sat busy at work. I took a deep breath and looked at the five other women, young like me, sitting in chairs lined up against the wall. All of them were busily filling out forms. The receptionist handed me a form and I went over to sit down with the others. I told Bobby to leave.

"Go, I can handle it," I said.

"Are you sure?"

"Yes, I am sure," I said, and went back to filling out the form. The form became an unexpected trigger in itself because it was the first medical form I had ever filled out. I felt like an adult in some ways, filling out forms and making decisions. But I also felt like a lost child making grown-up decisions. At the same time, I knew I wasn't, and didn't doubt that this very difficult, well-thought-out choice was the right one for me. As I filled out this form that asked me a long list of questions about family medical history, I was reminded that I was most likely different from most of the women in the room. I was adopted and I knew nothing about my medical history. I can't even fill out this damn medical form, I thought. Medical history, in those days, was a privilege, not a legal right, for an adoptee. And in moments like these, the laws protecting the mother—not the child—felt like a gun barrel pointing at me.

I don't know if what happened that day in that room was typical. The pain was awful, perhaps because abortions were still primitive in the sixties, even in the clinics, or maybe the doctor didn't care about causing pain, or maybe the doctor was just emotionally off that day. Whatever the reason, he ignored my pleas for relief.

"God! That hurts," I said, as he placed larger and larger rings into my vagina.

"It will be over in a minute," he said as he added one more metal ring.

"I don't think I can take more," I said, tears rolling down my cheeks. But I had to and I did take more pain. And I haven't forgotten that the pain was excruciating. I tried hard to shut out the sounds of metal on metal and metal on flesh scraping my insides. I shut it out. And then it was over.

"You can leave in two hours," he said. "The nurse will instruct you about infection and cramping," he added, as he stood at the sink washing his hands.

He picked up a new form, scanned it, and walked out the door, turning to the nurse. "I'll be in room two when you are finished here."

We never had any eye contact, the doctor and I. We didn't exchange

156

any friendly words—and that only added to the growing sense of bleakness within me. There was nothing. Absolutely nothing. A nurse entered the small, empty room they had wheeled me into. "Here, take two of these pain relievers," she said, smiling and handing me a small cup of water and the pills. She covered me with a thin blanket and said, "Don't drink any alcohol with these."

I was pretty doped up by the time I walked out of the building to where Bobby was waiting. We headed toward the parking garage. Then I stopped.

"What's the matter?" he said. I was in a bad place emotionally, but I wanted to pretend that it was just another day and we were just strolling down the street in New York City. Whenever everything is falling apart, I always seem to come back to this city, I thought. I looked up at the familiar tall, dark buildings and searched for a bit of hope in the sky—a star—the moon—something beautiful. But it was drizzling and the sky was a dark, empty space. I heard the sounds of the stop-and-go traffic and smelled the wet city street, and all of a sudden the sounds, the smells, the day came crashing down on me. How uncanny was it that I had had to travel to New York to get an abortion? To sharpen my overwhelming anguish, the date was a significant one for me. December fourth is the day written on my birth certificate.

"I want to have a beer," I said.

"A beer?"

"Yes, damn it. Just one beer."

We found a local bar and both had just one drink. It helped break the tension between us, but we still didn't say much. What could we talk about? All I knew was that I wanted to forget everything. I wanted to get lost. The mix of meds and beer hit me hard, and I crawled into the backseat of the car and slept all the way home.

When we arrived home it was after midnight. Bobby helped me up the stairs.

"Good night," I said. He tried to kiss me goodbye. I turned away.

"Good night," he said.

I watched him walk away and I knew in my heart that I never wanted to see Bobby again. And a few weeks later I told him exactly that.

CHAPTER 25
Forrest
I Am My Son's Mom

A few years after that horrible day in New York, I became pregnant again. This time I had money from the inheritance and I could choose to be a single mom because I had the funds to raise a child. It was the best choice I have ever made.

The night my water broke, I was sitting in a moonlit room, alone and scared. I listened to music and waited for my contractions to increase to the point where I would need to call my friend to take me to the hospital.

I was going to have a baby and I had no experience with babies. I never told anyone that I was petrified at the idea of the doctor handing me my newborn child. I was not like one of those women who openly adored babies and kitchy-cooed over them. I never had the urge to hold a newborn. Quite the opposite. As I waited to go to the hospital early that morning, I wondered, what am I going to do? Will it be healthy? Will I drop it? Will I be a good mother? Is single parenting the right choice?

To calm my fears as I waited, I listened to Tina Turner singing "The Love That Lights Our Way," a song about Miss Jane Pittman, a historical figure in the civil rights movement whose courage and perseverance I had admired. As I listened to the words, "Lord just give me the sign, I'll be first in line," Jane Pittman's courage came through to me and helped me. Jane Pittman changed history with one sip of water. I had taken her leadership to heart, held onto the scene from the movie, *The Autobiography of Miss Jane Pittman*, where she gracefully holds her head high and walks step by step to the white persons' water fountain. While my act of becoming a single parent was not historically significant, in the early seventies I was making a political statement by becoming a single parent. I was trying to help change society's attitude toward independent, single women who chose to be mothers. Unlike my mother, I was not letting go of my child; instead I was holding on tight.

At dawn my friend arrived to take me to the hospital. A beautiful, fairy tale March sunrise splashed across the sky in front of us as we drove along. When I turned around to look back at the house, I saw the radiant full moon. It still glowed brilliantly and directly behind us–it was a perfect alignment.

No one had prepared me for the god-awful truth about labor pains. There seems to be a code of silence among women that states, "Do not tell an expectant first mother how much it will hurt!" Nothing made the labor easier in my mind, not even my Arapaho friend, who had carefully placed three sacred stones on the bedside table next to me, nor her native ceremony in the waiting room, nor my wolf's tooth pinned to my hospital smock. Nothing helped the pain that day. Not the nurses, not the labor coach, not my friends and not my prayers. Nothing. Birthing is a force that goes beyond reason. Luckily, Forrest, true to form, impatient as always, was born hours before anyone expected.

Amidst the dreadful pain, I experienced something extraordinary. It was the payoff, and it went way above and beyond the pain. When the doctor placed my wet and bloody newborn son across my belly and I looked into his little wandering eyes, which seemed to gaze dreamily up at me, I felt as if a miracle had happened. And even though it was hard–horrible–and in no way did I want to repeat the experience, I would never have traded that first glance Forrest and I shared together. A calming and karmic feeling flooded my heart at that very instant, and I felt as if everything in my life was exactly as it should be.

That night, as I lay in the hospital room alone, holding my child in my arms, I pondered whether my own mother had experienced the same powerful love that I was feeling when she held me for the first time and, if so, how she could ever have given me up. I walked over to the mirror and held my son in my arms and whispered a prayer like an ancient rite–*mother to child–child to mother–for all eternity. May you be happy and healthy.*

***

By the end of the first year I had adjusted to motherhood. I learned to interpret Forrest's subtle looks and gobbledygook language. I met and conquered the "what to does" and "what not to does." I learned about diaper rash, formulas, lullabies, and car seats. Besides zero intellectual stimulation– my life was good.

Throughout Forrest's early childhood I would have many flashbacks where I saw myself as an infant reaching out to my mother, which at times triggered painful feelings. But when he turned four, suddenly they stopped.

I realized that babies were not quite as fragile as I had feared. I hadn't dropped him or broken him in some way, as I had feared doing before he was born. I had only stuck him once with a diaper pin. Maybe, by the looks of his overstuffed snowsuits, I could be accused of overdressing him in the cold winter days, or perhaps I bought him too many gifts. And maybe giving him too many teething biscuits wasn't the best of ideas. But on the whole, I did a pretty good job of raising my child. To help create stability, I kept consistency in his life, and I tried to be a perfect mom. There were the normal exceptions of "You are driving me crazy!" statements when he became a teenager, and the "let's see how guilty I can make you feel" behavior when we engaged in power struggles. But I kept a close, protective watch over his emotional well-being.

But like the rest of us, I was not always perfect. Some events took place that I wish I could undo. One of these incidents happened when Forrest was around two years old. It has left an everlasting imprint on Forrest, and I am to blame. He has inherited my fear of spiders. I know exactly the day it happened. It was a late winter afternoon and I was taking a luscious hot bath. When you are a single parent, taking a bath at any time of day is tricky, if not impossible, when your toddler is still awake. That day I had given him a bottle of juice to keep him happy. He was standing next to the bathtub watching me bathe. His little round hand rhythmically tapped the tub, as he sucked his bottle, half in a daze. As I washed the sweet-scented bath water over my body, all was calm. I sighed with relief and settled into the warm water for a good soak. I happened to gaze up at the ceiling in a half-dream state, and I saw a very large spider descending toward my chest at a rather rapid pace. For me, there are some things that will forever remain a non-debatable truth and one is—all spiders are out to get you, no matter how big or how small, and you should run.

I rose out of the tub like Godzilla rising from the seas. I took half the tub of water with me and it splashed over Forrest, who was oblivious to what was going on. As I grabbed him, his eyes grew wide and he almost sucked his plastic bottle into a new shape. Screaming "spider!" I ran out of the bathroom with Forrest in my arms. To this day, as far as he is concerned, tidal waves, mother fears, and spiders are one and the same.

***

When Forrest was around four, by chance we created a family Christmas tradition. It began one snowy afternoon when we were cuddled together, sipping hot chocolate and admiring our newly decorated tree. Out of nowhere, Forrest turned to me and asked, "Mommy, how come Santa brings less presents every year?"

His question made me realize that over the years, he had noticed that there were fewer and fewer presents from Santa.

"Hmm, good question," I answered. I knew by the tone of his voice and the look on his face that a simple answer like, "I don't know, dear," was not going to suffice. As a matter of fact, as he stared up at me, with a whipped-cream moustache and a little-man look, I knew that Santa was in deep trouble. If I didn't think of something quick, Santa was going to be a goner.

"Hmmm, well . . ." I paused, searching for just the right answer.

"Santa teaches new parents how to do Christmas," I finally said.

"He does?"

"Yep, the first year he brings all the gifts and teaches grown-ups about Christmas. And he even tells them what snacks to leave for his reindeer."

"Oh, like when we leave them cookies?"

"Yep, then when the grown-ups learn what to do, Santa doesn't need to leave as many presents."

"He doesn't?"

"Nope, he has lots of presents to give away and he has to travel all over the world. So parents and friends become Santa Helpers."

"Oh, I see." He thought about what I had said, nodded, and then returned to licking the whipped cream off the top of his cocoa. Forrest was satisfied with my answer.

Phew, I have saved Santa for another year, I thought. Feeling confident with my answer, I decided to embellish the story a bit more. That was a bad idea.

"But," I continued in a louder and more confident voice. "Santa always brings one small, special gift for the family."

"He does?"

"Yes, of course he does. That's part of the magic."

"What does he bring us, Mommy?"

Uh oh, I had to think quickly–what could Santa leave? Something simple, I thought, and something that I could afford every year.

"He brings a very beautiful, special ribbon and places it at the bottom of a parent's stocking," I answered. It worked! Forrest's eyes began to sparkle. I could see the excitement and dreams of Christmas running through his mind once again. Santa was saved for another year, but now with a new luster. And that was how it began–the ribbon at the bottom of the stocking tradition.

In Forrest's younger years, I was determined to keep the magic of Santa alive. I loved Christmas and I wanted those special, magical moments to be a part of our tradition forever. Perhaps, for a while, Forrest was also determined to keep it going, or maybe he just went along to please me, but whatever it was, it worked. Whether he kept the myth of Santa alive for him or for me, it did not matter, because the magic of Christmas was alive in our home for years. Every Christmas morning Santa left a brightly colored ribbon at the bottom of my stocking.

Of course, things changed when my son reached the doubting age. He stopped believing in Santa Claus and, in time, we began stuffing each other's stockings. And yet by some Santa miracle, every Christmas morning, a beautiful, sparkling ribbon appeared out of the bottom of my stocking. The ribbons became a central event and grew fancier with the years.

In those years, Forrest, having stuffed my stocking the night before, knew that he *hadn't* placed a ribbon in it–so who had?

"Did you put the ribbon in there, Mom?" he would ask me each year.

"No, I didn't put it in there," I would answer innocently. And then I would smile and say in an all-knowing mother tone, "Santa must have left it, dear."

"Mom! You did it!" he would say, laughing, a bit frustrated by my response. And before we knew it, the yearly banter over the ribbon's origins became another part of our Christmas tradition.

In his teens, Forrest became more determined to find out whether or not I had placed the ribbon in the bottom of my stocking. How was I able to do that without him catching me? That was the big question. Over the years he tried many different and ingenious ways to trick me. But he was never successful–after all, it was Santa who brought the ribbon, wasn't it?

One Christmas Eve he was so determined to catch me stuffing my stocking that I found him fast asleep with his arms wrapped tightly around its overstuffed sides.

Then one Christmas it happened. It was the year before Forrest was to leave for college, and so it held a special meaning for us. We were both very busy. He was working late at a store and afterward he planned to go to a party. I was involved with an animal rights group, which was taking up a lot of my time. Christmas morning came and as we opened our stockings, I realized that I had forgotten the ribbon ritual. Oh no, I thought. This has been our one consistent Christmas tradition! It will never be the same. How could I have forgotten the tradition that has been in place for almost his whole life? I sighed and resigned myself to the fact that kids grow up–magic disappears–mothers fail and of course, Santa was going to be kaput.

"Come on, Mom, open your stocking!" Forrest said impatiently.

"Okay, okay." I knew it wouldn't be the same without the ribbon. I took a long time, stalling over each object–postponing the dreaded end. I could feel the loss of our tradition approaching. I was on the verge of tears.

"Come on, Mom. Why are you taking so long?"

I dug deeper into the stocking, reaching the bottom. And then it happened. It really happened! The Christmas magic–serendipity at its best–a changing of the guard of sorts happened. I felt a soft satin ribbon between my fingers. How did that happen? I thought as I pulled out a glorious silver ribbon. I stared straight at him, smiled, then looked down at the ribbon. The tradition was intact! Then in a very familiar, accusing tone, I asked, "Did you put this ribbon in here?"

He shook his head, looking serious. "No, I didn't put it there, Mom."

162

Then, with a twinkle in his eye and a chuckle, he grinned just like Santa at his very best moment. Forrest savored the glory of success. Teasing me, he leaned over and whispered, "Mom, it must have been Santa."

How did he know I had forgotten? It was at that very moment that I realized Forrest had the magic–the dreamer inside–the touch of the Feys running in his blood. He was his mother's son. And to this day, I find a beautiful ribbon at the bottom of my stocking each Christmas morning.

***

I became involved in the woman's movement and led workshops across the country while Forrest was in his teens. I kept my personal life mostly private because I did not think it was relevant to my work. But now I believe differently. I began to change my mind because of those who come to retreats that I'm conducting with a strong preconception of who I am. People make snap judgments about me all the time and those who do are often wrong about me. An incident that occurred on a retreat I was leading with a number of other women will illustrate my point.

We were seated around a long table having lunch, and I was lost in my thoughts, concentrating on eating the fresh green salad and the fine homemade soup. I ate slowly, absently listening to the table conversation and paying little attention to the large woman who had seated herself beside me. Looking back, I believe she sat next to me because I was the leader of the retreat and she wanted to impress me with her importance. In the process of doing this she eventually took over the table conversation, loudly making points on a variety of subjects and generally becoming a bit of a nuisance. She interrupted others when they tried to talk to me and after awhile began to sound off on male stupidity. I admit, I'd only half listened to what she'd been saying.

Then, leaning toward me, she said, "As far as I am concerned, there is no place in my life for men." She laughed loudly again, drowning out all private conversation.

This remark caught my full attention and I glanced up from my plate. She saw my look and grinned, as if she'd been making her pronouncements for me in particular. Now I looked at her thoughtfully. She had a harsh demeanor and was definitely a smoker. I found the stale smell of her cigarettes offensive. I think that she might have been a businesswoman, an executive of sorts, a woman accustomed to running the show.

As I tried to eat my salad, she continued her diatribe about men. At one point she said, "The male is a species I can do without."

The group laughed uncomfortably at her remark.

"Oh?" I said, since she was clearly looking for a response from me. But I said nothing more. I didn't want to engage in a long pro and con talk about men with her. I'd just led an intense morning workshop, and I simply wanted to sip my soup and chill out.

She then reached over me and grabbed a roll out of the basket, buttered it, and took a big and aggressive bite. She made her next remark with conviction. "Being a mother must be ghastly when you've got boys," she said, dipping her roll in and out of the soup. She boasted that she was a staunch lesbian/separatist, and it was clear that she had misconstrued my self-confidence and power as evidence that I shared her perspective of men. Apparently she thought I was a man-hater, fighting male domination and in sympathy with everything she was saying. In reality, the more she preached at me, the more I backed away.

She was wrong in everything she thought about me. I am a feminist, but I care deeply about men. I'm also a stickler for table manners, for good manners in general, and hers were beginning to grate on my nerves. Still I nodded politely, while she went on and on, slurping her soup and chewing the roll savagely and loudly. She had no idea how different we were. How could she know? There was nothing about me that reflected my formal childhood upbringing, except for my composure and perhaps my table manners, which included breaking and buttering my bread one piece at a time. I can still hear my Neilson mother's voice instructing me: "Marcy, never, never butter a whole piece of bread," she'd say firmly and add, "It simply shows a lack of breeding."

And that's how the woman appeared to me. She not only lacked manners and breeding, she lacked judgment. I reached for an almond cookie and continued to listen to the woman expound her opinions.

The woman went on and on. "I feel so strongly about my decision about men . . . that I didn't dare have a baby at all, because I was afraid it would be a boy."

For a moment there was an uncomfortable silence, and then I couldn't help saying, "I have a son. And there is no one I love more in the world."

She gazed at me, dumbfounded. "You have a son?"

"Yes. I have a son. Actually," I added, "I'm continually surprised by how vital my son is to my spiritual growth."

She looked at me incredulously. "Really?" she said, and stopped chewing, leaving a bulge in her cheek. Not only was I saying that I had a son, I was also stating that he was vital to my spiritual process.

"Yes," I continued, boasting a bit. "My son is a Gap man." The whole table laughed out loud, intrigued by the idea that I had a son who worked for the Gap. The Gap? When I, his mother, was dressed in my priestess garb, adorned with pagan jewelry and wearing an African wrap. I watched them put the pieces together. There was no way that I looked like a Gap mom—no way at all.

"But that is only half of him," I went on. "Actually, my son is a lot like me inside." I went on to tell them that I had raised my son on my own, right from the beginning.

"Wasn't that hard?" one of the women in the group asked.

"It was hard. Really hard," I said.

"I bet it was." The lesbian separatist gave me a pitying look. "You mean the father left you to raise the kid alone?"

I couldn't help laughing. "No, the father did not leave me."

"Then you left him?"

"No, I didn't leave him." I paused. "To begin with, I never married him."

"But you have a son?"

"Yes. I have a wonderful son. And I am glad I chose the single-parent route."

"You're not divorced, then?"

"No, I'm not divorced. I'm simply a single mom."

"I get it. When the kid's father heard you were pregnant, he wouldn't marry you."

I could see her processing the information and I smiled inwardly, knowing that I love moments like these, when I blow someone's theory right out of the water. I smiled as I made the next statement, knowing it would be a slam-dunk.

"You're wrong again. He would have married me. He wanted to from the beginning. But I didn't want to get married. So I never told him I was pregnant with his child."

The woman stared at me, speechless. For all her lesbian separatist views, this woman was still ultra-conventional. At last she asked, "You do know who the father is?"

I looked her straight in the eye, and my tone matched hers.

"I know exactly who Forrest's father is. He is a poet. And he was a sweet, dear man when I knew him. But I wanted to be free, and there was no doubt in my mind that if we had married, we would have ended up divorced."

All the women were drawn to the story of Forrest's father and me. They wanted to know more about what he was like. What did he do? I answered the questions as best I could. I explained that I'd met him in the early seventies and at that time I wanted to be a single mother. To have a baby without having a husband took courage.

"Forrest's father was a nice guy—but for me, in those days, he was too much of a dreamer," I said. "He was incredibly handsome," I added, "a tall blond man with blue eyes, a dead ringer for my father, and I was drawn to him like a moth to a flame. But he was also an alcoholic, like my father. I nicknamed him 'the wandering poet' because after a few drinks, he would repeatedly telephone me in the middle of the night. 'Hi, Robin,' he would say, as excited as a little kid. 'Listen to this piece I just wrote,' and then he would spout off the newest poem to me. Maybe if the time had been different I would have fallen for this romantic outpouring, but in those days I was driven by an internal force that was taking me somewhere else. Somewhere far from a married life with a station wagon, two-point-five kids, and going to weekend cocktail parties.

"So when I became pregnant, I decided it was time to send my handsome poet out of my life. And I did.

" 'Goodbye,' " I said to him one night. 'I can't do this anymore. I am sorry, but I really need to be alone.' It wasn't quite that simple, but it's close. A few weeks later he moved away, never knowing that I was carrying his child."

"My God!" one woman said. "You never told him?"

"No. I never told him. To this day he doesn't know that he has a son, and I am sure that if he did know, he would be furious with me."

"I bet he would be," someone said.

"The truth is that I wanted to make sure that my child would be safe growing up. I couldn't imagine co-parenting. I made sure not to put a father's name on the birth certificate."

"You did?" said the same person.

"Yes, I was seriously afraid his father would be too strict a parent or even violent."

"Why?"

"Because he came from a New York, Irish cop background and had told me that his father had abused him. And after he drank too much he got into fights. So I wanted to make sure that no one ever had a legal right to punish my child in any way that I disagreed with. I had to protect him."

Everyone nodded.

"What about your son?" another woman asked. "Doesn't he want to know his father?"

"Not yet. He hasn't asked. But if Forrest ever wants to find his father," I told all the women at the table, "I will help him in the search."

***

I think that at some time every mother worries about whether or not she has done a good job as a parent. I certainly did. At times I felt as if Forrest and I were leading each other though a complicated maze. The summer of his junior year in high school, I worried more than usual because we had had such a horrendous spring. It was full of high drama–lots of slamming doors and "I'll nevers." My solution was to send him to a Unitarian summer camp in the Berkshires, to work out some of his issues.

One night while he was at the camp, I got a phone call after midnight. Needless to say, I was somewhat worried. "Hello," I answered, half asleep.

"Hi Mom, this is Forrest." His voice sounded shaky and it was clear that he had been crying. In many ways I had expected a call like this from him, since the camp was for seniors and juniors in high school, and it was specifically designed to be intense and healing. For example, each night for three weeks, these kids paraded into a chapel and engaged in dramatic, soul-searching conversations together. Night after night, they shared heartfelt secrets and sometimes heart-wrenching moments from their lives. I knew the leaders and the type of workshops they offered. I trusted them and I was pretty sure that he would have a life-changing experience at some point during the three weeks. Although I hadn't expected it to happen quite so late at night.

"What's the matter, Forrest?"

"Mom," he said, and started to cry. "We just came back from our chapel meeting. It was horrible–everyone was sharing sad stories."

"It must have been intense," I commented, recalling the intensity of my own workshops, which used the same format.

"We were talking about our parents."

Oh God, I thought, here it comes–the moment I've dreaded. I was now going to have all my overcharged guilt and fear of being a failure as a parent heaped upon my head. To top it off, it was after midnight. I sat up in bed and sipped a glass of water, getting prepared for the onslaught.

"I see, so what happened?" I asked cautiously.

Then Forrest, in one sentence, without knowing it, was able to wash away my worry and say something that had a profound, healing effect on me. He said it with an intensity and innocence that propelled me into a new reality.

"Mom, do you know there are parents who actually do not love their kids? Can you believe it?" he said incredulously.

I think it was the way he said, "Mom, can you believe it?" But all of a sudden I realized, at that very moment, that I had succeeded as a mother, because he could not fathom a parent not loving her child. The cold grip that my Neilson mother had held me in for all those years, the one that began the day that she announced that I was broken and never would be able to love

167

someone, was gone! Forrest, with one affirmation, had made me feel real.

"Mom—it was so horrible. You should have seen this one girl crying."

"It must have been hard," I said. And then, in typical teenage fashion, his mood changed and he was happy again. He no longer had to worry about the world—no, in his mind, Mom would do that for him. Worry, that is.

"Got to go," he said. "I love you, Mom!" and off he went to the next event.

CHAPTER 26
Finding My Family
My Mother's Face

After the reading of my father's will, I spent many years looking for my birth mother. I wanted to see her–talk to her–tell her that I had survived and that I was okay. But she seemed to have vanished. No matter how many calls I made or how much research in city hall files and elsewhere I did, there was no trace of the whereabouts of Stefanie Muriel Lebow. I kept every name, every clue and every form that I had accumulated from my search in one folder. But after two years of dead ends, I grew frustrated and tossed the folder in a drawer. I stopped looking for her.

Four years later when Forrest arrived, the old longing for family returned. It was as if my mother was pulling me onward. Once again I felt driven to pick up the search. One evening, after I put Forrest in his crib, and I had the night ahead to relax, I poured a glass of Bordeaux and pulled out that old folder of clues. I neatly spread its contents on the coffee table. All I knew about my origins was on the table: my revised birth certificate, my father's will plus various jottings, bits and pieces of paper that contained every name, telephone number, and whatever I could find about anyone who might have known my mother, and a list of people who might know where she lived today.

The last person I had contacted was Joan, the social worker with the doe eyes and gentle demeanor, who had handled my case so many years ago. I had talked to her the summer before Forrest was born.

"Ah yes, I remember who you are," she said. Her voice still had the same soft, lyrical rhythm.

"What do you remember?" I asked, hoping she would remember it all.

"Your big brown eyes." She chuckled. "And oh, I remember you had a frightful time at the end."

"The end?"

She stalled, as if searching for soothing words. "You see, you had really bonded to your last foster mother."

"I had?"

She became silent, as if lost in some memory. "Oh, your cries were so chilling."

"I don't remember."

"I wish we could have done it differently but in those days . . ."

"What was her name? My foster mother, that is," I asked.

She paused, as if going through a file case in her head.

"My dear, I can't remember. I am sorry. It is so long ago. I just remember those big brown eyes of yours and the look you gave me at the end."

"Oh," I sighed, knowing I had just hit another wall.

It was that phone call to my old social worker that had made me stop the search for a long time. I didn't want to do it anymore. I felt too frustrated every time I came to a dead end. I couldn't handle it.

But I never seem to be able to just give up on something or someone. Damn, I can never just walk away! I thought. And so, there I was that night, once again obsessively looking for the clue that would change everything.

All the conversations and visits to strangers gave me bits and pieces, but none of it was enough. No leading clues. There were just many uncomfortable memories that led to nowhere. I searched marriage records, birth records, telephone books, Actor's Equity lists, old journals—but I found nothing. I looked everywhere for a clue, a lead, a hint—anything! I even employed two detectives who could have come out of a B-rated movie. True to form, they took my money, spent it, and came up with nothing. Every telephone number that I called, every letter that I wrote, every clue I came across, all possible leads to my mother ended nowhere. I was overwhelmed and sometimes I doubted my memories about my beginnings. At times I was afraid that my mother had never existed. But then I would remember a flash, a feeling, and I knew she had to be out there. Somewhere. I could feel her pull. Everyone has a mother, I kept saying over and over. Sometimes I felt as if I were chasing a ghost or even a crook with an alias. At other times I felt like a ghost myself—a wraith constantly chasing some clue, a story, a witness to my existence. I desperately wanted to meet someone who had known me when I had been with my mother and father. Someone who could say, yes, it had happened.

Nothing worked until that October night, when something changed. In the same way a gambler is driven to roll those dice one more time, I made one more attempt. It might come out differently this time, I thought. I felt like I was getting my fix. Then I heard a voice say, "Robin, go over that list. Do it one more time." I turned around to see who had said that. Of course there was no one there, except for Amber, my shepherd mutt, who was stretched out at my feet. Even she raised her head as if a stranger had entered the room.

For some reason in the years of searching for my mother, I had never been able to find anyone on the long list of names of cousins, aunts, uncles, and friends who were mentioned in the will. I don't know why, but these were names I never found listed anywhere.

That night, for what seemed the five hundredth time, I stared at the will, slumped into my wing chair, ready to get to work. Sipping the wine for courage, I read out loud from the second page. "Ann Drake, daughter of Frances Ryan." I shook my head. How the hell am I ever going to find Ann Drake? Or anyone else? I thought.

"Try your Great-Aunt Frances Ryan again," a voice answered.

Once again I looked around. No one was there. I dialed the information operator in Toronto. "May I help you?" she asked with a slight Canadian accent.

"Yes. Frances C. Ryan, please."

"Do you have an address?"

"No."

"We have a new listing for a Frances C. Ryan." She gave me the number.

Shocked, I said, "Thank you," and scrambled to find a clean piece of paper. I quickly scribbled the number on the paper. Even though this time finding the phone number had seemed so easy, I had no hope that anything would turn out differently than it had in the past. The possibility that I would actually be able to talk to someone who had known my father or my mother seemed faint and far off. "It's probably the wrong Frances C. Ryan," I muttered.

Where was this call going to take me? Most likely nowhere, I thought. But I was hooked on an unspoken hope. Why was I still clinging to an old, haunting memory, a time with my mother, with my father, when my mother really loved me? What was the point? Why make this call? I'll only end up hurting. I sighed, took another sip of wine, silenced my doubts and dialed the number.

The phone rang and rang. Just as I was about to hang up, an older woman answered. "Hello?"

"Is this Frances C. Ryan?"

"Yes."

"We don't know each other, but my name is Robin Claire Mulock," I said.

"Ah," she said, and paused. I could hear her lighting a cigarette. "I have waited for your phone call for years," she continued in a matter-of-fact tone.

"You have?" I asked, incredulously.

"Yes. What took you so long?" She laughed as if she didn't expect an answer from me.

"I never agreed with my sister's decision not to fight Steffi to get you," she said.

"You didn't?"

"No, I think it was appalling, and I told her so. It was not right for her to treat Alfred's baby, I mean you, like that."

"Do you know why she did that?"

"It was pure selfishness on her part. She was angry at your mother," she said.

"My mother, do you know where she is?"

"No, but maybe your great-uncle up here in Canada can help."

"Do you think so?"

"Yes, my dear. When will I meet you?"

A search that had taken years was over in minutes. It was that simple. One random phone call to Toronto information at just the right time, and just the right combination of names, and I had found my first blood relative, my great-aunt, the matriarch of the family. The first relative I had ever talked to—she was a voice out of my past. It was a simple thing in so many ways, just a phone call, but for me it was a milestone.

My reactions may have seemed extreme to those who have reached adulthood knowing who their parents are. But thousands of adopted children like me, with no knowledge of their biological history, have had, as I have had, the same intense desire to know where they come from. But it was much more than that. My years of searching were not only about knowing where I came from—they were about dreaming that a mother was waiting for me to come home to her. My search was about finding courage to face a truth that could hurt. When their children come to find them, some mothers might weep and welcome them with open arms. But there will be other biological mothers who might look the other way as they shut the door behind them.

There are thousands of us who have been left behind, who have searched for our mothers, the mothers who haunt us with their absence. As for me, after discovering the real facts about my mother, I found myself. I discovered that the intimate bond between mother and daughter does not necessarily need space or time to exist. It is a part of who you are.

***

I went to visit my newfound family. But still no one knew where my mother was. They had all met her and told me a few stories about her.

"Charming woman," my uncle Cawthra said. "Just charming."

On that visit, he handed me an old chest. It was a turning point in my search, and I have never forgotten the feelings that came over me when I saw it.

"Go through it and see if there is something you would like," my Aunt Julyan said.

"Thank you," I said.

I was delighted by the treasure that stood in front of me. I began foraging for something of value that might tell me something about my history. I rummaged through papers and letters and photos of grandfathers, grandmothers, uncles, aunts, and cousins who I'd never known. And then, for some reason, I pulled one particular photograph out of a pile of pictures. When I turned the photograph face up, I was startled by my reaction to the person I saw staring back at me. My blood surged through my body and a violent anger possessed me. The feeling was sudden and short. There was no outburst, no overflow, and, as swiftly as the anger came, the feeling vanished, leaving a dark, cold emptiness inside me. The snapshot did not remind me of a face. It was the face.

"Is this my mother?"

My uncle nodded.

I put the photograph face down on my pile of things to take home and went back to rummaging through the letters. Then, something more happened. I turned around, thinking I had heard someone speaking to me. My uncle was still standing there, but the voice I'd heard was a woman's. Could it be my mother's? I don't know. All I do know is that the voice seemed to come from far away. Without knowing why, I reached for a particular blue envelope in one of the scattered piles. It was as if my mother had handed me that particular letter and said, "Here, Robin. Read this one. It is important."

That letter was important. Out of the hundreds of letters in the chest, this one was from a Dr. Rothman, and it had a phone number and address. Looking at it, I knew in my bones that it was a vital link with my past.

"May I have this letter and photo?" I asked. My uncle nodded again. "Yes, yes, of course, take as much as you want," he said.

Dr. Rothman was my mother's family doctor. To my surprise, I learned that he was also the doctor who had delivered me. What follows is his side of our conversation. My questions are implicit in his answers.

"Yes, I remember your delivery. I have been the family doctor for years."

"No, your birth was an easy delivery."

"Well, I know your mother's sister, too. Oreilla. I delivered her daughter. . . ."

"Judith is her name. A good Jewish girl. Oreilla also has cancer, though I think she is still alive."

"Yes, I said, also . . ."

"No, I do not believe your mother is alive. She died in the late sixties . . . of cancer."

"Yes, she remarried a famous black musician. . . ."

"What was his name? It will come to me. Yes. His name is Luther Henderson."

"Yes, he lives in New York. They had one child. A girl, Melanie Claire . . . I delivered her, too. . . ."

"Sorry. That is about all I can tell you. . . ."

"Yes, I am sure."

"No, I am quite sure she is dead. There is no mistake. It was too late when they opened her up. They just sewed her back up. It was too late."

With this one phone call, my life changed. The years of searching and dreaming of a loving reunion with my mother, of having the pain of abandonment resolved, had come to an end. In a conversation that lasted less than five minutes, I learned that my mother was dead, that I was half Jewish, and that I had a half sister who was half black. And it was exactly at that moment that the dream of being in the same place once again with my mother, of being in her arms and telling her, "I've come home"—was over.

***

When I woke up the next morning I thought, "I will find Melanie." Melanie was now my closest blood relative. It was vital that I find her. She knew my mother and now she must know me. I began my second search.

It took me only a short time to find Melanie, and it wasn't one-tenth as grueling as the search for my mother had been. In the process of questioning people who knew my mother's second husband, Luther Henderson, I was soon put on the right path. I found Luther first. He told me that Melanie lived in Los Angeles, and he offered to telephone ahead and get back to me. He was cautious, polite, and acted very protective of his daughter. I found out later that my voice sounded so much like my mother's that it took him aback.

"I am not quite sure Melanie knows that you exist," he said.

"Oh," I said disappointedly.

"I am not sure she knows that she has a sister. I had better break the news to her. I will get back to you." I thought it would take days, but the phone rang only an hour later.

"Hi!" A loud, drawling, and very forward voice rang on the line.

"Hi," I answered, gathering my wits.

"This is Melanie. I guess I am your sister. You are my mother's other daughter. How are you?"

CHAPTER 27
Finding My Sister, Melanie
The Mother Fight

When I went to pick up Melanie at the airport, I was shocked when I first saw her. I did my best to hide my disappointment when I saw that we didn't look a bit like sisters. I could have been looking at a stranger. Even more disheartening was that in no way did Melanie resemble my mother. And since my mother was dead, I had hoped to see her face in Melanie's. I didn't. She was black; my mother was white. But that was the least of it. Her features bore no resemblance to my mother's. Actually, she looked more like her father. And I had to accept that I still would not be able to say, "Oh, there is my nose, my eyes, my chin. Oh, that's where I come from."

My newfound sister and I had never talked about the difference between us in any depth, and Melanie always insisted that she did not see herself as black. So, I suppose I expected her to look more like me, more like the mother that I had seen in photos. But as I stood there in the airport, face to face with her, I realized I had not dealt with the reality of how different from each other we might be. And what that difference might mean to me.

For one thing, I was not prepared to be confronted with the hidden racism my upbringing had instilled in me. Maybe it was inevitable, since I had grown up in a very wealthy, white Protestant family—a family that had unstated but very real racist feelings. Later, as a teenager, when I lived with Jock and Prudy, the social scene they embraced often was filled with the same hidden racist attitudes. After a great deal of work and soul searching, I see that in those days—the fifties, sixties, seventies—that they were embedded in many of the country clubs, the cocktail parties, and the neighborhoods that we had lived in. Much of this goes on even today.

So, between the Neilson family with its unstated racist attitudes, and Jock, with his blatant ones, I was poorly equipped for meeting my black sister for the first time. While she seemed a complete stranger, she was unequivocally my sister—my closest blood relative. Under the circumstances I had only one thing going for me and that was a desperate need to have a sister with whom I could bond.

When we arrived home that first day, I turned the key to unlock the front door, and as it went click, I was suddenly caught off guard and confronted with my own unresolved issues with racism. I was catapulted back to an incident that occurred years ago, with Jock, who was in those days a successful advertising executive. A stay in Jock's home came with conditions that I had to live by. I could not live there unless I abided by these rules. And, at the age of sixteen, I had no idea how to survive, where to live, or how to get the money I needed to take care of myself. So I agreed.

One evening, Jock had called me into his room to reprimand me for something I had done. He was standing in his walk-in closet, carefully hanging up his pinstriped suit and tie. I sat down on the bed to listen. What had I done now? I wondered.

"Don't you ever bring that guy into this house," he said, not even turning around to face me.

"What guy?" I asked, not knowing whom he was talking about.

At first he didn't say a word. He began carefully clipping his already short, clean nails.

"You know who I mean. That black kid," he said at last.

"My friend George?" I asked.

"Do you understand me?" He ignored my question, then added, "Matter of fact, I don't want you to see that guy at all." Then he left the room, not waiting for my reply.

As I listened to him, I felt terribly ashamed. I don't know now if I was humiliated because he reproached me for being friends with George or whether I was ashamed because I needed Jock's home to live in. And to live in his house I had to betray my friendship with George and accept Jock's values. I didn't understand or believe in them then, and I sure as hell don't believe in them now. But until that day when I put the key in the lock with Melanie standing beside me, I'd completely forgotten that long-ago incident and my friend George. I didn't understand the impact Jock's attitude had had on me all those years ago until that moment.

In some bizarre but very real way, I was fighting my upbringing. For the first time, those unconscious demons of subtle racism with which I had been raised were going to be addressed. I wanted to cry. I don't know if they were tears of joy or frustration. I was going to have to learn how to use new tools. But at that moment, I just felt very lost and ashamed.

Melanie's reaction to me was the opposite of mine to her. She absolutely saw our mother in me and told me so, as if she were angry about the fact. On the way home, I had been expressing my frustration in never getting to really know our mother. I'd been asking Melanie, "What was she like? What did she look like? What was the tone of her voice? What perfume did she wear?"

"Where's the mirror?" she asked as we entered the house.

"Over there in the bathroom. Why?" I said.

"Look in the mirror," she said. We both went into the bathroom and looked. "There is Mommy!" she said angrily, pointing at my reflection. "That is who she looks like." Hmm, now that I think about it, maybe that's why I can never truly recognize myself in a mirror. Is it too painful?

Most importantly, another piece of the puzzle that had been my sister, me, and our mother fell into place with Melanie's words. As we both stared into the mirror, I began to understand what it must have been like for Melanie to be her mother's daughter and not look a bit like her. How hard it must have been to not have that basic bond.

That evening, Melanie said, "Looking back, sometimes I feel Mommy was trying to see you in me." She waited for me to say something, and when I said nothing she added, "Mommy always treated me as if there were two of us. It was weird. I always had doubles of everything. And now I think it was because your ghost was always there."

As I listened to her, it occurred to me that both my mother and I had possibly shared a common experience with Melanie. I suddenly had an insight: I had an invisible bond with my mother and it had crossed all barriers of time, metaphysical realms, and realities. The bond was based on the simple fact that neither my mother nor I could ever be reminded of each other's existence vicariously through my sister. No, just as I couldn't look into my sister's face and see my mother, my mother could never have seen me by looking at her other daughter.

It sounds crazy, but I am convinced that there is a strange, unsettled energy, a mysterious barrier, that lurks between my sister and me. Is it my mother's unresolved issues in life? Is this the part that haunts both my sister and me? I don't know. My mother had a quick temper and it seems my sister's and my temper begin to flare whenever we try to get too close and deal with what I see as the real issues.

For example, my sister is black and I am white. My sister was kept and protected by our mother until she died when Melanie was nine, and I was let go of when I was three. My sister held on to memories of my mother—I never really got to have any. I was a giggling child, scarred by my trauma, while Melanie had asthma. I see the list of comparisons as sometimes overwhelming. When my sister and I try to bond, something stands between us and we lash out at each other, until we both can't take the intensity of the unresolved pain and we dramatically stop all of our contact for years.

What is doubly strange is that our breakdowns in communication happen whenever we try to place ourselves in the same physical space. Psychics would explain it as an unresolved spirit presence. I see it almost as a time warp. Have Melanie and I both stopped time to try to hold on to a living image of mother love? Do we cling so hard to it that we can't move forward in some way? I don't know, but I am sure what happens with us is bigger than the obvious outer differences between Melanie and me.

On one of Melanie's early visits, this weird barrier was present. Melanie had brought an old tape of our mother singing the blues. She'd said nothing to me prior to her visit about having such a tape. Strangely enough, rather than ease us, the tape only added to the tension of her visit.

At the time I was glad she had brought it. I was convinced that if I could just hear my mother's voice again, it would trigger buried memories of her and it would help me heal.

"You see, it is all I will ever have of her," I said.

Melanie said nothing, but nodded. She slunk into the living room clutching the reel to reel tape. Melanie moved slowly and noiselessly, quite the opposite of my heel-to-heel walk. She has told me that it is one of those traits that I share with our mother.

As Melanie moved across the room, I noticed again the sweater she was wearing. All week she had worn this white mohair sweater that had been our mother's. I think it was her security blanket.

"Mommy was always in this sweater," she'd said. "It was her favorite one to wear around the house."

As she talked about the sweater, a jealous, unloved child stirred inside me. I'd wanted to touch the sweater, stroke it. But Melanie and I always kept a physical distance from each other, so I could only look at her and try to visualize my mother wearing it. The sweater embodied my mother's spirit, and I felt that Melanie sat there with my mother's arms wrapped around her, warm and safe, while I had nothing.

But maybe hearing my mother's voice for the first time since the day she had left would help me heal, I thought. So I reached for the tape, thinking Melanie would give it to me to put on the recorder. But when I reached for it, she clutched the tape as if I were taking something that was hers.

"Let me have it," I said.

"No," she said, glaring at me.

"It's my tape recorder. I know how to use it."

"I don't care. It's my tape."

There was a dead silence. It was an unbearable moment in which an ugly truth rose up between us. The niceness was gone. We were locked in a sister-to-sister power struggle for our mother, as if she were alive and standing in the room.

"Fuck it. Can't you share anything?" I said.

"What the hell are you saying? I've brought you everything. Photos, stories about Mommy. Everything."

How do I know it is everything? With you, there are always new surprises, I thought.

"You had everything," I said.

"And I lost everything, too," she said.

"I just want this one thing. My mother's voice."

"What do you mean?"

"I want to hear her voice again. Don't you get it?"

"So what's that going to do?"

"I don't know." I sat down, overwhelmed with the grief that was rising inside me.

"I don't remember my mother's voice or her face or her touch," I said.

"I never forget her." Melanie sighed.

"You had her. You remember her," I said.

"Do you know what it is going to do to me to listen to this?" She was almost in tears. "Do you?"

"No."

"It is going to bring it all back."

"But you had everything."

"And you hate me for it," she said.

"No, I don't hate you. I just want you to share her with me. She's my mother too!" With that, I stormed out of the room. I went downstairs into my studio and threw things: paintbrushes, books, cans, anything I could find. I swore, and then I cried and cried.

It was too hard for me. That was the angriest I ever remember being. The incident ignited all my grief and bitterness about being left by my mother. I thought I was over that hurt, but I wasn't. My whole body ached and hurt more than I could have ever imagined.

Going from one foster home to another, being adopted by strangers, never seeing my mother again, not knowing where I belonged or if anybody wanted me, had squeezed all pride of self out of me. And now I was having flashes of new memories: of me begging and whining to different adults to tell me where my mother was. And at that moment in the living room, with Melanie clutching the tape, she became just another one of the people who stopped me from getting closer to my mother.

Eventually I went back upstairs and into the living room. There I found Melanie still sitting on the sofa as if frozen, hugging the tape to her chest. She didn't seem to have moved a muscle since I left. I wanted to say I was sorry. But I didn't. I was too confused about what the hell was going on with me. The one thing I knew at that moment was that I could give up the struggle over who ran the damn tape recorder.

"Just put it on. I don't care who does it. I just want to hear it." Hearing me, Melanie stood up and went over to the tape recorder. She said nothing, but it was clear she'd gotten her way. I thought to myself, is this what our sister bond will be—one sister begging for pieces of her lost mother while the other refuses, clutching whatever she has to herself—afraid to lose any more? I didn't want that. But maybe Melanie, too, is grasping for what she has lost and can never have again. Maybe she's no better off than I am, I thought.

Melanie turned on the tape recorder and we sat back in silence. Would we hear our mother singing to us, like a lullaby? Even if the singing would break our hearts, we were ready.

What actually happened was something neither of us expected. It was eerie, uncanny, a karmic moment. Was it our spirit guardians who stepped into the room and protected us from the enormous pain we would feel in hearing our mother's voice? Could they see that we were not ready to have such a precious and yet deeply vulnerable moment together? Or was it the spirit of our mother who had stepped in to take control of her two out-of-control children? I don't know, but first we heard nothing but the click, click of the tape going around and around, and then we heard a deep, distorted voice. Indistinguishable words came over the speakers. It sounded like an alien from a far-away planet speaking in another language. It was frightening. I felt as if an ancient spell of incomprehensible words of power had been cast on us. It was as if the tape had become possessed.

We realized that the whole reel had been put on backward. Who did that and why, I don't know. Melanie, clearly unsettled by the whole thing, said she had nothing to do with it. I know she didn't.

I still don't know why it happened. And to make matters worse, neither of us had the know-how to reverse the miles of tape back to its normal position. We tried, but no matter how hard we tried, it didn't work. Finally we gave up.

That was not a good visit. Melanie left the next day, and that was the last time we ever shared the same physical space in my home. In the future, we kept our physical distance. We continued to talk on the telephone, and write to each other, until we reached a point of such disagreement that we stopped communicating for over twenty years.

***

Our story wasn't over. For no reason I can explain, years after that last falling out, I telephoned her and we began another round—another page of our story. For a while we stayed connected with phone calls and e-mails, although when we did make contact, what we spoke about was filled with awkward tension.

But once again our relationship slowly eroded over time. And as I changed, I no longer was jealous of her closeness to our mother. Our final blowup occurred over a difference of viewpoint. That time we clashed over our differing memories of what had happened during our very first meeting.

And then she said something about our mother, acting as if she were still alive and in the room with her.

It felt crazy and uncomfortable. I wanted the arguing to end. I wanted my mother dead so I could move on. Let go. And although I wanted to rescue my sister from what I perceived as a sad, dead place, I didn't know how to do it. I saw that she was caught between realms. Lost in time. We were always talking about our mother—and, though we were talking about inconsequential things, suddenly I couldn't take it anymore. I snapped at her. She answered in kind and soon our talk escalated into a horrendous argument. Thoroughly impatient with her and with what she was saying, I lost my temper and yelled over the phone, "Melanie! You have to face reality. You've got to let her go. Our mother is dead. She's dead, Melanie, dead!"

That was the last thing I said to her in that round, before I hung up. Once again, our sister bond had broken. Forever? I thought. I doubted it. I love Melanie in a strange and haunting way.

That last angry conversation with Melanie accented the uncanny energy I often feel when I talk to her. In many ways, Melanie seems to me to be stuck at the age she was at our mother's death. Her use of language is from the sixties. "That's groovy!" is a phrase she uses regularly. But the strongest evidence for me is that she still refers to our mother as Mommy. And when she speaks of Mommy, her voice becomes childish—even though she describes our mother with the kind of brilliant insights one expects from an adult.

***

Our relationship remained difficult and strained for many years. I was afraid this would be our pattern for years to come, until we learned to let our mother go. Or until we learned to take hold of our sister love and explore together our mother's imprint on us. I didn't see any other way.

***

I waited for the next meeting of our souls. It did happen. Melanie and I currently have a peaceful acceptance of each other. We are older and more accepting of each other's frailties. I recognize and honor the fact that my mother's memory is a blazing fire in my sister's heart. And it is a deep pain. In many ways my mother's spirit is my sister's life force. But for me, standing in a different place, I've begun to believe that my sister, Melanie, has become my mother's living ghost. They are one and the same.

I did not have much success in my long hard search to make a family and to feel that I belonged somewhere. It is ironic, but I come from two families that have a history of turmoil and disconnection among their members. My father's family is scattered across the country, busy with their lives, living comfortably with their wealth, and they do not seem to talk to each other—let alone me.

The few family members I met and tried to establish a relationship with have now died, except for my cousin Sarah. She is the daughter of Frances C. Ryan, the great-aunt who first received my phone call that October night years ago. Sarah is a very good person and I enjoyed visiting her in Toronto every summer, until she moved across country. Now we only share a phone call every once in a while. But Sarah is the kindest and most generous of all of my family members, on both sides. She has shared herself in ways no other relative has.

For example, one day a few years ago, I received a small box in the mail. Three beautiful handmade woodcarvings that she had whittled herself were carefully wrapped inside. They were a mother and baby elephant and a carved statue of the Goddess Maat—The Egyptian Goddess of truth. I was very moved by this gift and in a very down-to-earth way she was passing on my families' spirit in her choice of Goddess. My father's side has many writers and artists—something we share in our blood. In fact, this gesture of hers was the first heartfelt gift I had ever received from a family member. The time and care that she took to make the carvings for me were evident, and that is deeply precious to me.

I also kept in touch with Kate, my father's second wife, whom he met in the theater world after he left my mother. According to Kate, they had a violent marriage that only lasted for two years before my father killed himself. According to family gossip, Kate was nowhere to be found then. The family thought this was dreadful and said she was off having an affair on that sad day. But no one ever said anything to her. Instead, they smiled and gave her the inheritance. She inherited financial comfort for life and lived in a fancy hotel in Chelsea Square. Her yearly income was probably equal to my entire one-time inheritance. We stayed in touch with sporadic calls, but she lived in England, so we did not see each other. She had a flair for gossip, politics, and the eccentric. She was a brilliant woman who read a great deal and saw me as a Jane Austen character whose life was unfair and tragic. I, on the other hand, saw her as the bridge to my father's ghost, but it was hard because most of the time she told me how she was spending my father's money or that she was dreadfully broke—"skinned" as she put it. But of course for her, being broke meant she couldn't get her nails done or have a facial that week. She wanted to pass on my father's trust fund to me and she said she would try to arrange it but the Mulocks refused to consider it.

On my mother's side there is really only Melanie and a cousin, the daughter of my aunt Oreilla (who has died). We seem to have a hard time of it. I have found that my mother's side of the family has intense, dramatic flare-ups. These blowups are usually filled with chaotic endings that make me want to withdraw and look for a peaceful place to hide.

I have tried to figure out what I have learned from these unsettling family episodes. Maybe some of my family has accepted me. Maybe I am now experiencing what I didn't get to have growing up. Maybe the dream I carried all my life was wrong–the feelings that I had thought I had missed out on, in some great family bonding experience, were never really there. Or is the struggle I experienced with my sister, or the lack of communication and rejection by my father's side of the family, exactly what family is all about? Perhaps families are all about broken pieces of coded DNA tablets–a puzzle at best, and everyone in their own way is trying to figure out where they fit.

Mother V
Becoming Eclipse
1983–Present

I who am the beauty of the green earth
And the white moon among the stars
And the mysteries of the waters,
I call upon your soul to arise and come unto me.

–Starhawk, *The Spiral Dance*
Adaptation of Doreen Valiente's
"Charge of the Star Goddess"

CHAPTER 28
Finding The Goddess
Another Type of Mother Love

One night in late September, when I was thirty, I attended a lakeside concert led by Kay Gardner. The evening was described as music to the Mother Goddess. I had done a lot of work with Native American tribal traditions, but I had never experienced a Goddess celebration. I was curious to find out what Goddess music might be like and so I went with a friend.

The group gathered at the entrance of a lake house and it was apparent to me, as we filed down a wooded path to the water in silence, that something ancient was stirring.

***

Years ago I had come to this same lake and had experienced an extraordinary vision from what I believe now to be the Anishinabe spirits. While I was sitting near the water that long-ago night, light beings came out from the dark, tall forms of the trees. One by one they surrounded me. They asked me to make a vow to them. They asked me to acknowledge them with my work and help return honor to their ancient spiritual presence on the earth. I have kept my vow since that day.

***

As we entered the open space, a full harvest moon was beginning to rise over the lake. Across the water, silhouettes of tall pines lined the horizon. The smells of the night forest in the crisp air added to the magical sensation. The moment was timeless and the setting was strangely familiar.

Kay Gardner was a talented musician as well as a skilled priestess. She shared her knowledge of ancient musical scales and instructed us in simple rituals. As she sang in her haunting voice, tears welled up in my eyes more than once, although I did not know why. I felt as if we had traveled back in time to a place where all that had ever been–still existed. As we honored the land and the spirit guardians of the place, I could feel the ancestors emerging from the forest to join us. I felt like I had come home.

Kay stood on a picnic table and played a simple lyre, made from the back of a chair. The moon had just risen over the trees, and it seemed to rest above her head. She looked like she was wearing the ancient Egyptian headdress of the moon.

"What a great painting that would make," I said to my friend, who stood next to me, lost in her own bliss. This is incredibly beautiful! I thought, as I began to sway in time to the music. Every cell in my body was coming alive.

Soon a Celtic tune began, and someone played the spoons. We began to dance in place. It was fun. The music went on for a while, and we sang Goddess songs from all over the world. And then, as the concert came to a close, Kay turned and looked up at the stars and, while gesturing to the moon with her arms spread wide, she invoked the *powers that be*. I had never seen a woman do this before, but it sparked some deep memory within me.

"We have rising for us the Harvest Moon, where all comes into balance," she said.

"Draw Her down!" someone called from the crowd.

"What's that mean?" I asked my friend.

"Oh, it is an ancient rite of calling the energies of the moon into yourself," she said.

"Oh," I said.

"It's really powerful and people say it brings a sensation of bliss."

"The Goddess has many forms," Kay said. "In the same way the sun is attributed to the God, the moon belongs to her." Kay smiled. We all looked up at the moon with reverence.

"Her smile is sweet for us on this night of balance."

"My whole life needs to be in balance," I said, laughing. "I need this," I whispered to my friend.

"Me, too," she answered.

"Now get your keys out of your pockets," Kay instructed us. "And if you don't have keys, get some change or anything else that you can shake."

We could hear the sound of metal rustling in the dark and people whispering.

"Shush," Kay said gently, guiding us back into silence. "First, let's listen to the night and honor the spirits that are present in the forest." The jangling stopped.

"Take the hand of the person next to you. And listen. Make a prayer for the earth and for yourself."

Far away across the lake an owl hooted, and then there was silence. A strong sense of anticipation was in the air. We were all quiet for what seemed a long time. Then the chant began. Slowly, we joined Kay, as she called out the many names of the Goddess. Our keys became like the sound of bells. I envisioned what it might have been like a long time ago, in a temple somewhere. I imagined blue and white mosaic floors, and then I saw the bare feet of dancers with bells on their ankles, swirling around. I also saw flaming torches, and I could smell burning incense for a brief moment. Before I knew it, my head was spinning and I was overcome by an energy that made my whole body tingle and my heart beat faster.

A bit worried, I turned to my friend. "Do you feel that?" I asked. She turned to me still singing and nodded. I noticed a soft light glowing around her. Then I looked around at the other people. They too had this light! I was scared, and I wondered if I had lost my senses. But I quickly realized that it wasn't the case. In actuality, my senses had been heightened. I felt the feeling of ancient power moving through me. How incredible this is, I thought as we *drew down the moon*. It seemed as if all of us at that moment were having a similar experience. "Church never felt like this," I whispered to my friend. Her eyes were shut and she did not answer me. I continued to shake my keys and sing. Even though I wasn't singing in perfect tune, it didn't matter. The voices grew louder, and I heard harmonics above the crowd. I knew that in some mystical, magical, sacred way we were reenacting an ancient rite that priestesses had performed centuries ago. We were calling the Goddess to ourselves. It was a joyous experience–a simple act of faith.

"Yes, this is it!" I gasped. "This is for me." A strange passion filled my body as I repeated the names of the Goddess in the chant. Suddenly, I was singing in full voice. There was a clarity happening inside me that I had never felt before. I had fallen in love with the Goddess.

I have often thought about that night at the concert and wondered why it had such an impact on me. Some people believe that it was the effect of the full moon, or the energies of the fall equinox. I think it was the extraordinary power of the chant. As we sang the goddess names under the stars and moon, it awoke my priestess soul.

The next morning I went to the bookstore and bought my first goddess book. After that I bought more books and I began to read everything I could find. I learned from my research that the goddess movement was diverse in its beliefs and origins. I was happy to discover that there were no hardcore rules, dogma, or hierarchal systems; it was described as a spirituality that is based on the mother principle. I learned that contemporary goddess spirituality grew out of consciousness-raising groups from the early seventies. Mostly inspired by the principles of the Old Religion, which predated the Judeo-Christian era, it branched out into many different forms.

The Mother Goddess reflects women and is revered in all her aspects as young, old, beautiful, ugly, fearsome, wild, sexual, compassionate, and even as a raging force of nature. Above all, the Goddess is personal. "We all come from the Goddess!" I heard people sing over and over, until I understood on a heartfelt level that everyone is the Goddess. "Look into the eyes of your friend," a priestess once said to me. "Look deep and there you will see the Goddess staring back at you."

***

I explored a career in expressive therapy in my late twenties and employed many techniques drawn from Native American traditions. I was drawn to use my intuitive skills to help autistic children and I worked in a place for children with special needs. My techniques were effective and I won awards for my projects. I presented in mental health conferences. In those days the work I did was cutting-edge. Holistic healing had not yet emerged. I never mentioned the name "goddess" or my spiritual orientation to anyone. I was aware that I was working in a closed-minded society and so I was careful to use acceptable terms to explain what I did. In other words, without knowing it, I, too, had joined the many people, silenced throughout history, who hid their belief in the Goddess because they were afraid. Without even knowing it, I was reenacting the sad history of the Goddess's demise.

The story of goddess spirituality is about overcoming invisibility and loss. It was easy for me to relate to the story of the Goddess from my own childhood experiences. The Goddess who had been revered as The All Powerful, The Beautiful, The Great Mother, was reduced to the image of a beauty queen or demon. Whereas once her traditions had empowered women and had honored the sanctity of mother love, now they were mostly ignored and seen as a primitive religion.

It saddened me to discover that a beautiful tradition had become lost among spiritual politics and social change. I learned that there had been a time when spirits of all kinds—fairies, angels, and guardians—thrived and weren't so quickly dismissed or debunked. There had been a place for visionaries and for mystics like me to coexist alongside the philosophers and rationalists of the times.

As I changed, I saw my friends' resistance—some got very angry and others laughed behind my back. It didn't take long before these experiences made me understand why the ancient traditions and the people in goddess history were forced to yield before the new religions, which did not tolerate female power. I saw how the Goddess became the Motherghost of our times.

In the same way my mother's love could not completely be erased from my heart, the distant memory of a loving mother deity was also not completely lost from humanity. Even though her worshipers—the people of the land—were forced to deny her existence and were killed in her name, her icons remained and her power symbols were reflected everywhere in nature. The goddess spirit was never far away and her memory could not be destroyed. Throughout the centuries, generations secretly held onto the Goddess in the same way that I as a child had held onto my mother, through the sun, the moon, and all of the nature spirits around me.

190

The propaganda against the ancient traditions that was spread in those times still exists. And even though I knew that I would face the harsh reality of our society's lack of religious tolerance toward the Goddess, I chose to face this wall of fear and hatred and embrace the beauty that I felt in my heart. My truth was that the Goddess, The Mother of All, was calling me home.

CHAPTER 29
My Name Is Eclipse
The Mother's Priestess

I found an important piece of my true self the day I discovered my name. This happened during my initiation into the Goddess culture. Though it took me a long time to tell people about my priestess name, and it took longer to actually take it on as my everyday name and to have others accept me as Eclipse, it was one of those decisions that changed the course of my life.

One afternoon while napping, I had a mystical dream. Mystical dreams are different from psychological ones; one remembers them very clearly, and they always have a spiritual message. This was my dream:

An old man with a long white beard, wearing a long, dark purple robe, greets me as I exit a cave. I am holding an old love letter from my recent lover.

"Are you Merlin?" I ask.

He laughs at my question and says, "No, I am much older than Merlin. My name is Taliesin."

He then motions for me to follow him. He leads me to a beautiful open field.

"Go to the center and wait," he instructs me.

I do so. It is nighttime, and I am standing in a shimmering wheat field. It feels like an ocean. I am a little scared, and don't want Taliesin to leave, but he turns away.

I am standing there alone, in the middle of the field, waiting, when I hear a voice. It is not a man's voice, nor is it a woman's voice. It has multiple tones and sounds like many voices in one.

"We have come to give you your name," it says.

As an adopted child who struggled with the names I was given, I had wanted a new name ever since I started studying native traditions back in my twenties. There is a practice of taking on a new name when you come of age and go on a vision quest. But nothing had felt right for me. I had waited a long time. Marcy and Robin did not fit me anymore.

"Is this my vision quest?"

"You are standing in the place of the Sacred South," they say.

The Sacred South is the power of fire, and in many nature traditions, is a symbolic place of innocence and of the power of taking action.

"The South?" I ask, feeling more like I am in the sacred place of the West, the power of water, where loss and letting go are symbolized.

"Are you here to help me with my breakup?" I ask, holding up the letter I had received that morning.

"No, we are here to give you your name," they say.

"I don't want my name right now. I just want my lover back."

"We are here to give you your name," they repeat.

"You are?" I resign myself to the inevitable.

"You are Eclipse."

"Eclipse? I can't call myself Eclipse! People will think I am crazy."

"You are Eclipse."

"You've got to be joking. Can't I call myself something simple, an herb or an animal or something else? I don't want to be named after a natural phenomenon. People will think I am pretentious," I say, resisting.

"You must wear the power of Eclipse. You are Eclipse," they say again, and then I suddenly see them in front of me—two very tall bald-headed beings dressed in white robes. I step back. Their presence feels so soft and healing. They have unusually large hands, with long slender fingers. They show me the sign of eclipse as they bring their hands across each other, like a winged bird, over their heart centers.

I copy them. "Eclipse," I repeat, and I can feel the power as I make this gesture. I feel calmer—centered—and I feel a sense of purpose. It is frightening and exhilarating at the same time. I feel called to use this name and petrified to do so. I feel inspired by my own name.

"Believe what you see here, and make this sign when you doubt who you are."

I look up at the sky and I see a beautiful eclipse. It has a pink lavender glow. It is not like any eclipse I know. There is no darkness, no ominous signs. Instead it feels like the in-between moments of dawn and dusk—moments of stillness.

"You will carry the two lights in your heart. The light of the moon and the light of the sun will come together in your heart."

When they say this, I automatically make the eclipse sign over my heart.

"Good. You will learn the many healing powers of your name. The teachings will come one at a time." And then they are gone. I feel humbled.

I awoke that afternoon, every moment of the dream very clear and imprinted in my consciousness. I was lying on my bed, very still—almost stiff. My hands were over my heart, in the eclipse sign that they had shown me. I didn't move. I just lay there thinking about what had happened. Then as I looked over my body stretched out in front of me, I noticed that my hands were folded on my chest in the exact same way in which the Egyptian mummies were laid to rest. It was the same sign. The great wings of Isis had become my hands across my heart. As I lay there, I realized that the first teaching or challenge I would face with the revelation of my name would be to embrace the sacred power of Isis—the Mother of all.

CHAPTER 30
The Daughters
Healing Broken Mother Bonds

The first day I met Maggie, I was taken aback by her looks. She was an absolutely vibrant woman, with a defiant way of standing and sharp bursts of energy when she moved about. She coolly scanned my office and found her place to claim. She strutted across the room, flopped down into the overstuffed chair, and waited for me to speak first. It was a power game for her. I smiled. Despite her slight stature, she was a tough-looking woman with dark red hennaed hair that sprung out in every direction. It dominated the delicate features of her face, where the most beautiful blue-green eyes revealed her Irish background. Her pierced nose, flower tattoo, and worn leather jacket wrapped tightly around her frail body all underscored her rebellious, angry nature. She was a twenty-year-old freckle-faced Medusa in all her modern glory.

We sat silently together as I looked over her astrological chart. It was the way I always liked to begin a new session. Silence gave me time to pause and just be present with someone.

"I see that your Leo moon is in the twelfth house," I said as I pointed to a little moon symbol up on the left-hand side of the chart.

"The twelfth house? What does that mean?"

"It is a part of the chart that represents what is hidden in your life."

"Ha," she laughed sarcastically at my statement.

"The moon is a mother symbol and, in this house placement, it can mean that your mother might have felt absent to you."

I looked up from the paper to see what her response to what I had just said might be.

"Is this correct?"

"Yeah. You are right on." She nodded as she gave me a nervous half-giggle.

"Good. I'll go on." I leaned back.

"I was what you call a 'locked-up child'," Maggie said.

"Oh?" I sensed the bitterness in her voice. "I don't understand. What does 'locked up' mean?"

"Oh, it's simple," she said as she fidgeted with her keychain. "I was too wild for my mother. So, when I was eleven, she turned me over to the authorities."

"That's a tough one to accept."

"Yes, my mother sent me to jail," she said.

I could feel her anger, and I looked straight at her. I wanted to let her know that I was not intimidated by her rough manner.

"That must have really hurt," I said, returning her stare.

"I don't know," she said, looking away.

"You don't know?"

"No, I don't remember a damn thing."

"I see," I answered, and then looked back at the chart.

Her voice had a tone that was familiar to me; it was the voice of children everywhere who have lost their mothers. I knew that I was getting too close to her vulnerable spots, so I gave her some space and started looking for more clues. I could feel her pain as if it were my own. Even though her demeanor was different from mine, like her, I, too, had been betrayed by my mother, and like her, when I was young and finding myself, I, too, had used sarcasm as a way to shield myself.

"Your Leo moon dramatizes the mother energy," I said.

"Well, I have a lot of drama," she said, smiling.

"Possibly you acted out your mother's wildness?"

"My mother wasn't wild," she said, and laughed.

"Exactly. That is what I mean. Women often act out their mothers' hidden desires."

"What do you mean? I don't get it."

"It looks as though, from the Saturn conjunct the Moon, she was not able to be free."

"You are right! How did you know that?" she asked.

I saw that I had sparked her interest, and some trust.

"Because I am an astrologer, and it's my job to know."

"Well, you are damn good at this."

I could see that I was getting somewhere with her.

"Good. Now, let's imagine what your relationship with your mother would be if you were both on the same team in a relay race."

"That is an interesting thought." She leaned over to look more closely at the chart.

"Look at her and see when and where she became stuck in her life. Where she couldn't go any further with her visions of herself." I pointed once again at her Moon in the twelfth house.

"Hmmm," she said.

"Wherever she was emotionally stuck becomes exactly the area in your life where you will pick up the symbolic torch of hers and begin to run onward."

Maggie's eyes widened as she thought over what I had said.

"Well, my mother was trapped at home. She was dirt poor, with five kids and a drunk husband."

195

I noticed that her voice was becoming animated and I asked, "What do you think she dreamed of?"

"I don't know."

I could see a light appearing in her eyes; perhaps a spark of feeling and connection with her lost mother was beginning to happen. I was actually asking her, in a subtle way, to touch the human frailties of her estranged mother and to see her as a human being–not a wicked, callous woman whom she blamed for everything bad in her life. In doing so, she would probably feel her own wounded heart. It would help her heal, but it was a big challenge.

"I spent years trying to understand her, and I don't understand her at all," Maggie said, looking down at the floor.

"I have an idea. Close your eyes for a moment."

She leaned back into the chair and closed her eyes.

"Now imagine that your mother and you are on a beach somewhere. She is holding a torch."

"Okay," she said. A few seconds later, she began to smile.

"Can you see her? Is she with you?" I asked.

"Yes."

"Ask her what her dreams were for herself."

A long time went by. I watched as she relaxed deeper into the meditation.

"Is she still holding the torch?"

"Yes."

"What does the torch symbolize or represent to her?"

"I don't know."

"Ask her what she is passing on to you."

There was silence. Her smile left, and her lower lip began to quiver, until one tear, like a raindrop, trickled down her cheek.

"Tell me, what is she saying to you?"

"She's telling me . . ." Maggie became still.

"She's telling you what?" I pushed.

"That she dreamed of . . ."

"Of what?"

"Of her freedom." Maggie gasped.

"Her freedom?"

"Yes, her freedom. She says she so wanted to be free–a young girl again. But she can't be . . ." More tears came. Maggie was feeling her mother's struggle. I could see that her mother had become real for her.

"Perhaps it's the same freedom that she wishes for you now?"

"I don't know." Maggie sighed.

"She can't carry the torch of freedom any further for you, but she wants to," I said.

Maggie opened her eyes and her tears were silently streaming down her cheeks.

"She wants to, but my mom can't do it," she said.

"I know, but you can take the torch for her. It's your turn to be free and to carry that torch."

Maggie stared right at me, her green eyes piercing the energy around us. I stared back and would not look away. It was one of those moments—a karmic shift had occurred. She nodded her head as if she knew what I was going to say next.

"It's her precious gift to you. It's your torch now. Take it."

"I will," she said and as she walked out the door she turned around—and gave me a big grin.

CHAPTER 31
The Mother Ritual

After Maggie left, I thought about the different ways that mothers and daughters heal their broken bonds. I knew that even though I had spent years working with others on healing the mother-daughter relationship, I still needed to resolve my painful feelings about my birth mother.

This type of healing is a process that I knew I couldn't rush. I see many women in my work who compensate for a fragile or nonexistent mother-daughter bond by becoming overzealous caretakers–super moms. They become the "mother fix" for others. When I meet women like this, I often feel as if they can't give enough of themselves, as if their giving becomes the way they satisfy the beast inside them that says, "You are not enough." But whom do these women go to when they need help? These women often feel guilty if they take for themselves. If they do not find mother love, these women often replace lack of mother love with addiction.

Sometimes the motherless daughter experience evolves into the opposite behavior, and a woman will constantly reach out, seeking a mother connection, saying over and over, "Love me! See me! Help me!" Sometimes their mothers have not been able to protect them when they were children, and these women cannot shake their constant feelings of vulnerability.

I know that the "mother energy" created by the initial bond with our mothers does not go away. It has a magnetic pull to it. It will be manifested either within the search for the mother, the act of mothering, or the connection to the mother. Our mothers, with one glance, one word, and even with silence can empower or cripple us in our adult lives. Mothers haunt their children no matter what has happened between them.

***

I attended a ritual honoring mother love back in the early eighties. We were in a meadow on a spring day, and the scent of sweet blossoms surrounded us. There were about a hundred and fifty of us that day. We came from all walks of life, women of all ages and orientations. We were young girls, old crones, mothers and daughters, single privileged heterosexuals, married women, gay women, women of color, ex-nuns, Jews, Christians, and neo-Pagans. We were sharing our mother experiences, and our stories were deeply moving.

I lay back on the grass and listened as each woman spoke. I gazed up at the blue sky and felt how soothing the gentle voices of the women were, like a waterfall of soft voices trickling over me as I baked in the warm sun.

But the more I listened, the more I realized that I had nothing kind to say about my own mother. What was I going to do? I thought as I turned over onto my belly and hoped someone would say something that could serve as an opening for me.

Women spoke from the heart, saying things like, "I am Anna, daughter of Sarah. I am one of eight surviving children. My mother had three miscarriages. But she was a strong woman. She did not say much and she never stopped." There was a pause and then, like a confession, the woman continued. "The day my brother died, she just kept washing the floors over and over, and I remember her humming as if it would make her feel better."

"Blessed be the power of Sarah," we all responded when she was finished.

"I am Mary, daughter of Catherine. My mother kept us clean and made us feel special."

"Blessed be the power of Catherine."

Another woman rose. She was in her late forties, tall, with a scarf around her neck and deerskin boots on her feet. I noticed that the wind picked up just as she stood. She had an English accent.

"I am Brigit, daughter of Margaret. My mother was a strong Catholic woman. I don't remember her ever missing a Sunday Mass." We all nodded. Each of us had known someone like that. She continued. "When she died, I ignored her wishes and I brought her ashes to Stonehenge–to my Goddess." Tears streamed down her face. "I took my mother's ashes and spread them at the harvest moon," she said, and then she knelt on one knee and hid her face as if in shame. She wept for what seemed a long time. Her tears touched our own hidden pain and guilt, and some of us began to cry. Had we also betrayed our mothers? Finally, she continued. Her eyes were red and her face was pained but strong. I saw the mask of the Goddess. "Mother, I am so sorry." And then she screamed, "Mother! I ask you to forgive me!"

We chimed in with, "Blessed be the power of Margaret."

The ritual went on for hours.

"My mother was powerful. She fought the patriarchy and left my father with his money and his secretaries. She took my brother Billy and me to a small, shabby apartment. We gave her a hard time for it."

"My mother was strong and she never gave up. It was her way to love us."

"My mother had a laugh that let you know that her power was in her humor–blessed be."

It was getting late, and I knew it was my turn. I knew that I had to speak my truth. I got up and said, "I am the daughter of Stephanie, and the adopted daughter of Frances. Both of my mothers were driven by power. One wanted to be a movie star, and the other manipulated me into submission." I sat back down.

An uncomfortable silence followed. Was it because no one, until that moment, had spoken about the wrongs that some mothers can inflict on their daughters? Was I turning the wheel—changing the theme? Would my truth be part of the whole truth of mother and daughter love? Or would I once again be silenced and denied my reality? My words hung in the air as the group held in their hearts what I had said. The group became the Goddess's heart holding my sorrow.

A little bit later, a short, hefty woman with a very sweet freckled face stood up and broke the silence. She seemed very shy and a little bit shaky, as if she had never spoken to such a large group before. She stared at us, and then down at me. She spoke almost in a whisper, and we strained to hear her.

"My name is Catherine, daughter of Mary. My mother didn't care either. She drank until she killed herself."

Once again there was a long silence. This woman was clearly going through an internal struggle, and it was deeply moving to witness it. Then in a very, very, soft voice, a voice that cut across time and reached into eternity, she simply said, "Mommy, I forgive you."

CHAPTER 32
Saving the Matriarchs

I dream that I am walking through a narrow tunnel that is descending into the underworld. The only sound I can hear is a broken heater that rattles loudly above my head. I am shivering and know that I am afraid. There is an eerie feeling about the place and I am heading toward an open doorway. I can hear heavy breathing coming from it and I am sure that there is a monster waiting for me. I try to prepare myself for the worst as I enter the room, but instead of a monster, I discover a large, overweight, and unkempt elephant, chained to a wall. I recognize her as the elephant I saw years ago in a broken-down zoo in the town next door. She is rocking back and forth as if in terrible pain. "Oh, you poor thing," I gasp in horror. But the elephant is unaware of my presence and seems lost in a trance.

She periodically pulls at her chain and the sound of the iron clashing loudly echoes in the small space. I hear screams but I cannot decipher whose screams they are—the elephant's or mine. That is when I realize that the two of us are merging together in some strange way. I am overwhelmed by it all and I cover my ears and close my eyes. I begin to rock back and forth along with her. Something causes me to open my eyes again and to look at her. But this time when I do, I see the elephant is an ancient being, a Goddess, standing in front of me. I start to cry, knowing we are both imprisoned inside this small cell together, and I suddenly am reminded of myself in the foster home. I notice tears trickling down the elephant's wrinkled face, and I remember reading that elephants weep from sorrow. She speaks to me in a raspy voice, but I can't make out what she is saying. So I move closer to her and listen. She can only say, "Help me."

As I sipped my coffee the next morning, reviewing the dream, I realized that I was profoundly moved by it. Clearly, the Goddess was calling me to do her work in some way. But how? I knew that I had to do something about the elephant. But what? Free her? That seemed way too big a task.

Forrest entered the room just at that moment.

"I'm off to school," he said.

"Forrest, do you remember the day we visited Fanny when you were five?"

"How could I forget? It was one of those depressing childhood moments."

"We are going to have to do something. I've had a dream about her."

"No, Mom. You are going to have to do something. Not me."

"Right, I am going to have to do something."

"Oh, Mom, it was just a dream," he said, looking a bit worried.

"No, it's real. It feels like a cosmic call."

Forrest rolled his eyes. "By the way, I am working tonight," he said as he came over and kissed my cheek.

"Seriously, Forrest, I have to do something for her." I could feel myself almost in tears as I talked to him.

"I know, I know. Just don't do anything that will embarrass me, Mom, okay?" he said as he walked out the door, laughing.

"I won't," I called after him. Then I began to wonder what rescuing an elephant would entail.

After breakfast, I headed off to the zoo, wondering if Fanny was still there. It was a bleak, damp, September morning. Not a good day to go to the zoo. The place was pretty empty; there were no visitors, no children squealing, and no vendors. It was strange; I did not see or bump into anyone the whole time I was there.

I first came to the monkeys, who hovered together on a bare limb in the middle of a cement moat. They watched me very carefully as I walked by their exhibit. Next I was accosted by the stench of urine as I passed a bear cage no bigger than a small bedroom. The two bears were sprawled lethargically on a cement foundation. I noticed sores on one bear's foot. I cringed at the sight and quickly continued on. Only a year before, I had read that a group of drunken teenagers had let out a polar bear, and the only way the zookeepers could retrieve him was to shoot him.

The place was as dreary as it had always been. I found the elephant exhibit in the same place it had been years ago. When I opened the door to the room, I was shocked at the place's dingy appearance and rancid smell–the energy was simply overwhelming. My heart sank as I looked at the lonely beast, chained by one leg, standing in front of me. How many hours–days–months–years had she waited alone?

I knew that Fanny had come from India and was a victim of a culling when she was around five. During a culling, hunters kill a whole family of elephants, except for the young calves, who can be easily transported. As I read the news clipping on the wall that told the story of her arrival from the circus, I realized that Fanny had been alone and chained for over thirty-five years. She rocked back and forth as if oblivious to her surroundings. She seemed trapped in time.

"I want to help you," I said as I walked over to her cage. I reached my hand through the bars to touch her. Her rough skin felt like the earth, dried and caked from the sun, but it was softer. Few people know that elephant skin is actually quite tender, not rough hide, as the trainers with their metal hooks would like the public to believe, as they poke and prod helpless elephants into submission. I rested my hand near her cheek, and sent her loving energy. She stopped rocking.

For a moment, as we became very still together, I closed my eyes and felt the warmth of her soul resting with mine. In some strange way, deep in my heart, I knew that Fanny and I belonged together and that we had shared many lifetimes.

Then she began to rock again, and a vibration that is called infrasound—a rumbling that elephants make—came from her and filled the room. I had read that elephants make this sound and that it comes from the soft spot on their foreheads. In the open plains in the wild, other elephants can detect this sound from miles away. I closed my eyes again and let my whole body be filled with her energy.

At that moment, as I looked at Fanny I knew that I was going to embark on a piece of Goddess work that would be like a karmic swirl. I pulled out a small healing quartz crystal and wedged it in a crack in the wall near her cage. I said a prayer for protection.

I knew that Fanny and I were soul mates, joined at the heart. I had never felt such a strong mystical connection before. I was compelled to rescue her. The task ahead would not be easy, but I knew that this battle was bigger than one woman and one elephant. I felt that we were, in some cosmic way, ambassadors of our species. Could I make a change? I didn't know. But I had to try.

As I looked at her standing there alone, trapped and forgotten, I couldn't help but identify with her. I began to remember the hopeless moments from my childhood. I could see the similarities in our situations. I ached for both of us and I began to cry. She suddenly pressed her large cheek next to the bars of the cage as if she were trying to reach me. I looked up at her large brown eye, with its long eyelashes, and saw a tear roll down her cheek. Elephants are known to weep real salty tears. Fanny was crying.

I joined the local animal rights movement the next day. Even though I had never thought that I could cope with the onslaught of despair and pain that many animal rights activists experience, I knew that I was going to have to try.

I did a little bit of research and learned that other groups and individuals had failed in their attempts to rescue this elephant. The larger animal welfare bureaucracies, which often looked for the big stories—the ones that bring in big money from PR—saw her as a lost cause. Fanny's story was too small and her cause would most likely fail. Quests to end her plight had been tabled.

I was reminded of the day my Neilson mother said to me, "You are what they call hard to adopt. That is why it took so long." I, too, had been tabled because I was not a cute baby.

"She is a lost cause. Fanny won't do," representatives from the larger animal rights organizations said over the phone to me when I inquired about her liberation.

"Well, I am going to try," I kept saying.

"It will never happen," they declared.

I did not listen, and decided to organize my own group, called the Free Fanny Committee. I wrote an article, a plea for Fanny, in the local paper. I was astonished by the enormous amount of replies that came pouring in. The letters ranged from being angry with me for accusing the zoo of abuse, to being grateful that I had the courage to speak the truth.

The fight for this elephant opened my eyes to things I had never wanted to see. The blatant exploitation of her plight went across the board, with a lot of backdoor wheeling and dealing from radio talk show hosts, councilmen, small business owners, large animal welfare organizations, and some individuals—all of them took advantage of Fanny's pain in different ways. It was only as her story made the news, and as we began to have small successes. that these powerful people and organizations stepped in to help and take credit for the cause. Clearly, they all had an agenda besides rescuing one elephant. It seemed as if everyone in power wanted to make money from her suffering. As I spoke to people across the country, the ugly political reality became glaringly obvious. I discovered that, when it came to rescuing animals, exploitation and politics were intertwined.

The small local groups are the ones that do all the work, and then the big people often come in and scoop the story. But it is important to support the local animal rights groups; they are the ones whose hearts are boundless. They spend whatever they have on the animals in need. They take in the stray cats and rescue the dogs in pounds that have reached the end of the line. They are among the many gods and goddesses of our times.

"They are doing nothing to relieve her pain or change her deplorable conditions," I said to one such activist, who had been fighting these types of causes for years. She laughed and shook her head. "Welcome to the world of politics. It is everywhere," she said.

As I continued my fight, I learned a great deal about small towns, bureaucracies, and corruption. The committee I formed grew into a strong network. We were ready to fight. We wrote letters to the mayor and the local media and made many phone calls to councilmen. With time, I got better at navigating through a world that was seemingly corrupt. I encountered many conflicts and obstacles in others and within myself—childhood flashbacks were constantly being triggered. On a cosmic level I felt I was warring against the indifference and cruelty of the world. I was fighting not only for Fanny but also for all the vulnerable ones who are trapped in the world and have no voice. Sometimes the obstacles overwhelmed me, but I held on to my dream. My Goddess-fired rage inspired my sense of purpose. I was going to fight for Fanny in every way I could.

I did not tell anyone about my mystical practice. I knew that the media would misuse that information. I was afraid it would undermine my cause. Prejudice against the Goddess is still a very real force in this world.

One Christmas Eve morning, the phone rang.

"Hello, this is Jonathan from the *Journal*."

"Yes?" I said.

"I need a heart-touching Christmas story and Fanny seems like a good one."

"Yes?"

"Can you meet me in an hour at the zoo, before it closes?"

"It's snowing." I hated to drive in snow.

"I promise to write a good story."

"Okay."

"Meet me at the zoo in an hour."

It was snowing harder by the time I got to the zoo. The parking lot was covered with an inch of snow and was completely empty. The zoo felt eerie that day. It felt as though I were walking through the corridors of an empty tomb. The lights were dim and the sound of my footsteps echoed against the cement walls. It reminded me of my dream.

I went to Fanny's cell and waited. Jonathan was late. Damn, I hope he is coming, I thought. I looked at Fanny and she was again rocking. By now I had done a lot of research about elephants in captivity, so I knew that this was either a sign of distress, or a way elephants have to keep from getting arthritis from lack of exercise. I noticed that her bucket of water was empty. I had also learned that elephants need a great deal of water and need to bathe daily or their skin will itch unbearably. Fanny, like many other circus elephants, wasn't getting what she needed.

I suddenly turned around and saw that three men had entered the space. I recognized them as the zookeepers, and I knew they did not like me because they saw me as someone who was threatening the zoo and their jobs.

"She needs water," I said, smiling politely, while pointing at the empty bucket.

They ignored me and started to surround me. One lit a cigarette, another leaned up against the wall, and the third came very close and stood beside me. They still said nothing. It was as if they were coordinating a scene in a movie. I would have laughed, but I was feeling very uncomfortable with them. But they said nothing. It was clear that they wanted to intimidate me. It worked. I was scared, but I held my ground, and turned back to look at Fanny. Finally Jonathan arrived.

"Hi. Sorry I am late."

"Yes, you are!" I said angrily.

"You must be Eclipse Neilson." He reached out to shake my hand as he looked around at the three men.

"Let's get out of here," I said.

We left and grabbed a cup of coffee at a nearby diner.

"They always put me on these types of stories," Jonathan said, seeming a bit disgruntled by the fact. "I studied history in college," he added.

"And you? What do you do?" he asked, looking at my attire, which was pretty tame, except for a Tibetan jacket that I was wearing. I could tell that he was trying to pick up my field of work and was fishing for another story—something more interesting than an elephant in a zoo.

"What did you say you do for work?"

"I didn't say."

"Eclipse is an interesting name—did your parents give you that name?" he asked, searching for an opening.

"No, they didn't. This article isn't about me, right?"

He smiled.

"I know it isn't, but it would give the story a good angle."

"Please don't do that." I stared straight at him.

"Why?"

"I just want this elephant's suffering to stop. I don't want the focus to get sidetracked. Please help me."

Jonathan listened, and as I pleaded her case, I think he felt the elephant's plight. As I talked to him and looked into his eyes, I saw that even though he was trying hard to look indifferent and to act like a reporter, he was being pulled in by the story. I knew that he, too, would end up swirling in the magical mystery created by this cause. I knew this because, as he talked, I looked into his soul and I saw a compassionate being sitting across the table from me. He did become pivotal to our cause as time went on. He kept the story alive.

Months went by, and I became obsessed by this political action. I worked day and night, making calls and organizing meetings, researching elephants, appearing on talk shows, writing letters, and raising money. The battle lasted for over a year. In private groups, and with like-minded groups of healers and caring people, we called upon Ganesh, the elephant God, before each meeting, and Tara, the Goddess of compassion, and Kali, the Goddess of rage. I asked the angels to surround Fanny, and the fairies to play tricks on those who opposed us. I asked everyone, Christians, Buddhists, Quakers, Unitarians, Pagans, and whomever I could find, to pray. We needed the whole army at work. Our group went to city hall and marched in the parks, and we spoke passionately at city council meetings. We were outraged and we got good media coverage. Soon other animal rights groups joined in, and other individuals fought for the freedom of this one elephant. It was wonderful. A community of caring souls was formed. The city kept hoping that we would go away. But we didn't go away. Instead we became a national story.

Jonathan called me for a sound bite one day.

"Can you believe it, here I am reporting on a variety of big stories about crime and politics?"

"Yeah, what are you saying?"

"Well, I am hoping for a byline on one of these stories so I can be big time, and would you believe it, it is this one elephant story that makes the national news and gives me my byline," he said, and laughed.

"Great!"

"How do you explain it?"

"Elephant magic?" I didn't bother to elaborate. That is the secret of the great Mysteries, I thought. But it is written that Ganesh rewards those who care.

"Whatever; got a comment I can use?"

Throughout the entire effort, I wondered why the officials were resisting Fanny's release. I kept asking myself why they were so passionate about keeping her. In the administration that had previously governed the town, the last mayor had been sent to prison for embezzlement. Was there something else going on? Was it tied to this elephant? Did that explain the numerous threatening calls I had received throughout the winter? I also believe that my phone was tapped (not an uncommon experience for an activist). Was money involved? Or were government funds for the zoo being misused? These were the questions I kept asking.

I had a connection to a man of some rank who worked for the FBI. He helped me in his own way by giving me simple directions and a few names to research (unofficially, of course). He directed me and taught me how to find information among the back halls of city government files. And in time, and with luck, I finally found what I needed–damaging information.

I was excited and that afternoon I went directly to the mayor's office. I asked lots of provocative questions and dropped a few names of important, corrupt individuals. I let the people in the office know that I would ask those same questions in front of cameras, which would raise more questions. Investigation was something the town dreaded. I also hinted that the public would be outraged if they knew what I knew.

It worked. The mayor, who had vetoed our cause and put so many obstacles in our path, gave up his fight the next day. Now Fanny could be released. Coincidence? The mayor would never say there was any connection between his giving up the fight and my visit, but that did not matter. We had won the first big battle.

"I am throwing in the towel," was what the mayor said that day. To put icing on the cake, this victory happened on my birthday. CNN radio called early that morning.

"How does it feel to win the battle for Fanny?" the reporter asked.

"It feels great!" I said. "Just great."

The battle was far from over, however, because Fanny's exploitation would continue. Fanny needed a home. She had made national news and was a hot story. Soon many theme parks sent flashy videos and photos, boasting that they had the best elephant trainers for her. Breeders offered the town money to take her.

"She still has a few good years," they said.

Other individuals bargained with the town, wanting to buy her. Lots of money was being talked about, and it became a bigger nightmare. Once again the horrors of my foster home experiences returned to me, and the pain in my heart was overwhelming. I can't give up, I kept saying to myself. I can't give up!

The Free Fanny Committee wanted Fanny to go to a sanctuary called Black Beauty Ranch, in Texas, a place where there would be no chains, no demands for tricks—just freedom and a companion for her and, above all, a pond. But things looked bad. A large theme park in California became our biggest threat. This theme park believed in animal entertainment, giving elephant rides to people, having the elephants file in line, holding tails, and making them work, dragging logs: things elephants don't do naturally in the wild. Even though they claimed to have a large space, the truth was that their family of elephants was chained in a line at night by both legs. It looked like we might lose Fanny to a place no better than a circus. Of course, the argument theme parks and zoos use is that they are educating the public about the species. They sent their trainer, and when it looked like we were going to lose, I was heartbroken.

The next morning, the trainer from the theme park brought his videos and props to show how wonderful his park was and how much they were doing for the Earth and the plight of endangered species. He talked about training elephants, and he mumbled something about aversive techniques used for problem elephants.

"Aversive techniques? Could you explain what that entails?" asked someone asked from the crowd.

"Oh, it is used for unruly elephants—a little jolt from an electric prod. Or a poke with this type of hook," he answered, showing the crowd the small metal hook he was holding. The crowd was silent.

"But of course, your Fanny is not one of those elephants," he reassured them.

"What I mean is that we won't hurt Fanny if she doesn't comply," he said as he smiled and patted Fanny on her side.

Can we trust him? Did everyone hear what he said? Electric prod? Hook? I thought.

Then something otherworldly happened. As I looked around, I saw the mystical realm open. Luminous white elephants came from behind the trees and surrounded the space. At that very moment, Fanny picked up some sand and threw it at the trainer. He looked around, a bit disgruntled.

"Can we move over here?" he said as he brushed the dirt off his sleeves. Everyone moved. Fanny did it again. The crowd laughed. He pointed to another area of the cage. We moved again. It was clear that he was becoming pissed. I looked around and I saw the white luminous elephants surrounding the crowd. I knew at that moment that the two realms of the earth plane and the mystical world had merged.

"Fanny loves to throw sand," a woman said fondly, and giggled. Everyone nodded.

"Yeah, it's the way she plays."

"Hey Mister, what's the matter? You don't like sand being thrown at you?" someone called out.

"No," he said, defending himself. "I don't like elephants that throw sand."

"That's our Fanny. She thinks it is a trick," the first woman said.

"She has been doing this for over thirty years," someone else called out.

"Well, we will have to change that trick," the trainer said as he brushed the dust from his sleeve. The crowd was silent.

It was a blessing. Magic at its best! Fanny's timing was impeccable. I think she knew. I saw at that moment that even though the townspeople were in denial about Fanny's conditions, and many had fought to keep her in the zoo, and others had been seduced by the glamour of the theme park idea, they really did love her, and when they heard the trainer talk about disciplining her with aversive techniques, they worried about what would happen if she playfully threw sand.

"How do you suppose this trainer from the great theme park will stop Fanny from throwing sand?" I wrote and asked on talk shows and television. "She has been doing this for thirty-three years."

The townspeople knew the answer to that, and they came to the rescue of their elephant and voted for Black Beauty Ranch. Fanny had stepped in and had rescued herself from the fancy theme park. The next week in city council, when the town official read the results of the committee's vote, tears began to stream down my cheeks.

Black Beauty Ranch, which is sponsored by the organization Funds of Animals, is a six-hundred-acre sanctuary in Texas, home to six hundred animals. And every single animal has a story as powerful as Fanny's. They come to this sanctuary and get to live the rest of their lives in safety. And never again are these poor wounded animals forced to do something that is against their own instincts. In my heart this place is a Goddess temple.

The day before Fanny left, I went to a farewell party for her that the town held at the zoo. The crowd that gathered was mostly hostile to me and my group of activists. I believe that they needed someone to blame, and we were the targets. There were nasty signs with my name and the names of other activists posted on walls. Some people saw me as the evil one who had stolen their town's elephant. But I could not let this deter me. I had one last, secret task to accomplish. I was worried that Fanny would not make it safely to her new home. In my research I had discovered that sometimes traveling across the country in a small truck can be too traumatic a trip for elephants, and they will die. I had a small bottle of sacred water from the rivers of India, and I needed to get it to Fanny.

"This water will protect her," a Hindu priest told me as he handed me the small brown bottle. "Take it to her."

As I pushed my way through the crowd, approximately three thousand people were there that day to say goodbye. But I was driven by the gods to get that water to her. A journalist saw me and stopped me. He asked about the hostile stares I was getting. I acknowledged it and went on. I saw the zookeeper handing out apples. He was the same man who had sworn revenge on me only a few weeks before. I knew I was taking a big risk. It was like walking into a fire, but I had to get this water to Fanny.

"Excuse me," I said to the zookeeper.

He spun around and looked at me. His look told me that he hated me and that I had a lot of nerve to ask him anything.

"Please, I want you to place this sacred water on her for protection for the trip," I said to him.

He stared at me. My heart pounded. I would have burst out in tears if he had said no.

"Please," I said again. I stared deep into his soul and mustered whatever power of prayer I could. Please, Tara, show him compassion, I prayed. In the turning of a moment, it felt like we aligned and forgave each other. We made peace.

"It's not poisonous, is it?" he asked.

"No, I promise it's not."

He took the bottle, pulled out the cork, and sprinkled it on Fanny's side. I sighed with relief.

"Thank you," I said, and walked away from the noise of the crowd. That night Fanny left for her new home.

Fanny arrived at the ranch three days later. She would live the rest of her life there, free from chains, with a new companion, whose name was Conga. She was the first elephant Fanny had seen in thirty-five years. Conga had been in a circus for most of her life, but was now free. One of the crueler ways circuses train elephants is to take them and stretch their four legs down to the ground, and then hose water over them and use an electrical cattle prod on them. The most common intention in training elephants is to break their spirits.

"She'll be okay when we break through her feistiness," the trainers say. Break their spirits. This is what they do to elephants in circuses. Break their spirits.

When Fanny arrived that day, it was near sunset. They brought her into the enclosure where Conga waited. Everyone was afraid that maybe the elephants would not get along. Some people, including a few journalists, were there watching. To keep each animal calm, the lights had not been turned on. When Fanny saw Conga she went right over to her, and they both touched, and wrapped their trunks around each other. The only sound in the space was the sound of elephants touching and reaching out to each other. Fanny was crying.

I received a call from the ranch a few days later.

"Fanny came out to her yard this morning, where there is a big pond, and she got down on her knees and started banging the ground!" they said.

"What does that mean?"

"We thought something was wrong."

"Oh no! Is there?"

"No, but it looked like it. She was going berserk, so we called up an Asian elephant specialist, who knows all about elephant sign language."

"What did they say?"

"They said how strange it was that she was doing that."

"Strange? What does that mean?"

"They said that it is a very rare gesture for an elephant to make in captivity."

"Really? What does it mean when an elephant makes this gesture?"

"It means–absolute joy."

"Absolute joy," I repeated.

"Yes, absolute joy."

***

After I hung up, I went outside into the garden, and I wept from a very, very deep place. I could feel a breeze rustling in the trees, and I could feel the spirits of the luminous elephants close by. It was a perfect moment in my life.

For Fanny
here is the deepest secret nobody knows
(here is the root of the root and the bud of the bud
and the sky of the sky of a tree called life; which grows
higher than soul can hope or mind can hide)
and this is the wonder that's keeping the stars apart

i carry your heart (i carry it in my heart)

—e e cummings,
"[i carry your heart with me(i carry it in]"

CHAPTER 33
A Son's Gift for His Mother

Over the years I have come to accept that I am an orphan at heart, and that, no matter what, I will always feel compelled to rescue all the ruffled-raffled woebegones of the world. The Charlie Brown tree—the one that has a crooked top or a hole in its side—that's the one I'll bring home for Christmas. Predictably, I will always choose the unwanted one: the orphan tree, the throwaway plant, the ugly cat, the screw-loose dog. Charlie Brown trees and scraggly dogs have become the calling card of my free spirit.

Another reflection of my childhood is my never-ending struggle with feeling like I do not belong anywhere. At times, I secretly long for the Norman Rockwell family or the Queen's summer cottage somewhere in England. Either one of these is, in reality, starkly incompatible with the rebel in me, who thrives on being the independent one, the one who goes up against social expectations and all pretentiousness.

Most people see me as a self-confident, strong, and independent woman who doesn't let society dictate her actions. I often hear: "Eclipse, I want to feel free like you do." Or, "You have such inner strength." And, "It takes a lot to throw you off your course." While this is true most of the time, not too long ago a silly comment from Kate did just that: threw me off course. I can still hear her voice booming over the phone: "Rrrobin," she said with arrogant drama, left over from her theater days with my father. "I've got Gawd-awful news for you."

"What is it?"

"Now, Rrrobin, don't kill the messenger who brings the message," she warned me.

"I won't."

"You've done it again!"

"Done what again?"

"Your great-uncle and great-aunt are upset with you. They are saying you are rude and go on about yourself. You know, they are never going to accept you into the family if you keep this up!" she said.

***

Over the years I had attempted to maintain a relationship with the grand patriarch of the Mulock family, my great-uncle Cawthra, who was now an eighty-year-old man but still had enormous wealth and intellect. Cawthra and my aunt Julyan Mulock had had an aristocratic English upbringing, and it showed in subtle ways. I desperately wanted them to like me and to accept me as one of them, even though they saw me as the newfound American black sheep of the Mulock family.

"Rrrobin, English people do not act like Americans. They say that you utterly exhausted them with your multitude of questions and ideas," Kate continued.

"I did what?" I said, incredulous. "I had no idea."

"That's what they said."

"Look how Cawthra himself goes on and on. It's in the genes. Are you sure?" I asked, totally taken aback by the news.

"Yes, I am sure."

"They seemed so pleased," I argued.

"Well, it doesn't look like it, my dear. English are always polite. Now listen, Rrrobin, you must learn some manners and don't try so hard to please them. Try to keep a low profile for a while."

***

I had thought that my aunt, my uncle, and I shared a common understanding of what many people would call a "far-out philosophy." They were both fascinated with the mystical teachings of Rudolf Steiner and had donated an enormous amount of money to preserve the anthroposophic dream. And Dinah Mulock Craik, who wrote *The Little Lame Prince,* was our ancestor. The world of fairies, fantasy, and mystics was in our blood. I felt connected to them in a special way. How many people can say that they have had a profound conversation with their great-uncle about communicating with the dead? Not many, I believe–but I had had just such a conversation with Uncle Cawthra the last time I visited him. During an ancestor ritual, I had been given a message a few days before from my dead father, who had said, "Ask Cawthra about the golden eagle."

"Tell me about the golden eagle."

My uncle looked surprised. "How do you know about that?"

"My father told me. He said to ask you."

"As you know, the golden eagle is related to the Egyptian God Horus, even though some call it a falcon."

"Yes," I nodded.

"Your father and I would always say, 'Oh, look at the golden eagle' when we wanted to let the other one know it was a grand moment." I saw his eyes begin to tear. "I suppose your father is telling me he is okay."

***

215

After the news from Kate, needless to say, I lost all self-confidence about my acceptance into the Mulock family. I began to withdraw from them, thinking that I would never belong to a family.

A few months after that horrid phone call, I received another phone call, this one from my cousin Sarah, letting me know that Cawthra had died.

"What can I do?" I asked her.

She assured me that flowers would be enough. After I hung up the phone with my cousin Sarah, I knew that I wanted to make sure, very sure, that there would be nothing wrong with whatever I did this time. Absolutely nothing! I kept thinking about the mess I had made the summer before. Just this once, I wanted to be like everyone else and "keep a low profile." At the same time, I was appalled at my own behavior. How could I, who had spent years as a rebel, now want to do everything just right? I felt as if I were completely tossing my free spirit out the window.

Unfortunately, my Neilson upbringing, despite all its shoulds and shouldn'ts, had not prepared me for the procedure of proper funeral etiquette. Mother had somehow forgotten that. I was just going to have to wing it.

Even though I knew it was seven o'clock in the morning San Francisco time, I called my son.

"Hello." A sleepy voice answered the phone.

"Forrest, this is your Mom," I said. I used my mother tone, which I don't often use anymore, but we were 3,000 miles apart. So I couldn't use the mother stare, which always worked when I wanted to get a point across. I was desperate to make sure he understood the importance of the instructions I was about to impart.

"Now, listen to me very carefully. It is of utmost importance that you send some flowers, right now, to your great-aunt Julyan," I said in that same exacting mother tone.

"Why?"

"Cawthra has died."

"How sad," he responded, yawning into the phone. "Poor Julyan. I wonder if . . ." he started to say.

"Listen to me. Get out of bed and go right now and buy some flowers. Do you understand?" I said to him sternly.

"MOM! I know! I got it. Okay?!" he replied. I felt him beginning to revert back to his fourteen-year-old reactive self.

"Good, let me know what you buy. Love ya," I said, hanging up the telephone.

After talking to Forrest, I went to the florist and searched for the perfect basket of flowers to send, but I could only find a small pot of violets and tea roses. Would it look like I didn't care? I didn't know. These flowers weren't exactly what I wanted, but they would have to do, so I sent them to the Mulocks' home. I decided to call Forrest again and tell him to send a bigger bouquet, from both of us. Hoping to catch Forrest before he left the house, I rushed home. It was too late, but I left a message in that mother voice that all children know means business. I said, "Forrest, send a large bouquet of flowers and I will help pay for them. Also, make sure you say that they are from both of us."

That was quite the runabout for a Saturday morning; now all my social duties were complete and I could relax, I thought. I made myself a cup of coffee and collapsed into my favorite rocker. As I rocked, I began to think about my great-uncle Cawthra. He was a small, dramatic man who looked a lot like a regal Jiminy Cricket. Cawthra loved an audience and often was in the company of eccentric people, telling great tales of glory. The last time I had seen him, we were at the family country home outside of Toronto. We were on a beautiful deck, which overlooked a rolling landscape of herb gardens and a sprawling green lawn. It was an unusually warm summer day for Toronto, and we sipped tea and wine and chatted.

Then, out of the blue, in his typical dramatic style he began to tell me about a great spiritual teacher who once had a meeting with a young female student. "This teacher was going to be delayed," he said, sipping his wine as he continued, "so he sent someone ahead to relay a message to her and to give her a rake. She was instructed to rake the leaves in the garden until the teacher arrived. The student started raking and began to approach her chore in a philosophical way, making all kinds of intricate spiritual connections. Finally, the teacher appeared and asked her, 'What did you discover raking the leaves?' " At this point in the story, my uncle leaned over, tilted his head and stared at me, pausing for a moment. Then he grinned and continued. "She answered the teacher with a great deal of gusto, elaborately describing the interconnections between the leaves and the patterns of the universe. This response irritated the teacher and he abruptly interrupted her, 'You fool! You should have just been thinking about raking leaves!' he yelled, and then he sent the student away to learn more," Cawthra said with a dismissive wave of his hand. The story was over, and my uncle laughed, and coughed spasmodically, and promptly lit a cigarette. I politely laughed along with him, only understanding some of the meaning of the story, and wondered why he had chosen to share this one with me.

***

A few weeks before Cawthra died, I became obsessed with the idea that my sole purpose in life at that time was to ask my uncle to pass on the mystical legacy and history of the Mulock family to me. I worked up the courage to write to him:

> *I hope I am not being too bold as I speak to you, but I believe I am here connecting with you now so as to help continue our family's unique spiritual legacy. I am not here for the family money or name; rather, I am here seeking the special energy and mystical gifts that many of the family members have carried throughout generations. I believe it is coded in the genes and I know that I have these genes too. I want very much, when you are willing and it feels right, for you to share with me what you believe this legacy to be.*
> *Much love and respect,*
> *Robin*

***

He didn't respond. Perhaps he was insulted by my letter, or perhaps he died before he could answer it. Maybe my words implied that he was mortal, and I think in many ways Cawthra didn't like that fact. I would have to accept that he had died without passing on the information that I so desperately wanted. I would never know why.

The phone rang, interrupting my reminiscing.

"Hi Mom, it's Forrest."

"Forrest, I know it's you. Who else calls me Mom?"

"You're right, Mom."

"Did you send the flowers?" I asked nervously, even though I knew that I had covered all my bases.

"I did better than that!" he said excitedly.

I sat down with that comment, knowing I probably didn't want to hear what he was about to tell me.

"Mom, you are going to be so proud of me!"

Now, every mother knows that when your child exclaims, "You are going to be so proud of me," there is a fifty-fifty chance that she may not be.

"Why, dear? Why am I going to be so proud of you?" I said, taking a deep breath. I am already stressed, I thought, so please don't tell me something I don't want to hear.

"Well, Mom, as I was going to the florist, I thought about all the things you have ever taught me. You know, I've listened to you all my life, and I've learned a lot. I know you love trees and the environment, and I know Aunt Julyan does, and Uncle Cawthra did too, and also, since you are now in the middle of a political action for the forest . . ." he said, and paused for a second.

"What did you do, send a forest?" I hurriedly asked.

"No, Mom, I sent a tree!" he exclaimed proudly.

Oh my God, I thought. At that moment, I did not know whether to weep with pride or scream from exasperation.

"You did what? You sent what?"

"A tree," he said.

"Forrest, it is winter. What the hell are they going to do with a tree?" I asked, distressed. All I could imagine was one tall bare-branched tree in a burlap bag, but deep inside, despite my current anguish, I was really proud of him and I did praise him.

"Mom, I started tearing up when I thought about it. I wanted to get something special for Cawthra," he explained.

"That is really nice of you." By this time, I was feeling a bit guilty about my heavy-handed response. Then I asked the dreaded question. "Where did you send this tree, Sweetheart?" Then I added, as if by stating a fact I would somehow magically make it a reality, "You *did* send it to their home–right?"

"No, Mom," he answered, annoyed. "You told me to send it to the funeral home. Remember? I did exactly what you said, and I didn't forget to put your name on it either."

At that moment, I died a thousand deaths. I experienced both heart-bursting pride for my son and an absolute panic over what the outcome of his one single act would be. What a nightmare! I could hear Kate's voice ringing in my head, "Rrrobin, what have you done again?"

I could see the Mulocks' disapproving faces and hear them all saying, "There she goes again, not knowing the proper way of doing things." Hadn't Kate just lectured me a few weeks ago about this, saying that I was too pushy with them? Now, one bare-branched tree in a burlap bag stood tall, among the flowers, on the altar, with our names in bold letters glaring out at everyone. What could I say? Hadn't my precious son listened to me all his life? Hadn't I explained numerous times about the importance of acting from a heart-centered place? And had I not told him, over and over again, "Just be you, be yourself, no matter what"? Was that not Spirit's truth?

As I struggled between my own people-pleasing side and my self-confident adult side, I saw that my son had *walked my talk*. He had boldly held our spirits high for all to see. In other words, when I was too scared to stand up and be me–he did it for me. Yes, he was my son–myself.

A few weeks later, I was driving down a country road at night, noticing the dark bare branches of the trees against the moonlight. Suddenly, I heard my uncle's voice booming in the car.

"You fool, you should be thinking about raking the leaves!"

At that moment, it came to me what he had meant that summer day. I got it! I realized that I had what I had wanted my uncle to pass on to me. I didn't have to be accepted by the Mulock family, nor did my son. I carry the ancient blood inside me, and so does Forrest, and our spirit connection, when we are aligned and loving each other, is what is alive in us. It is the mother and child bond—an energy that only a mother and her child can experience. Then all of a sudden I felt a rush of energy, and I swore I could hear all the trees singing to me in full splendor, like angels' voices. It was the Anishinabe's si-si-gwa-d—the gentle song of the trees. It felt as if they were saying to me, "Forrest is your legacy and he is standing in his heart. . . . It is all so simple."

When the forest weeps, the Anishinabe who listen will look back at the years. In each generation of Ojibway there will be a person who will hear the si-si-gwa-d, who will listen and remember and pass it on to the children.

–Ignacia Broker,
Night Flying Woman: An Ojibway Narrative

The Motherghost VI
The Mystical Realm
2000-Present

And you who seek to know Me, know that your
Seeking and yearning will avail you not, unless
You know the Mystery:

For if that which you seek, you find not within
yourself,
You will never find it without.
For behold, I have been with you from the beginning,
And I am that which is attained at the end of desire.

–Starhawk, *The Spiral Dance*
Adaptation of Doreen Valiente's
"Charge of the Star Goddess"

CHAPTER 34
At My Mother's Grave

I had always been afraid to visit my mother's grave. There were too many feelings. Too much confusion. Too much sorrow. I had been grateful that she had remained lost to me for all the years I searched. But something had changed. There was a calmness inside me—a taking-control-of-my-life type of feeling. At the same time, I could feel my apprehension growing as I drove slowly up the hill of the cemetery where she was buried. It was a strikingly beautiful place, with large fancy statues, ponds, fountains, and meticulous landscaping. The stillness of the energy was uncanny.

I knew this endeavor was not going to be easy. It can get more complicated when you are psychic. The dead were calling me to come home to my mother. But why? I didn't know exactly what had shifted inside me, but it seemed to coincide with getting the news about my mother's whereabouts. I had tried to find her for years and, as strange as it seemed, no one could tell me where she was. And then all of a sudden, one afternoon, with one phone call from a stranger, everything changed and opened up and what was lost was found.

The question I kept asking myself was, why now? Why was I being led to exactly this moment in time and place? I was booked to lead an evening workshop that was out of state and, strangely, scheduled on the anniversary of my mother's death. The route I needed to take would take me by the town where she was buried. Seemingly, this was a strong message that the time was right. Had she called me back to her after all these years? Was this another one of her divine schemes to orchestrate my life in the way she wanted? Who knows? I just know I was compelled to be there.

My intention was to get some kind of resolution. If I could resolve my conflict with my mother, maybe then she'd rest in peace and I would be released from her grip. She had haunted me in so many ways. I could feel her presence occasionally, and it always felt like being hit by the recoil from a gun, like the times when I would be looking in a mirror and suddenly I could feel—with the same dread I felt on the day she walked out of my life forever—her staring back at me, in just the same way. Or maybe her haunting would come when I heard the sound of a baby crying. Sometimes it was the smell of a certain perfume or a sad lullaby or the sound of high heels on pavement. In those sudden moments I knew my mother was present and wanting something from me. And that was the problem: I didn't want to give her anything. I was still angry with her, and she was not letting me go. But when I thought I could just walk away from it all, Robin—the weeping child of my heart whose only dream has always been to return to her lost mother's arms—would take over, and I would be compelled to keep searching.

"Fourth row in, up the hill, by the tower," the groundskeeper said, directing me to my mother's plot. I found it easily and walked slowly over to the spot where a bronze plaque in the ground read *Stephanie Muriel Henderson*. No one was around and so I sat down right on top of the grave. I waited. I began to stroke the grass and I waited some more.

"This is as close as I'll ever get to you," I said, feeling the loss of my long journey's dream to finally have a happy mother-daughter reunion. I waited again. Nothing happened. She haunts me, I thought, almost grabbing at me, wanting my attention, and I finally come to her grave, and then there is nothing.

How macabre and strange it was, after so many years of painful, heartfelt searching and holding on to daydreams of a mother welcoming her lost child home, to come to this. Here I was alone, sitting on what now would be a box of bones. To know that my mother was under there—the woman who had hurt me so terribly and who I had loved so desperately as a child— just didn't go together in my thoughts. It was creepy. There had to be more than this silence. It was empty. A period at the end of a sentence. I wanted more. I needed more.

"I've come back. I found you."

Silence.

"I made it. You've wanted me here. So what do you want?"

More silence.

I closed my eyes and started to meditate. I took a deep breath and imagined going into the ground toward her coffin. It became very dark and damp. I knew that I was approaching the other realm, and I could feel my discomfort as I sensed her close by me. It was like being in a pitch-black room with an undefined creature somewhere nearby waiting and watching. But I still did not see her.

"Why are you not appearing?" I asked, frustrated.

"I can't," I heard a voice answer.

"Why?"

"Because you are sitting directly on my grave."

"What's that got to do with anything?"

"When you are so close physically, like this, you are directly aligned to my body."

"So?"

"When you do this, I can only appear to you the way I looked at the moment I died."

"People see spirits at graves all the time," I argued.

"No, that's not true. The dead always appear some distance from

226

their grave," she said with authority.

I looked around to see if she was behind me. Nothing. "What is wrong with showing me the way you were when you died?" She was quiet again. I waited.

"I was not beautiful that way," she said.

"I don't care."

"But I do. I care," she said.

This is strange, I said to myself. I am arguing with my dead mother about looks and appearing or not appearing. I was beginning to feel like a teenager.

"Look, Mother, I came all this way and it's taken all these years. Can't you understand? This is so hard for me. Please, just appear."

She became silent again.

A long time went by. Nothing. I realized our power struggle was going nowhere, so I went back into the meditation and to the darkness, but I couldn't find her this time. Resignedly, I finally just relaxed in the calm, dark space. I don't know how long it was, but at some point I began to hear singing in the dark distance. It was my mother. It was like a lullaby.

"*Hello, darkness, my old friend. . . .*" Her soft voice grew louder and filled my thoughts. I had completely forgotten the gentleness and the warmth of her singing voice. I had forgotten about the comfort of the lullabies that she had sung to me. I could feel the years roll back since she left me, and as I sat on my mother's grave, I recognized how much I had longed for her voice. How many nights I had cried for her. Especially when I was scared or felt lost. It brought back the grief of losing her. A lump formed in my throat and I was very, *very* sad.

I realized that I had followed my mother's voice back in time, into the late sixties, and as I looked I saw that she was singing to herself in her own thoughts as she lay in bed dying. She hadn't let me see her, but she had let me be there at the moment of her death. As I sat listening to her singing, I could feel her sadness, the sadness she had carried all her life. I realized that it was something we had shared together. It was the sadness of a torn mother bond. And at that moment it occurred to me that she was leaving, once again, another child–it was my sister Melanie at age nine. But most of all, I realized that she was the other side of my wound. That she had suffered the same pain I had. In the sweetness of her voice I saw that I had not been forgotten and we were connected. We were mother and daughter forever.

I sighed. So much time had gone by in my life since I had first set out to find her. Here I was now, sitting on her grave. It was as if I had time-traveled back into the sixties and stumbled into the day she died. I was looking into the past and seeing her, lying on her bed, alone in the room, staring out a window to her left. Her sorrow was overwhelmingly palpable. The radio was playing Simon and Garfunkel's "The Sound of Silence," and she was softly singing to herself, almost as if she were singing herself to sleep. I began singing with her.

Maybe, in a cosmic way, I stepped into my healing power at that moment. Maybe I transformed into an angel for her. Maybe I brought her heart ease, at last, about our torn relationship. I could see myself holding her like any adult daughter would at her mother's death. I had heard stories of daughters holding and rocking their mothers as they left this world. This felt right, as I imagined myself holding her and singing to her. The song became a lullaby. I kept my heart open. I told her what had happened between us was okay. I was okay. She could be at peace. I could feel the journey of our souls come full circle: where once she had held me and then let go, I would now do the same. I knew that I was putting my mother's soul to rest that day as I sat on the grass on her grave.

For the first time I felt her humanness; and, as weird as it sounds, sitting on her grave, I finally could feel her as if she were alive. No longer was she a figment of my imagination, a mother figure I raged at and ran from. She was simply a sad woman dying too young.

We shared a long, quiet time together.

"I still want to see you. Talk to you," I whispered after awhile.

Silence again. Nothing.

"I am more stubborn than you," I said, crossing my arms as I did as a child. "And I want to stand face to face with you like I did when I was three." I felt tears of exasperation welling up.

"I've dreamed of this day."

No words from her.

I sighed.

After awhile my sense of humor kicked in, and I began to tease and try to coax my mother into appearing. "And anyway, I am taller now. Taller than you," I said. I imagined my five-foot-two mother staring up at me. I wiped a tear from my cheek, really grateful that I could once again make jokes.

Nothing was happening, so I started thinking about the workshop on spirit guardians that I was going to be leading in a few hours. My mind wandered to thoughts of what truly gave me joy—the glorious beauty of nature, the fairies and the angels, those precious beings who had been with me and had filled my life from the beginning—that had not changed. Even though angels had played a large part in my life and had rescued my broken heart, it was the ancient Celtic fairies that had saved my joy and preserved my humor. After all, I had Irish blood running through my veins, and the legacy

228

of that side of the family was mine to claim. I felt like I owed everything to the fairies, because their lightheartedness had gotten me through so many difficult incidents. I needed a bit of humor right then. I had been overwhelmed with gloom.

I started calling the fairies with an ancient invocation. As I finished this mystical act, I heard a crow in a nearby tree cawing at me. The crow, in many traditions, is seen as the lucky trickster. I opened my eyes and cawed back at him. I laughed at our interchange. "What do you want? Have you got a trick for me?" I asked.

Then an ant walked by, climbing the grass as if it were in a jungle. It finally reached me and I watched it climb even more diligently up and over my leg. The ants have been special to me all my life. As a child, I had always wanted an ant farm, but I never got one—Frances Neilson said it could break and scatter ants everywhere in the house.

As I sat there, the ant reminded me of one of my favorite spiritual moments. It had happened a few years before, while I was sitting in the sun anxiously waiting to hear from the vet about my dog Moonwheat's health. The future looked bleak with the loss of my old dog, and I had a constant, dull ache in my heart every time I looked at her. Moonwheat had been my soul companion for over twelve years. She had been sick for a while, but I could see that she was not yet ready to leave me and so I was hoping beyond hope for good news. She was old and failing, with wobbly legs and cataract eyes. My heart was truly breaking, knowing it would only be a matter of time before she would be gone forever. As tears began to roll down my cheeks, I happened to look over to the table, where my iced tea was sitting, and I saw an ant coming toward me. As I reached out to grab my glass, I knocked it over, and the iced tea spilled, drowning the ant. I was deeply moved by the useless death of this little creature, which seemed to foretell such doom and gloom. I quickly picked it up in my hand and began to breathe on it and give it CPR. As I did so, I thought about all the little ants in the world that merely live for the sake of living. Soon I realized that I had merged in my mind the survival of my most beloved dog and the survival of this ant, so that they were one and the same.

"Please live," I whispered.

I was pleading with this tiny, black body, whose lifeless little antennae had dropped onto my finger. Maybe it was the fairy magic, maybe it was the sunlight, but within a moment the ant's small antennae moved as I stroked it and breathed onto it. Soon it was up and walking across my hand. I was thrilled and I carried it to a flower.

"I have shown you that Moonwheat will be all right," I heard the ant say.

I began to weep.

Moonwheat lived for two and a half more years. After that ant moment, at Rowe Conference Center, where I have led a summer retreat for over twenty-five years, I gave my most favorite morning ritual in honor of this one ant. (The participants now often lovingly refer to it as The Ritual of the Ant That Eclipse Resuscitated.) Each year since then, I stand in the circle of many women in a beautiful meadow surrounded by glorious towering trees that sway in the wind as we sing. I tell the story of the ant, and then I instruct each woman to go find something in the woods that one most likely would walk by and ignore, something insignificant—a small plant, sapling, flower, bug, mushroom, rock, and praise it—sing to it. Sing ah-leluia and tell it with your heart wide open that it is the most glorious being of this earth. This is truly the ritual of my heart.

As I sat on my mother's grave, I could feel my heart open, and I was glad the little ant had made its appearance.

"Have you got a message for me?"

The ant said nothing and continued on its way.

Then to my right I saw a very old woman dressed in a navy blue suit. She was being led by a younger woman, who was also dressed in a navy blue suit. They must be mother and daughter, I thought, noticing that both wore a string of pearls and walked in unison. They passed by me, acknowledging my presence with a smile and a slight nod of their heads. They continued down the path to a sitting area nearby. I had been so wrapped up in my dilemma that I hadn't heard them drive up.

I sighed and then started laughing at my situation. Here I am at my long-lost mother's grave. The grave that for years was nowhere to be found. Here is the mother who has haunted me forever, and now, when the opportunity is ripe for her to appear to me, face to face, she becomes coy and says that she won't appear because she feels ugly! It was all too bizarre. Any sane person would have thought that I had lost my mind. I would have thought so too, if I hadn't been trained in paranormal experiences and the unexpected.

I was getting bored, and I glanced over at the car that the two women had arrived in. I couldn't believe what I saw.

"Is that an antique Morris Minor?" I exclaimed.

I have a bit of a thing for cars, and all my life I had wanted a classic Morris Minor. In my moment of angst, just seeing it felt like Christmas. I immediately went over to admire this beautiful rare car, and, to my glee, it was in perfect condition. I forgot my mother ghost dilemma.

"You made that happen," I said to the fairies, as I slowly circled the car, peering in at the old-fashioned dashboard and admiring every inch of its well-kept beauty. "You did that just to distract me and make me happy." I started laughing, feeling lighter than I had all day. I could feel all of me enjoying the moment. I was here, present in this time and place: Marcy with the Neilsons' upbringing and classy taste, Robin longing for her mother, and me, Eclipse, using ancient invocations to the fairies. It was a perfect integration of the different experiences of my life.

I realized right at that moment that I didn't really care if anyone thought I had lost my mind. Maybe I had. I took my shoes off and began a little jig, pressing my feet into the soft green grass. It felt luscious. Just then, in the middle of a spin, my thoughts were suddenly interrupted by a booming voice right behind me. It was so close that it startled me, and I jumped.

"There! That's what I have wanted!" the voice said loudly and in an absolute manner.

I spun around to see who had said that. And there she was—my mother—standing life-sized in front of me. Face to face. And she looked breathtakingly beautiful. A little too much makeup for my taste, but still beautiful and full of energy.

"Robin, that's all I ever wanted from you."

"What do you mean?"

"I wanted to see those brown eyes sparkle again. For you to be happy like the little Robin I knew. I wanted you to feel free and alive."

"That's all you have wanted from me?"

"That's all," she said, and smiled.

I thought about what she had just said and about all the times in my life that I had wished someone would have said to me, "I just want you to be you." I thought about how much I had run away from her ghostly spirit only because I was afraid that she needed something from me. For so many years I had been too angry to give her anything, and now she was saying, "I just want you to be you, the Robin I dreamed you would become."

"How perfect and how ordinary," I said.

I laughed and she laughed. It was a perfect mother moment. A perfect mother statement.

"Okay, I think I can do that," I said, as I thought about what being me really meant.

"Good." She smiled.

"Anything else?"

"Yes, be patient with Forrest—he struggles to be himself—but he will find himself, and yes, take care of your sister, Melanie—she needs you," she said.

"But we are not talking," I said.

"You will be soon," she said, "because, remember, you are my daughters."

As we stared at each other face to face, I finally understood the mother-daughter connection. It felt like the time we had stared at each other in the mirror so many years ago. Neither one of us said anything. It was one of those cosmic moments.

It started to rain and I looked at my watch.

"I've got to go," I said, and I turned away to look at my car. When I looked back to say goodbye, she was gone.

Who would have guessed, I thought as I got into the car and drove away, that a pale blue Morris Minor arriving after I called in the fairies would have saved the day? The radio was playing one of my favorite Aretha Franklin songs. I turned it up full blast and joined in, singing freely. I was being me. I was happy. I was tapping the steering wheel, swaying back and forth with the windshield wipers as they swished the raindrops away. I was just being overall "cool" and enjoying every minute of it. And I kept it up all the way out of the cemetery and down the road toward the retreat. I was getting a second chance at life. My mother had guided me back to myself. She was not letting me go this time. Instead, she was setting me free.

CHAPTER 35
The Ancient Mother's Light

That night, as I stepped into the circle of three hundred or more women, each holding a candle, I stared up at the stars and out at the outline of the trees surrounding the field. I felt deep inside that something very sacred was about to occur. I walked around with my djembe, keeping a slow rhythmic pulse.

"Before we enter the sacred realm of the Goddess," I said, "just like a tree who spreads its roots deep into the dark, rich soil of earth, we need to ground ourselves in this world–plant our feet firmly in what we know is real." Some women nodded.

"Keep your hearts open. Remember, the heart is a symbolic mirror that reflects the world." I smiled as I passed by a very old woman standing next to a young girl, who stared up at me.

I looked into the eyes of the women as I walked by them. I could feel their excitement and trepidation. I smelled the incense burning and I felt centered.

"We must stay grounded in this realm," I continued. "This work is not about leaving Earth, it is about bringing magical moments and healing to our lives and to our planet." I paused to give people time to find their centers and ground.

"Think of one thing that you absolutely know is true about yourself," I said as I headed toward the center of the circle, where the beautiful face of a Goddess sat on a large round mirror, surrounded by crystals and flowers that were strategically arranged in a pattern on a dark red cloth. "Think of one thing that no one can take away from you. It can be as simple as 'I love chocolate chip ice cream,' or 'I love my child,' or 'my husband,' or 'my teddy bear,' or whatever."

"Whatever works for you. Whatever it is, know that absolutely no one can take this identity from you. Let this become your symbolic lifeline to yourself," I said.

We closed our eyes and searched for that one simple truth about ourselves that no one could take away.

"Just be you–that is all I ever wanted." I could hear my mother's words again as I searched for my one truth to hold on to.

What is it? What do I know about myself without a doubt, and what is it that makes me happy? I thought about everything special in my life, everything that I love in this world: the trees, my child, my dogs, the birds, the Goddesses. As I had instructed the women in the circle to do, I also had to choose only one thing to anchor me. I continued to scan my life and then suddenly, I knew what it was, the one thing that no one has ever been able to steal or damage inside of me. My belief in the fairy beings, those gentle spirits who have been with me in my most painful moments. And whose only intention for all eternity is to be the subtle life force that feeds our earth. The love I have for them is boundless. It was such a simple truth for me to arrive at. I could feel the Robin in me stir as I whispered, "I belong to the Feys."

Just as I envisioned the gentle spirits, I felt a wind come from the edge of the field. In response, I raised my arms to the heavens, calling in the beautiful powers of nature. I could hear the rustle of dark leaves in the night. Many women gasped in wonder.

"Now think of something or some place in nature that you love and anchor this image into your heart. Hold on to it." A flash of me as a little child letting go of the memory of my mother at sunset on the Captiva beach appeared. My eyes filled with tears.

"I am holding on to the first rays of sunlight," I said out loud to the circle, remembering how I had thought my mother would return with the rising sun.

"I am holding on to the image of the trees," someone else called. "The still lake in the mist . . . the meadows . . . the mountains . . . the Indian pipes in spring . . . the squirrels . . . the birds . . . the old oak in my backyard . . . my cat . . ." The voices of the women filled the air with what each had chosen to hold on to.

The drums began a beautiful syncopated rhythm and the women started to chant softly, "The earth is our mother—we must take care of her." We held on to our images as we swayed rhythmically like a turning tide in a dark sea. We were becoming a microcosmic reflection of earth. Each one of us in our unique way was finding what we loved. We were like the vastness of the desert and the depths of the forest. Our hearts opened like the arms of the sea—the rush of the river—the pebbles on the beach. We were the beast and the bird—the reptile and the insect—the sunlight and the storm—the snowflake and the mudslide. The energy was palpable and it grew as our voices grew stronger into a wordless chant. We were the root that holds on and the petal that opens. . . . I knew at that moment that in the future some of us would become powerful leaders in a new form. It might take time. But each of us—step by step in our lives, circle by circle in our communities, life by life—would make a difference.

As I listened, I could feel the ancient text that was coded in my blood run through my being. As I led the circle that night, a very old power was rising inside me.

Walking among the women, I saw their ancient souls in their eyes. I could hear the whispers in each one of their hearts. I saw a mystical web of

234

energy, diverse and resilient, connecting each woman to the other.

"I have become in the becoming the form, who came into being the first time." This ancient Egyptian invocation, written thousands of years ago, settled in my heart.

The stars seemed brighter, and I felt magnificent. The little soft lights of joy that the fairies have brought for centuries to the lost children of the world now filled the circle. Many of us saw this magical moment as mist came over the field. It felt like an extraordinary gift from the Great Mother herself. I closed my eyes and smelled the grass, the pine, and the birch. I felt the soft blanket of the night mist. It was like a mother's arms wrapping around me, ever so gentle and safe. I let the little Robin–the seed of my truth–go to the arms of the Great Mother Goddess, where I saw the fairies and all the spirits who had been with me from the beginning. They gently welcomed this sweet courageous child into their light. And I knew Robin had finally come home.

I knew, too, that I had finally found my destiny, as I felt the heart of the Goddess embrace me. The feeling was so recognizable that it startled me at first. It is that special type of love that we all have reached out for in our most vulnerable moments. This love is a power that permeates the planet and is seen in images in every culture, in every town, city, and village. This love is strong, resilient, and courageous. It stands up against war and brings peace to the weary. It opens in fragile moments to strangers and gently strokes the wounded and grieves for the losses of the orphans standing alone on dirt roads. This loves soothes the old ones who are hunched over in wheelchairs in retirement homes. It is a love that embraces the simple tasks of giving– spoonful after spoonful, diaper after diaper, day after day. It is a love that is diligent in a struggle to teach spelling, math, and manners, and will not give up on the angry teenager who has lost hope. It is a love that weeps and laughs and is proud and is fearful. It is the love that does not rest when a child is dying and will not let go out of fear. It is a love that is alive and growing every moment across this planet and is spreading like a veil of healing light. It is happening every time a mother pauses and holds her child close to her heart and whispers, "I love you."

EPILOGUE
Prayer for the Future

May we be calm.
May we rest in each other's heart.
Me we bring peace to our lives in a gentle way of knowing.
May we see each other.
May we feel the warmth of the sun rays like a sheath of wheat
opening to the land of plenty.
May there be more.
May we praise those we love, and may we be praised by those
who do not know us.
May we see each other.
May we sing songs that have no wonder, but gently still the
shattered heart.
May we survive our moments of uncertainty.
May we smile.
May all possibilities embrace our lives.
May we thrive and may we be sheltered.
May we dance until the land thunders beneath our feet.
May we awaken the knowing ones below.
May we rise like wings of light to be exactly who we are.
May we see each other.
May we dream of a world of kindness.
As it is spoken–it will be seen.
As it is seen–it will be spoken
As it is–it will be.

–Eclipse Neilson
January 2012

ABOUT THE AUTHOR

Eclipse Neilson is a visionary artist and political activist for both human and animal rights. She has led workshops on eco-feminist spirituality for over three decades and is the director of WomenCircles at Rowe Camp & Conference Center. She is the founder of the Magaian Way, a program that teaches visionary practices and offers lectures nationally. She has received numerous grants for her programs and work with children and adults within educational communities. Her programs, under the auspices of Project A.W.A.R.E. (Awareness With Art Related Education), bring hope and new perspectives to communities about the powerful beauty of our earth. She has recently designed C.O.P.E. (Circles of Peace Education), a cutting-edge program that addresses bullying in schools by inspiring peace within the hearts of our children. The future is now! She teaches youth to learn how to empower themselves so that they will grow up to become leaders and citizens of the world.